THE LIFE OF

Max Mallowan

THE LIFE OF

Max Mallowan

ARCHAEOLOGY AND
AGATHA CHRISTIE

Henrietta McCall

THE BRITISH MUSEUM PRESS

Henrietta McCall has asserted her moral right
to be identified as the author of this work.

First published in 2001
by The British Museum Press
A division of The British Museum Company Ltd
46 Bloomsbury Street, London WC1B 3QQ

A catalogue record for this book is
available from the British Library

ISBN 0 7141 1149 X

Designed and typeset in Fairfield
by Martin Richards

Printed in Great Britain by The Bath Press, Avon

Contents

Acknowledgements

A work of biography would be impossible without the assistance and encouragement of the family. Mr Philip Mallowan, whom unfortunately I have never met, has given me great help in the course of many letters in which he carefully recalled the past. He searched his memory for recollections of family events, some of which occurred over a century ago, before he was even born, and for which he had to draw on hearsay. The sight of his erudite handwriting on an envelope always evoked pleasurable anticipation. Mr John Mallowan, Max's elder nephew, remembered his uncle with great affection and clarity and I am deeply indebted to him for many anecdotes and much information, as well as for a huge number of letters and photographs and an early diary kept by his uncle. To Frances, John's wife, I am also grateful.

Agatha Christie's family have also been unceasingly generous. Rosalind Hicks, Agatha's daughter, has made available to me a fascinating archive of material including letters, diaries and photograph albums. She and her husband Anthony have been the kindest and most considerate of hosts at Greenway where I have had the pleasure of staying on several occasions. They were able to tell me so much, and never seemed to mind the time and effort involved. Rosalind has also been one of my severest critics, and I am truly grateful to her for saving me from making mistakes and for putting me back on the right track when I have wandered off it.

I am most grateful too to Mathew Prichard, Agatha's grandson, whom I have consulted on many points where his considered advice has been much appreciated.

I would like to record my gratitude to the staff of the Department of the Ancient Near East at The British Museum, in particular to the Keeper, Dr John Curtis. I am most appreciative of their kind advice and help on a myriad of points, small and large, as well as personal recollections and anecdotes. From the wider world of the ancient Near East, I am grateful to colleagues in London, Oxford, Cambridge (particularly to

Professor David Oates and Dr Joan Oates) and Birmingham. It was a great pleasure to meet Professor David Stronach and to hear his recollections of working with Max in the field.

I also very much enjoyed meeting Janet Morgan, Agatha's biographer, and talking to her about both Max and Agatha. Mrs Janet Pennington, the archivist at Lancing College, spent a day helping me to search the records of the College, and also kindly dealt with a number of enquiries about Max's schoolfellows. Mrs Caroline Dalton, the archivist at New College, Oxford, was also most generous in helping me to research Max's career there. She also allowed me to consult a notebook kept by Max, *Notes on Greek Texts*, and helped me to trace some of Max's contemporaries.

Foremost among these, and alas the only one remaining, is Rodney Kannreuther with whom I spent a delightful afternoon recalling Oxford in the early 1920s. I am very grateful to him for his memories and to his daughter Lady Cassells for arranging my visit.

I very much enjoyed meeting Reginald Campbell Thompson's son John and his wife Ann. Richard Quick, the nephew of Algy Whitburn, came to see me at The British Museum, bringing some fascinating memories of his uncle, both actual and descriptive. Professor Donald Wiseman remembered well his long association with Max and was kind enough to share those memories with me. I would particularly like to thank Rachel Maxwell-Hyslop, an invaluable source of information about Max. Her loyalty to his memory and affection for the man were a great inspiration as well as an enormous help in confronting some difficult issues. She was also a great friend and colleague of Barbara Parker, Max's second wife.

Nina Shandloff at British Museum Press is a model of what an editor should be: patient but firm, and I am truly grateful to her for working so hard with me on this book and being so encouraging and helpful. John Banks read the manuscript in its first draft and made most useful suggestions.

None of the above deserves any blame if I have made mistakes; they are entirely mine!

Lastly, I would like to thank my husband Christopher for his loving support at all times and for not protesting when work on the manuscript took precedence over the normal ordered routine of our lives.

Henrietta McCall
London, July 2001

CHAPTER ONE

An Ability for History

There was much about the young Max Mallowan that suggested the man he was to become: an inquisitive, assertive, bossy little boy who kept his younger brothers in thrall by a combination of charm and threats; a natural leader with a loyal heart towards those whom he loved; recalcitrant, but ready to be distracted and amused. He was a child who liked to have his own way, to collect things and to tell people about them, and he was devoted to his mother.

This may have had something to do with the state of his parents' marriage, which was troubled and at times stormy, leading to violent arguments. Frederick and Marguerite Mallowan were very different in character. Frederick Mallowan was disciplined and correct, and had been well educated. He had been born on 29 August 1874, at Kaiser Ebersdorf, about seven miles from Vienna on the Danube Canal. His father owned a large and profitable flour mill, which supplied most of the Viennese bakeries. The family lived in a pleasant house set in a garden just beyond the steam mill. During the 1890s, Frederick served in the Austrian army as a conscript, and twice saw action in the Balkans. At about the turn of the century, he decided to come to London to seek his fortune. In 1902 he married Marguerite Marie Duvivier, a Frenchwoman, and started a successful business which traded in oils, fats and dried coconut. He described his profession as being that of a produce broker.

Max's mother had been born on 12 August 1876, the daughter of a frustrated inventor and a well-known opera singer of the time, Marthe Duvivier, who had achieved her greatest moment of fame in the first production of Massenet's opera *L'Hérodiade* in Brussels on 19 December 1881. In *Mes Souvenirs 1848–1912*, Jules Massenet recalled that glittering evening, attended by royalty, nobility, government ministers, generals and leaders of fashion, not to mention four hundred honoured guests brought by special train from Paris: 'En tête de ces artistes étaient Marthe Duvivier, que le talent, la réputation et la beauté désignaient pour le rôle de Salomé ...'

Marguerite had had a romantic but unsettled childhood, wrote poetry and painted, and was spontaneous, vivacious, sentimental and loving. As a child and a schoolboy, Max adored his mother. She had been educated by Catholic nuns in France, and practised as a Catholic until about eight years after her marriage, when she became a Christian Scientist. After about five years she decided to return to Catholicism and went on a pilgrimage to Rome, where she was re-admitted to the Catholic Church. According to Max, his parents had very different ideas about the upbringing of their three children and this sometimes made the children feel 'gloomy', although the reality was probably more unsettling. By the time his youngest brother Philip was born in 1914, the marriage was beginning to disintegrate.

Frederick and Marguerite's first son was born on 6 May 1904 at Albert Mansions, overlooking Battersea Park, and christened Max Edgar Lucien after his Austrian grandfather and his mother's brother. The flat at Albert Mansions was a modest establishment, and Max was sometimes consigned to the care of the cleaning woman, kindly Mrs Pettigrew, who once committed the unpardonable sin of taking the new baby to her relatives in the East End, and was dismissed for her irresponsible behaviour. With the arrival of another baby boy, Cecil, in 1908, the family moved across the river to Kensington, to 52 Bedford Gardens, a street that runs westwards from Kensington Church Street, then as now a busy thoroughfare. Hansom cabs could be summoned by blowing a police whistle from a top-floor window. The house was well placed for nursery walks in Kensington Gardens, with nanny and the family dog, a chow called Choumi. During one of these walks, Max could not resist biting Cecil's succulent arm as it hung down from his perambulator, and found himself in serious trouble. When he was better behaved, he was rewarded with Batey's Stone Ginger Beer from the refreshment kiosk.

It was at Bedford Gardens that Max made his first excavations, in a flower bed at the bottom of the garden. He was rewarded by the discovery of some Victorian pottery sherds, which were ceremoniously cleaned and photographed. Seventy years later Max still possessed the photograph.

When he was eight, the family moved again to Wimbledon, to a house more suited to a growing family. There was a large garden with a tennis court on which Frederick taught his sons to play the game for which the area was famous, and he also took Max to the All England Club to see the great players of the day: Norman Brookes and Mrs Lambert Chambers. Max was enrolled at a local school, Rokeby, for which he retained a great affection for the rest of his life. This was in no small part because of Miss Vines, who introduced him to ancient languages, and opened the door on to a new world for the boy. There was a fierce mathematics master called Ferrier who had been forbidden to use the cane because he maintained that it was effective only if it caused a boy to groan. 'Ordinary cries counted for nothing.' Rokeby gave Max an abiding love for cricket.

In the summer holidays the family often went down to Bossington House in Hampshire. Their hostess was Molly Mansel-Jones, née Deverell, whom Max's mother had met when she first came to England at the turn of the century. Marguerite had arrived with letters recommending her as a teacher of French conversation and was engaged by Judge Deverell to teach his two daughters, Molly and Helen. They enjoyed their lessons so much that they kept in touch with Marguerite by correspondence and the three became lifelong friends, and met frequently. During the summer months, Molly, who was extremely religious, invited the vicar of St Michael's, Chester Square, to act as resident vicar in the church at Bossington. Everyone was expected to attend morning service on Sundays, but apart from that there were no rules. It was a 'real paradise for country lovers' with a long stretch of the river Test for fishing, swimming and boating, and the most delicious meals, especially breakfast with cold partridge and scrambled eggs. Molly had a devoted husband who was very kind to the three Mallowan boys. Bossington was sold after Molly Mansel-Jones was tragically run over by a bus outside her London flat in Onslow Gardens in 1928.

Probably on the recommendation of the Headmaster of Rokeby, G. R. Batterbury, Max was sent in January 1918 to Lancing College in Sussex. He was in Head's House, which was the name given to the

Headmaster's House, though the boys were for the most part supervised by the House Tutor. It was considered to be a privilege to be in Head's House, and parents paid an extra £10 a year in fees. Max was put into the Classical Lower Fifth and he was enrolled in the Rifle Corps.

Lancing had been founded in 1848 by the Rev. Nathaniel Woodard. He was the tenth child in a family of thirteen children, so money for education was scarce and he was taught at home by tutors. The boy decided early in life that he wanted to enter the Church, but it was impossible to take Holy Orders without a degree. Eventually two fond aunts found enough money to send him to Hertford College, Oxford, and he was ordained in 1841, aged thirty. In 1843 he went as vicar to New Shoreham in Sussex, and was shocked to find that many of his parishioners could neither read nor write. In 1847 he started his first school in the dining-room of New Shoreham Vicarage. It was such a success, and so inspired its founder, that he began to think about education in a much wider sphere. The early part of the nineteenth century had seen the foundation by the Anglican Church of public schools such as Cheltenham, Marlborough and Radley. Woodard wanted the Church to found other boarding establishments; he believed that boys needed to leave home to find public spirit, integrity and self-restraint. He also believed that religion should be a vital part of everyday life.

In 1848 Woodard published *A Plan for the Middle Classes*, a document which expounded his theory that the profits made by a school for the sons of professional men and gentlemen of limited means could reduce the fees of a second school, for the sons of tradesmen. But both schools would provide the same sort of education; the boys of professional parents would have better accommodation and food than that of their poorer contemporaries. Woodard sent his pamphlet to influential people in all walks of life, to Cabinet ministers, officers of the Church, heads of Oxford and Cambridge colleges, and it raised enough money for Woodard to realize his dream. Lancing College, his flagship, was founded in 1847 with twenty-four boys and two masters. The magnificent site on which the college was built, on 230 acres of Lancing Hill, was bought in 1852 and the first stone of the new buildings was laid in March 1854 in the Lower Quad. The college was then laid out on a long-established model for educational establishments, around two quadrangles edged with cloisters, the whole built from local stone faced with the flint from the nearby seashore. Woodard had always believed firmly in the educational value of good building.

The first boarding house, Head's House, was opened in July 1857 to accommodate forty boys. Woodard had a great contempt for luxury and in those early days the dormitories were crowded, the water ran cold, and windows were kept wide open in all weathers. Food was plentiful but grim: a suet roll with a very occasional currant was called 'milestone pudding'. The only project on which money was spent lavishly was the chapel, which was begun in 1888 and intended by Woodard to be the collegiate church of the whole Woodard foundation. It is the largest private chapel in Europe, and the great graceful golden mass of it soaring above the green promontory on which it is built still dominates the landscape.

Max was fourteen when he arrived at Lancing in January 1918. He was immediately immersed in the harsh regime and complicated systems of ragging and privilege which were the custom in public schools. He had to learn at once a complicated code of unwritten rules: for example, new boys could walk only in certain parts of the school grounds, could not put their hands in their pockets, could wear only certain colours of ties and socks. In a building without any heating at all, boys had to leap out of bed at 6.30 a.m. and plunge straight into a communal cold bath. It was said that the first boy in had to break the layer of ice that covered it. There was no time to dither: the first lesson was at 7 a.m. Breakfast was at 7.45 a.m. and consisted of porridge, fish (kippers or herrings) or pressed beef, occasionally a poached egg or a sausage. There was plenty of bread, and sometimes margarine, but not always. If available, there was jam or marmalade. Then there was Chapel, lessons, luncheon, games or Corps, first tea at 5 p.m., more lessons and Chapel, then second tea at 7.30 p.m., after which boys could read in the library or rag about in the houseroom before going to bed in large stone dormitories with open windows. Boys would put every available piece of clothing on top of the bedclothes in a vain attempt to keep warm. There was absolutely no element of cosy domesticity, and the only woman, apart from the Headmaster's wife, was Matron, whose role was fiercely to enforce discipline.

The normal harsh regime was made harsher still by the War. On still days, the boys could hear the guns in France and all around them were reminders of what was going on. From Lancing they could see a temporary army camp and an airfield dotted with little double-winged aeroplanes. Within the school, a blackout in coastal areas at night made the school deeply gloomy and a German submarine blockade in the Channel had enforced food-rationing. The boys themselves waited on each other at table, as the school servants had been called away on active service. Each House had an allotment where they tried to grow vegetables and supplement the rations available. Even the tuck-shop known as the 'Grubber' stocked only fruit and that only occasionally. Food parcels from home were forbidden. On Sunday evenings after Chapel the names of Old Boys killed during the week were read out. But perhaps most demoralizing of all was the absence of most of the younger and more inspirational staff, leaving, with one or two exceptions, only the more hopeless ones, and those who had been prised out of retirement.

The Headmaster at the time was the Rev. Henry Bowlby. He was a tall, lean man who had gained a hurdling blue at Oxford. He had come from Eton, where he had been a housemaster, and because his manner was somewhat aloof he was thought rather to look down on Lancing. None the less, in his five years before the War he had achieved a great deal there, increasing the number of boys in the school, building a proper sanatorium with a resident doctor and nurse, and embarking on further construction works to complete Woodard's plans, the most important of which was the completion, after forty-three years, of the enormous chapel. It was dedicated in July 1911. Another most worthwhile achievement, in the eyes of the boys at least, was his instigation of the levelling of the upper field, a large area where football and cricket could now be properly played, and on which Lancing could challenge schools such as Eton and Charterhouse, and frequently win. As an athlete himself, he took a keen interest in games and instituted House teams with a proper competitive team spirit.

Max's arrival at Lancing coincided with one of its bleakest periods because of the War. His letters home to his mother, written in a clear rounded hand in black ink, said little about the privations. There were descriptions of the masters, the ragging and practical jokes, his stints at fagging (which he loathed), the work he was doing, but most particularly of the other boys. Max's contemporaries at Lancing included several boys who became well known in later life, not least of whom was Evelyn Waugh. He made an immediate impression. In a letter to his mother dated 7 February 1918, Max told her,

> There is a jolly clever chap in my form (you can see he looks it) called Waugh, but he is a terrific slacker and of course doesn't get any high places through that, but keeps down low. And the other day when I hadn't yet got any books, I asked him to lend me his Algebra, as we had been set 7 sums to do for Tommy [Mr Tomlinson the mathematics master] and he lent me the book on condition that I didn't do more than 4 sums ... Waugh is really an awfully decent chap.

Evelyn Waugh regularly appears in Max's letters home. There was a friendly rivalry between them, and he was pleased when he beat his 'rival Waugh' in examinations at the end of his first summer term. It was particularly satisfactory to be able to report in October 1920 that he had gained a higher mark than Waugh in his Roman History essay; 'that is a triumph!' Evelyn Waugh's memories of Max are usually connected with vast toast teas, a vital part of postwar schooldays. They remained in touch for their first year at Oxford, and then drifted apart, their paths never to cross again.

Other contemporaries were Roger Fulford the historian, Gino Watkins the Arctic explorer, Hugh Molson the Conservative politician, Tom Driberg the Labour politician, Dudley Carew the journalist, Humphrey Trevelyan the diplomat and Rupert Fremlin, a popular figure looked up to by all his contemporaries as an expert on matters of art and taste. It was a golden age in the annals of Lancing; Evelyn Waugh speculated on why in his diary on 11 February 1921: 'The more I see of Lancing the more convinced I become of the fact that our generation, and in this I include all who came in the terms on either side of Fulford's and mine, was a very exceptional one. One day I must try and work out the many influences which contributed to this. I think that if I do I shall find that the war is directly responsible...'. And years later, in 1950, J. F. Roxburgh wrote to Dudley Carew, 'What a remarkable lot you were.'

Probably the most important influence on that generation was J. F. Roxburgh himself. In February 1919 the Lancing College Magazine announced the return of Mr Roxburgh 'from the wars'. He had already made a name for himself as Sixth Form Master before finally being allowed to join up in 1917 after several rejections because of a suspected heart defect. His war service, though short, was distinguished and he had been recommended for the Military Cross. That alone would probably have marked him out for hero-worship but the very essence of the man himself was an inspiration to anyone, let alone growing schoolboys stultified by terms of second-rate teaching. Roxburgh was a luminary. It was partly his appearance: he had fourteen (carefully counted by the boys) elegant hand-made suits and countless brightly coloured large silk handkerchiefs which he kept in his top pocket but sometimes flourished. He also enjoyed putting on academic dress. Few forgot his entrances, slightly late but quite unhurried, into Chapel wearing the robes of the Licenciat ès Lettres from the Sorbonne. One boy remembered a whispered exchange: 'The Prince of Glory passes on his way!' 'Alleluia!' There was also his undoubted stylishness. When boys came to his study in the evening they were treated to a special mix of China tea brewed in a large teapot and assorted biscuits from a large tin lined with frilled paper. Not for him handwritten examination papers: his were specially printed, as was his personal writing paper. But most inspiring of all was his enthusiasm. He was enthusiastic about Greek and Latin poetry, about French prose and poetry, about literature, art and everything that was important or interesting. He was never dull, preoccupied or boring. He brought to his teaching the excitement of real erudition and profound knowledge which was his mission to pass on to his pupils and very few failed to respond. Max's letters to his parents contain many references to Roxburgh. Roxburgh had told them that to obtain a top scholarship to Oxford:

> you must absolutely live on your subject. He said that you must
> have no time for writing a letter or reading of any description
> except on your own subject – the only thing one should do was
> 1 hour's football every day to keep the body fit, and every single
> moment of the rest of the day to work! ... And he said that the

same applies if you want to pass the Senior Tripos with 1st Class Honours at the end of your course at the University. He said that it was highly probable that we thought such a thing not worth doing – and he himself questioned its value. But at any rate he said that such a period of work for 3 or 4 years in one's life meant a sure and good career in front of one.

As Max started thinking about going to Oxford, he frequently applied to Roxburgh for advice. Could he get in on Latin and Greek? What should be read next? Would he let him read Anacreon's poems?

He said that he would be delighted to give me any book in which I was interested but he told me that they are extremely difficult to translate beautiful as they are, but he gave me the volume which has only a Latin translation at the bottom, almost as hard as the Greek! However I am going to have a good try at them with the help of my Greek Dictionary, as the poetry is very beautiful … I ought to be able to read most of him as there are only about 40 poems which are all very short – mostly on Love, Wine, Music and Nature … At the end are the only two complete poems of Sappho which I have read before and also what is left of Alcaeus. Mr Roxburgh gave me the very book which accompanied him in the trenches and right through the war – a very small and old copy of the Greek poems.

There were of course other masters at Lancing who made an impression on Max. His House tutor, W. B. Harris, 'Dick', had also fought in France. He was a small, springy, athletic man who taught English literature and was responsible for reviving football in the College. He called boys by their Christian names, which was highly unusual. He was succeeded by E. B. Gordon, 'Gordo', an Old Boy of the College who had been physically unfit to fight. The boys in Head's House were fortunate with their House tutors because they encouraged originality of character as much as conventional academic success. This sometimes took the form of turning a blind eye to elaborate practical joking which doubtless made the long bleak terms pass more quickly. The houseroom in Head's House was a particularly friendly place with tables and chairs, lockers, notice boards, framed photographs of successful teams and silver House cups. Above the fireplace generations of boys had etched their names into the wood (some more decoratively than others) and in front of it was placed a long wooden bench called the Settle, which was reserved for house prefects and on which on Sundays the famous 'Settle teas' were held where records for the number of buttered crumpets a boy could eat were set. Eight was the average. Settle teas had of course been abandoned for the duration of the War.

On 11 November 1918 at 11 a.m., a flag was hoisted on Shoreham Church as the Armistice was signed. For the rest of that propitious day the College went wild: lessons were abandoned, the College fire engine was dragged into the Upper Quad and turned into a fountain, boys scaled the Chapel and hung out more flags, and glorious anarchy reigned. Of the Old Boys, 163 had been killed, 132 injured and 29 taken prisoner. Inevitably there was a profound reaction against all the tragedy, waste of young lives, personal privations and misery that the school had endured. Although the War Office urged the public schools to maintain their Officer Training Corps, Lancing went back to its pre-War programme which involved uniform parades on Fridays, and on Wednesdays a shorter plain-clothes parade after morning school. During those early terms after the War, field days were held about three times and there was an annual House Platoon Competition at the end of March. Head's House never distinguished itself in this, partly because of the disruptive influence of Evelyn Waugh but more generally because the boys wanted to put the War behind them. Gradually conditions in the school improved: the Grubber re-opened for business, its shelves laden with whipped-cream walnuts, cream slices, ices, buns and chocolate. 'Settle teas' were reinstated. Max reported home to his mother on what he had produced as host one week for seven boys: 28 crumpets, 42 small cakes and one large chocolate cake.

In the week of 12–16 July 1920, the School Certificate examinations were held. Evelyn Waugh recorded in his diary: 'One appalling result of nerves, I found, was that all my knowledge of spelling – slender at the best of times – left me and I had to avoid perfectly ordinary words through being unable to spell them: "succeed" and "subtle" and several others. Mallowan found the same.' None the less, Max distinguished himself by passing in more subjects than any of his contemporaries. He passed Greek (and Greek text of the New Testament), English, Latin, History, French (with an oral test) and Elementary Mathematics.

The following October, Max found that life in the Sixth Form was very much more pleasant than it had been lower down the school. Each boy had a private study, called at Lancing a 'pit', where he could work uninterrupted and talk to friends who dropped in. Mountains of hot buttered toast were usually consumed and work in progress discussed. Max was immersed in a varied reading programme which included H. G. Wells, Bernard Shaw, Austin Dobson and Rabelais, as well as classical texts for his New College entrance examination. He reluctantly decided not to take music lessons 'much as I would like to be able to play well', as he knew he would never get beyond being 'a dabbler'. Mr Lucas, the History master, had told him that the New College entrance examination was

> one of the *hardest* to pass in Oxford, although it will be easier for me as I have passed my School Certificate ... men of ability are often turned down in trying to pass the New College matriculation, as only a limited number of candidates that apply are accepted. I shall have to take Latin & Greek translation and have the choice of doing a Latin or Greek prose or I can take Roman History from 133 BC to the fall of Julius Caesar the period that I am now studying, and French. Mr Lucas says that he would like me to take Roman History as he says that I have an ability for history ... but I am going to ask Mr Roxburgh for his advice ... There is also a general paper containing Scripture questions, Natural Science, History and Political Questions.

No wonder Max asked his mother to arrange for extra tutoring in the holidays: 'I think 3 times a week from 9–10 in the morning would be the best don't you? What about having it on Monday, Tuesday & Wednesday as that would leave the rest of the week entirely free.'

Max took his Higher Certificate in 1921 and left Lancing that July, aged seventeen. Like his contemporaries, he would probably have stayed on another year before going to university, but there was a disagreement about Max being confirmed, and Frederick Mallowan, an atheist, decided to remove his son from the school. A school with a high Anglican tradition had perhaps been a strange choice in the first place, but it had provided Max with an excellent education, and he had done well. Max's younger brothers Cecil and Philip went to Stowe, mainly because of J. F. Roxburgh's appointment as Headmaster of the new public school.

In his *Memoirs*, Max described the transition from Lancing to New College in October 1921 as 'purgatory to paradise'. A contemporary, A. L. Rowse, (some forty years later to be a fellow of All Souls at the same time as Max), later described the atmosphere of that postwar world. 'The grim experience ... had reinforced the strength of idealism. There was a real belief ... in bettering the world ... the sacrifice of the generations before us must not be in vain. A better world must be built up.' Beside that idealism ran a stream of frivolity, eccentricity and excess, personified by Harold Acton 'that bird of brilliant plumage', Peter Quennell, Claud Cockburn and, when he arrived the following year, Evelyn Waugh. Max was neither very idealistic nor completely given over to dissipation. His friends were a mixture of his old Lancing contemporaries, such as Rupert Fremlin and Hugh Molson, and new ones who had just arrived in Oxford like him. Of these, one who had the most influence was Esme Howard, the eldest of five sons of Sir Esme Howard, at that time British ambassador in Madrid, though he was soon to move to Washington. Esme had been at Downside where, like Max at Lancing, he had received a classical education and had been a notable football and tennis player before coming up to New College to read history. He often turned from his work to nature study, strolling by the river and watching birds. He also wrote poetry and painted. He was seriously ill with Hodgkin's Disease, but few knew how hopeless the prognosis was. When he came down from Oxford, this exceptional young man ought to have had a brilliant future in front of him, but only months of pain and periods of utter despair, illuminated by his unwavering faith, lay ahead, and he finally lost his fight for life in 1926. After Esme died, his contemporaries put together a special book of remembrance. Max kept his copy all his life. In it, in moving tributes, his friends described what was so special about Esme: his lofty ideals put into daily practice, his fervent faith, marked unselfishness, indomitable courage.

Other close friends at New College included Rodney Kannreuther, who had been at Wellington and was reading French. Rodney's father died suddenly during his first term, and it was a struggle for his mother to keep him at Oxford; there was certainly no money left for the pursuit of pleasure. Max hit on a lucky streak gambling on horse-racing, and this enabled him and Rodney to enjoy several convivial Saturday dinners which Rodney recalled with pleasure many years later. He often stayed with Max in London during the vacation, and in their third year the two young men went on a cycling holiday in Brittany. They remained very close friends who kept in regular contact until Max's death. Rodney was a very good-looking tall young man who towered over Max and teased him by calling him a Lilliputian. 'In his serious moments', wrote Max, 'he is very serious indeed, when not bent with laughing he is bent with philology, but his most characteristic position and that by which he will be most remembered by his friends is to be seen when doubled up ... trying desperately to retain his balance and his pipe.'

In his third year, Max moved out of college, as was usual, and took lodgings at 6 Ship Street with the closest friends he had made. Apart from Esme Howard and Rodney Kannreuther, there was Richard Warner, who had been at Wellington with Rodney, and was the butt of all the jokes and ragging that went on, Ronald Boase who had also been at Wellington and was 'endowed with a truly Scottish caustic wit' (his father was a barrister in Edinburgh) and an old Etonian who also came from Wimbledon, Kenneth Headlam Morley, who was a Scholar. Two of them were to die young: Esme and Richard Warner. So was Max's old Lancing friend Rupert Fremlin, who died while working for the Nigerian Administrative Service in 1934. Seventy years later, Rodney Kannreuther still remembered those days in Ship Street: the parties they had held, and the taste for high living they acquired, the weekly trips to the theatre, the sheer zest for fun, unfettered by adult respon-sibilities, that bound them together. It was perhaps not surprising that of the six of them, only one, Kenneth Headlam Morley, distinguished himself in his final examinations. The rest achieved only Thirds, except Richard Warner, who left Oxford with a Fourth in History. It would be wrong to think, however, that in the 1920s any particular stigma attached itself to a young man with such a modest degree.

It is more surprising perhaps that Max, having been such a studious and academic boy intent at Lancing on passing examinations with the highest marks, and reading a subject he found engrossing, barely scraped through Mods in the Lent Term of 1923 with a Fourth Class and graduated after four years with a Third. He seemed to be working diligently if his 'Notes on Greek Texts' and the *Republic* of Plato day-book is any guide; in it, in his neat hand, he wrote out most of Plato's *Republic* in Greek, and translated it line by line underneath. On the facing pages, he made notes on passages to revise, though the word 'Difficult' underlined several times frequently appeared. He kept vocabulary lists and made himself a list of 'Propositions to Consider'. But having done so, he perhaps did not keep himself up to the mark. His private diary kept at the same time gives a rather different picture, of long days playing golf with his friends, tennis matches and frequent trips to the theatre. Several times he sat up overnight to write an essay, but this was not necessarily the best time to do it. On the other hand, it was clear that he had many intellectual interests as well. One entry describes a day spent studying Greek vases in the British Museum, and another looking at ancient jewellery in the Ashmolean Museum. He kept methodical reading lists which included all the novels of R. L. Stevenson, Dickens, Hardy and Walter Scott. And he was particularly fond of Keats, keeping copious notes on the poems he had most enjoyed. As for women, Mary, the daughter of the Warden, H. A. L. Fisher, wrote in her memoirs that 'girls were not yet considered a useful adjunct to college life'. Certainly there was no mention of any in Max's diary until after he had come down, when the name of a girl called Maimie occasionally appears in his diary. She seems to have been at Oxford too, at St Hilda's perhaps, and he certainly wrote to her from Ur to ask her to a commem. ball in the summer of 1927, but who she was is not clear.

Max's four years at Oxford were certainly not a waste of time. He was growing up. Although he was still very close to his mother, on whom he depended financially, he had made good friends and began making robust assessments about some of his tutors. He found most of them quite inspiring, but the Dean, Percy Matheson, who taught ancient history and of whose teaching he was later to say 'I felt I was entering a gold mine', was the recipient of one of his all-night essays, which perhaps explains his exasperated entry 'the dullest tutor I have ever struck, he is even duller than his own Sunday tea parties which is saying a good deal … I wish I was still under S. Casson'. Stanley Casson was an archaeologist and historian. H. W. B. Joseph, who provoked Max into thinking about the wider implications of his subject, merited a whole section in his 'Notes on Greek Texts' during the Michaelmas Term of 1923. Outside New College, Max attended lectures given by Gilbert Murray on Greek tragedies, S. G. Owen on Juvenal and Percy Gardner on Greek sculpture. It was to Gardner that Max owed his introduction to the British Museum, and ultimately to a career in archaeology. Max never forgot Gardner's description of the discovery of the statue of the Hermes of Praxiteles in the Temple at Olympia, and how this had led him to think of sculpture in its original setting.

The young men at Ship Street were inclined to keep rather erratic hours. They often seemed to be exchanging views about life and poetry, or less serious topics, such as golf, at three in the morning. Sometimes they related ghost stories to each other, and on one occasion tried to frighten Dick Warner by tapping on his window, which produced 'a violent stamping on the part of the landlady from upstairs'. One night Rodney made Max read him entries from his diary, and, though Max chose the most frivolous ones he could find, Rodney found them 'horribly serious'. On his twentieth birthday, 6 May 1924, Max wrote in his diary that at the time he felt nearer sixty than twenty:

> the reason being that I have passed the night of the 5th buried in books in order to turn out an essay on Greek colonisation … Herodotus, Thucydides, Plutarch and a few other of the ancients gave me for 15 hours out of 24 a wonderful and vivid picture … I read continuously from 1–6 at which hour I started my essay and wrote on till 7.30. Having refreshed myself with a bath and breakfast I continued from 9–11 by which time I had managed to write 10 closely written pages crammed with information … Having finished at 12 I wandered about bookshops from 12–1 wondering upon what to spend the £3 present from mamma.

Later that month Max decided he would cycle to Gloucester, and, as this meant a 5 a.m. start, he and Dick Warner tried to smuggle Max's bicycle in through the sitting-room window at 11 p.m. Unfortunately they were caught red-handed by the ferocious landlady, Mrs Kent, and it took Max two whole days of cajolery to make his peace.

How disappointed Max was by his poor showing in Finals, he did not say though forty years later, when he became a fellow of All Souls, he saw it very much as a vindication of his poor performance as an undergraduate. It was doubtless somewhat of a relief that employment so readily came to him, and that it should have been so entirely congenial to and consistent with his talents as they then were.

Max tells in his *Memoirs* how, after taking Schools in the summer of 1925, he was crossing the quadrangle at New College to find breakfast, when he ran into the Dean of Divinity, the Rev. Robert Lightfoot, who enquired, 'Mallowan, what plans have you for the future?' Max immediately said he wanted to be an archaeologist, inspired by the finds made by Percy Gardner at Olympia. 'I want to go to the East and look for things there.' The Dean told him to go and visit the Warden, who might be able to help him. H. A. L. Fisher, the Warden, gave him a letter of introduction to D. G. Hogarth, the Keeper of the Ashmolean Museum, who, as luck would have it, had just received a letter from none other than the distinguished archaeologist Leonard Woolley from the site of Ur in southern Mesopotamia, where his discoveries had been exciting great interest. Hogarth sent him to see Woolley at the British Museum.

Max prepared himself for the interview by studying as much of the published material on Ur as he felt would make a good impression. He knew absolutely nothing about Mesopotamia, even though the excavations at Ur itself had been quite widely published in journals such as *The Illustrated London News*. He bought a pamphlet published by the British Museum about Woolley's excavations of the temple of the Moon God, and tried to memorize it. His reading list included Koldewey's *History of Babylon*, Budge's *Babylonian Life and History*, L. King's *History of Sumer and Akkad*, and he read some of Gertrude Bell's books about the country and its people. Stanley Casson wrote a letter of recommendation about his former pupil. The day of the interview came and Max found he was being considered by not one but two people. With Woolley was a beautiful but somewhat formidable woman, a Mrs Katharine Keeling, who had been at Ur during the previous season of excavation as unofficial artist and assistant, and who, it seemed to Max (rightly, as it later transpired), had subjected Woolley to her considerable charms. Max always said afterwards that had he not passed Katharine's scrutiny, even though Woolley seemed to have taken to the enthusiastic young man he saw before him, he would not have found his future prospects secured. As it was, he was engaged to start work the following season, beginning in October.

This Most Important Cradle of Civilization and Religion

M ax's new mentor and the man who was to secure his future in the world of archaeology, Charles Leonard Woolley, had been born in 1880 in Hackney. He was the third in a line of eleven children. Their father was vicar of the nearby church of St Matthew's, Upper Clapton. Woolley was educated at St John's, Leatherhead, and in December 1898 won an open scholarship to New College where, like Max, he read Classical Greats. Rather as was to happen to Max, it was the Warden, the Rev. W. A. Spooner, who decided that Woolley should become an archaeologist, and he was appointed as a junior assistant keeper at the Ashmolean Museum in Oxford in 1905. In 1907 he had his first brief experience of excavation at the Roman site of Corbridge in Northumbria, where a minor find brought him a moment of fame. He liked both the experience of digging and his moment of fame, so much so that the following year he resigned his post at the Ashmolean and set about finding permanent employment as a field archaeologist.

Woolley's first assignment abroad was with Randall MacIver in Nubia. MacIver was the curator of the Egyptian Section of the University of Pennsylvania and had just been appointed as Director of the Eckley B. Coxe expedition to Egypt and the Sudan at the sites of Areika, Buhen and Karanog. He was a former assistant to Flinders Petrie at Dendera and Abydos, so he had learnt his methods and site management from a man who was considered to be a master. Woolley was an apt pupil. When MacIver went on alone to Buhen, he felt confident enough about Woolley to leave him in charge at Karanog, a large necropolis and city site about 60 km south of Aswan, which had been in occupation in Meroitic and post-Meroitic periods (c. 300 BC – AD 500). Woolley did not disappoint him, and in the process gained much valuable general experience: organizing the local workforce, being the one responsible for making precise records of finds, drawing plans of excavations at all stages of progress and taking useful photographs. He also wrote his first full field report, which was duly published in *The Philadelphian*, the magazine of the University Museum of Pennsylvania: 'Karanog, the Town' (1911).

Meanwhile, David Hogarth, who had been digging at Carchemish (modern Jerablus) on the west bank of the Euphrates in Turkey, had been appointed the new Keeper of the Ashmolean in succession to Sir Arthur Evans, and contacted Woolley to see whether he would be prepared to take over as leader at Carchemish. Woolley was enthusiastic and spent the remaining seasons from 1911 to the outbreak of the First World War excavating at Carchemish with T. E. Lawrence as his chief assistant. Woolley and Lawrence were responsible for recruiting Hoja Hamoudi, the man who was to play such an important role in Middle Eastern archaeology. He was a tall, thin, bearded Arab, who soon became highly skilled in organizing and controlling the workforce, and made himself indispensable in a number of ways. His talents even extended to medical matters and he was deemed to have saved Lawrence from certain death from typhoid fever. Lawrence's special favourite was Dahum, the desperately handsome camp photographer whom he taught to read and write. In June 1913, Woolley and Lawrence invited Hamoudi and Dahum to England: they were taken to a show at Earls Court, and given a tour of Oxford where Dahum sat for his portrait by Francis Dodd at the Ashmolean. The two Arabs caused something of a sensation, not the least part of which was exactly what was Lawrence's relationship with Dahum. At the start of the following season, soon to be curtailed by the War, Woolley overheard Hamoudi talking about his visit to Oxford. 'There is a big public park, with little metal chains to keep people off the grass. They could easily step over the chains, but they don't. It was the most wonderful thing I saw.'

It was not until 1919 that Major Leonard Woolley returned to Carchemish. In that unsettled postwar climate, it was not the place it had been. He no longer had Lawrence to help him, there were incessant skirmishes between the French and the Turks, the site was being damaged by unauthorized digging and plundering. Woolley went back to Egypt and worked for the Egypt Exploration Society at Tell el-Amarna.

His old friends, the University Museum of Pennsylvania, then decided to fund another expedition to Mesopotamia and, with the British Museum as joint sponsors, brought up the possibility of excavating 'Ur of the Chaldees'. Leonard Woolley was the obvious prospective leader of such an expedition. So in October 1922, Woolley once again found himself in Mesopotamia, some 480 km south of Baghdad, at that evocative place Ur, which during the course of the next twelve years was to be the making of him, and with which his name was permanently to be associated.

Ur, modern Tell al-Muqayyar, was a large walled city, encircled in antiquity in the north and west by the Euphrates river, and having at that time two quays. Settlement had begun at the site in 4500 BC during the Ubaid period and remained in occupation until the end of the fourth century BC. Ur had had its times of supremacy and its times of destruction, and the unravelling of the different fortunes of such a large site was both complicated and challenging. Sir Henry Rawlinson had identified the city as early as 1850, after he saw the inscribed bricks brought back by W. K. Loftus from the site, and in 1854 the Trustees of the British Museum commissioned J. E. Taylor, the British Vice-Consul in Basra, to begin excavations. He found four large inscribed cylinders, each one deposited at a corner of the ziggurat or temple tower, commemorating its restoration by Nabonidus c. 550 BC. Nothing at all had happened since then until 1918 when Captain Campbell Thompson had made soundings there during one short season, from February to the end of May, and published a brief report of it in *The Illustrated London News* on 1 April 1922. H. R. Hall had worked at Ur, Eridu and Ubaid in 1918–19. Some of the objects they had found were exhibited in the Assyrian Galleries at the British Museum, but it was more or less on a blank sheet that Woolley was to draw his plans and ultimately his conclusions. It became obvious early on however that, as Woolley put it, 'it is with the Third Dynasty of Ur [2112–2004 BC] that connected history begins, and from this date the record of our buildings is virtually continuous right down to the later Persian period, about 400 BC'.

There was still some building visible above ground, not least of which was the massive ziggurat, some 64 m by 46 m at its base, and originally probably about 12 m in height with four storeys. The summit was approached by a triple staircase, of three converging flights of stairs, with squat tower-buttresses between the angles of them. In the north-western part of the site stood the walls of an extensive religious precinct, the *temenos*, enclosing temples, palaces and other associated buildings. The city wall could be traced for nearly the whole of its circuit. It was a double wall with internal chambers constructed of unbaked brick, about 10 m across, and still standing in some places to a height of some 3 m. The wall was pierced by gateways set back into the wall face, with towers to either side, and covered entry. These gates turned on hinge sockets made of hard stone which was inscribed with the names of the kings who had been associated with restoration of the city wall. The earliest of these was Amar-Sin (2046–2038 BC), the grandson of Ur-Nammu, founder of the Third Dynasty of Ur, and the latest Babylonian king Nabonidus (555–539 BC).

The excavation team that first season, 1922–3, had, apart from Woolley as Director, F. G. Newton, an archaeological architect who had worked at Tell el-Amarna in Egypt, and at Knossos with Sir Arthur Evans; Sidney Smith of the British Museum as epigraphist; and A. W. Lawrence, brother of T. E. Their first task was the building of the expedition house, with fourteen rooms and an attached guard house. That done, and the indispensable Hamoudi welcomed back (with two of his sons in tow) to recruit, organize and control the local workforce, investigations began: first at the ziggurat, begun by Ur-Nammu and completed by his son, Shulgi. The core of this colossal structure was faced with mud-brick with a skin of baked brick which had been set in a very thick layer of bitumen. The temple platform was the best-preserved part of it, but much of the upper part was crumbling. Nabonidus had faced part of the outer walls with bright blue glazed bricks, but these had fallen away. Woolley was convinced that the Third Dynasty building covered a much earlier and more modest construction.

The main work of the season, however, was the complete excavation of the temple of the Moon God, Nannar, and his consort. H. R. Hall had begun the excavation of the sanctuary of the temple in 1919, but now Woolley began a more thorough investigation of the whole building and found that it was of much earlier date than previously thought: fragments of inscribed stone vases embedded in the earlier layers were dedicated by kings of the Dynasty of Akkad (2324–2154 BC). Below that there were layers of unbaked brick and 'green' bricks (i.e. bricks laid while still damp) dating back to a 'very remote antiquity'. Nebuchadnezzar was responsible for radically extending the temple, with the construction of a wide brick-paved courtyard, 'the lower court', and the construction of another court at a higher level, 'the upper court', though he had left the original five-roomed inner sanctuary intact. According to Woolley his own reconstruction of the temple of the Moon God owed a great deal to Herodotus, whose description of the contemporary Marduk temple at Babylon was so helpful.

Woolley also spent some weeks digging at the sites of Eridu to the south and Tell Ubaid to the north-west, where he concentrated on collecting pottery samples in an attempt to establish a chronology for Ur.

At the end of the season, he was able to report that the work had been 'remarkably rich in results', and that the earliest object found dated back to 2900 BC although he thought many of the painted potsherds and stone implements might be many hundreds of years older. The site was producing rich objects, including a finely carved statue of the *ensi* (city governor) Entemena from the débris at the foot of the ziggurat, a hoard of neo-Babylonian jewellery from beneath the sanctuary floor, and a second smaller hoard from the same period in a trial trench dug across the ruins of another temple. A great number of inscribed clay tablets had been found, mainly dating to the Third Dynasty of Ur, but some to the time of Artaxerxes (464–424 BC). A brick-lined well within the *temenos* had produced a quantity of clay foundation cones dating to the Larsa Dynasty (2025–1763 BC).

Before he left Baghdad to return to England, Woolley gave a lecture to an invited audience about the latest discoveries, at the request of Gertrude Bell. Woolley had first met Gertrude Bell at Carchemish and they had met again in Cairo during the War where they were both working for the Intelligence Department. She then returned to Mesopotamia where she worked behind enemy lines gathering information for the British. She was a remarkable woman: a pioneer in desert travel, a brilliant cartographer who had drawn the only maps of

Arabia available at the time, an author, a mountaineer, an archaeologist. She was also an intensely feminine woman in a man's world, immaculately attired in dresses she ordered from Worth and Molyneux in Paris. Legend had it that an unmistakable green-and-gold Harrods delivery van was once spotted in the middle of the desert; it had come to deliver a hat. In 1922 King Faisal of Iraq, whose path to the throne she had helped to smooth, appointed her as Honorary Director of Antiquities and thereafter, until her early death in 1926, she was to play a great part in western museums' excavations of that country. She was responsible for the building of a new museum for antiquities in Baghdad and for a far greater share of objects found by foreign excavators being allocated to it. Under her supervision, division of finds at the end of each excavation season was generally considered to be fair, though predictably the excavators and their museum sponsors often felt disappointed as prize pieces went to the national museum.

Even with the unfair competition in the archaeological world of the sensational discovery of Tutankhamun's tomb, as well as the royal wedding between the Duke of York and the Lady Elizabeth Bowes-Lyon on 26 April 1923, Woolley had every reason to feel pleased with the coverage given to his first excavation season at Ur. His end-of-season reports were published in *The Illustrated London News* on 17 March and 21 April 1923 and *The Times* on 14 May 1923, and he was able to look forward with enthusiasm to several more seasons at 'this most important cradle of civilization and religion' for he felt that only a very small fraction of the great ruin had so far been touched. It was these reports, and perhaps a remarkable aerial photograph of the site taken by the RAF and published in *The Illustrated London News* on 28 July, that had come to the attention of the young Max Mallowan at Oxford.

The following season, 1923–4, Sidney Smith was replaced as epigraphist by Cyril Gadd – to the relief of Woolley, who had not found Smith congenial – and work went on very much as before. There was a new face, however, in the excavation house that spring, that of a beautiful young widow called Katharine Keeling. Her precise reasons for being at Ur were not made clear, nor how she had met Woolley in the first place, but she had a talent for drawing and was put to work drawing objects that were being uncovered. It was most unusual for there to be any women at all on excavations, apart from the odd hardy wife who came out to help and to run the house-keeping. An unmarried and unattached woman was a subject for speculation and gossip, although it was some time before the Director of the University Museum of Pennsylvania felt he had to draw Woolley's attention to this, and put him on his guard. For the time being, Katharine's presence gave Woolley great pleasure, as she took such a keen interest in everything that was going on.

Katharine Keeling was and remains somewhat of a mystery and there is much about her life before she met Woolley which is open to much speculation. Her father, Carl Theodore Menke, came to England from Germany some time in the 1880s and settled in Kings Norton in the Midlands. Katharine was born in 1888 and in 1910 she went to Somerville College, Oxford, to read Modern History, although because of ill-health she came down after two years without taking a degree. During the First World War she worked in a prison camp at a place called Stralkavo in central Europe. It was here that she met her first husband, Lieutenant-Colonel B. E. F. Keeling. They were married on 3 March 1919 in London and shortly afterwards left for Baghdad and Cairo for their honeymoon. They began their married life in Egypt, but it was to be short-lived. On 29 April, Colonel Keeling was appointed Director-General of the Survey of Egypt and a director of the Cotton Research Board. On 20 September, he shot himself through the head, rumour had it at the bottom of the Great Pyramid. The exact details of why he did so, and how and where, remain sketchy. The suicide might well have been as a result of developments from the highly secret intelligence work in which he had been engaged during the War, but most people who came to know Katharine believed that it was because he realized that he had married a woman who wanted marriage in name only. Although she possessed a compelling physical presence – Agatha Christie was later to describe her as an *allumeuse*, someone who lit a flame in the heart of even the most confirmed bachelor – she had no interest in intimate relationships. It was said that the sole sexual moment of her marriage to Woolley (which was to take place in the spring of 1927) was his being allowed to come into the bathroom while she was having her bath. He apparently spent his wedding night in an armchair. None the less, he adored her and supported even her most illogical vagaries. Max came to know much about this strange marriage, but he never committed it to paper.

Woolley's second season at Ur was also the subject of two articles in *The Illustrated London News*. The first of these, published on 4 October 1924, was written by Cyril Gadd and Sidney Smith and attempted to establish a stylistic relationship between objects found at Mohenjo-Daro and Harappa in India and Mesopotamian objects. They also pointed out a close relationship between brickwork excavated at Mohenjo-Daro and Ur, though it must be said that much ancient brickwork is indistinguishable from any other, at least in black-and-white photographs. More significant and indeed dramatically exciting was a further four-page report on 25 October entitled 'A Second Tower of Babel: the House of the Mountain at Ur'. Two pages of the report were taken up by a very fine coloured reconstruction of the ziggurat drawn by F. G. Newton and William Walcot. Woolley reported that the work that season

> had for its main object the clearing of the ziggurat ... and for months a gang of about two hundred Arabs was busy carrying off the thousands of tons of broken brick and sand that concealed what was left of the ancient building. When we started, there was only a mound higher and steeper than the other mounds ... now there stands up four square a huge mass of brickwork which may claim to be the most imposing monument in the land.

Woolley reported to H. R. Hall (who had excavated at the site in 1919) at the British Museum on 3 February that

> We are now cursing you! For three weeks I have been carting away your dump in front of the south-east face of the ziggurat ... incidentally it is a great improvement to the landscape to have the ziggurat ... not masked by that mound of rubbish: in the course of the work we have found two excellent 'antikas' – good pickaxes buried by your workmen which we are now using ourselves!

In case Ur should slip from the public mind before the end of the third season, 1924–5, Woolley made sure he kept sending reports and photographs to London. He was well aware of the value of publicity. For a general article on 'Memorable Events' (*Illustrated London News*, 24 January 1925) he submitted a photograph of the newly excavated 'Hall of Justice' found at the south-east side of the ziggurat, and three weeks later he dispatched another article from Ur about the current season's progress. 'The two months ... during which we have been at work at Ur have yielded much of interest.' He went on to describe the excavation of the boundaries of the great ziggurat terrace, which was formed by a heavy wall of crude brick, steeply sloped and relieved by shallow buttresses. In that wall face they found at regular intervals nail-shaped clay cones stuck into the joints of the brickwork: these bore the name of the first king of the Third Dynasty of Ur, Ur-Nammu. On top of the terrace they could trace a sequence of shrines of the Moon God erected by various kings. Nebuchadnezzar and his later successor Nabonidus had surrounded the whole complex with a quadrangle of double walls, enclosing a broad courtyard, and Woolley describes a fortress building with towers at each corner. In the walls they found foundation cones of Warad-Sin (1824–1823 BC). He also described excavations to the south-east of the ziggurat. An 'unpromising looking mound' concealed one of Ur's most important constructions, a gate-tower leading to the ziggurat terrace: this was the 'Hall of Justice' called E-dub-lal-makh, originally founded by Amar-Sin. This article was well-illustrated with views of the site, and some objects, including the foundation cones of Warad-Sin, terracotta figurines, a beautiful shell-plaque engraved with two male figures – wearing ceremonial robes and crowns, with long locks of hair hanging over their left shoulders, holding hands and stepping forward – and the fragments of an ivory casket in the Egyptian style.

On 18 April, there was more: 'A Great Work of Sumerian Art'. 'This month [March 1925] we have found strewn over the floor of the courtyard [in front of E-dub-lal-makh] ... fragments of ... one of the greatest and most splendid works of art in stone that Mesopotamia has yet produced.' It was indeed a magnificent colossal limestone slab, when complete a little short of 2 m wide and 5 m high, depicting Ur-Nammu and his achievements as architect of the Temple of the Moon

God and as pastoral king of the sacred land of Sumer, as builder of canals and irrigation trenches, and taking part in an animal sacrifice. It was much broken and damaged but it still ranked as one of the finest works of Sumerian art. In August 1925 the stela was in London at the British Museum where it could be viewed by the public, and Woolley himself was now referred to as 'the distinguished archaeologist'.

Woolley could now look back on the first three seasons at Ur and sum up what had been achieved: 'we have covered between a third and a half of the area of the walled enclosure which was the *temenos* ... and our plans ... for the various periods between the sixteenth century BC and the sixth ... are fairly complete ... so that we can already form a tolerably coherent and truthful picture'.

The season had been much enlivened by the arrival of a new epigraphist, an American Jesuit called Leon Legrain, whose interests, apart from archaeology, were in cricket and claret. He spent much of his time in the excavation of E-dub-lal-makh, and even Woolley was impressed with his powers of application, writing to Dr Hall at the British Museum: 'so excellent, he's never tired of working over the inscribed material ... and he is a most charming companion ... I'm sorry I can't have him out every year'. There was a new general assistant called Linnell, who 'shapes well and works hard, and I hope to keep him on regularly: altogether it's a pleasant house-party'. Katharine Keeling was, however, not present and Woolley missed her. It was an unusually hard winter at Ur and the expedition house was cold and bleak. Everyone was saddened by the news of the death of F. G. Newton in February: 'a great loss in every way'.

Legrain was still part of the team when Woolley interviewed Max for the post of general assistant in the summer of 1925. Woolley also engaged a War veteran called Algy Whitburn, who had been recommended by the Royal Institute of British Architects, to replace Newton. And he invited Katharine Keeling to come out to Ur again as a volunteer assistant. Algy Whitburn was a delightful man with whom Max remained in touch throughout their lives. Some ten years older than Max, he had been very badly injured during the war, and afterwards walked with a severe limp. He spent two years in hospital after which he resumed his career as an architect at a firm in London. The senior partner was a friend of Woolley, and he suggested Algy

Whitburn might go to Ur, as he was a single man. He had a great sense of humour and was a fount of amusing Cockney stories. He wrote an evocative account of Ur about which he lectured in England in later years, describing how the city in its glory, set in green fields dotted with date-palms, was now but a giant molehill rising above the level of the melancholy desert guarded at its northern end by the great ziggurat which had defied both man and nature.

Max described in his *Memoirs* the excitement of that journey into the unknown that October, and in an article in the journal *Iraq* published in 1960 in memory of Leonard Woolley he revealed that Woolley had obtained for him a free passage as a seaman on an oil tanker sailing from London to Port Said, impressing upon him the constant need for strict economy. Max and Algy Whitburn became good friends travelling overland from Beirut; they were met at Ur Junction, the station some 3 km west of the site of Ur, by the expedition motor car, an original model T Ford, and swept off to the expedition house, their luggage grabbed by the men who rushed off from the station across the desert with it balanced on their heads. For the time being, it was just the three of them in the expedition house, which Max described at some length: entry through a walled courtyard with the Antiquities Room and the Architect's Office to each side, the main living room, the bedrooms and one bathroom – later two so that Katharine could have a private one of her own. (Agatha Christie, who was to visit the site for the first time in November 1928, described the house in her novel *Murder in Mesopotamia*. When it came to the bathrooms, Nurse Leatheran, who was based on Agatha herself, was scornful: 'when you've got used to taps and proper plumbing, it seems strange to call a couple of mud-rooms with a tin hip-bath in each of them, and muddy water brought in kerosene tins, *bathrooms!*'). The roof of the house was mud-plastered but not always watertight, the walls were also mud-plastered, and the floor was of burnt bricks, some of them inscribed. There were few luxuries, but Mallowan described the effect as pleasing, though austere. Woolley soon made it clear that they were there to work and not to have fun. On one occasion Max and Algy Whitburn settled down to a game of cards after dinner, and were curtly told by Woolley that if they did not have the energy for work they had better go to bed. Woolley was fundamentally kind and helpful; he was rather a suave man with a certain charm of manner, not often wasted on younger colleagues. One of them, Richard Barnett, described him in an unpublished memoir as having 'rather a feline confiding manner', self-contained and self-sufficient. At Ur, he drove himself hard, setting a punishing example: up before dawn and seldom in bed before three in the morning.

Certainly no time was wasted that first morning after their late arrival: everyone was expected to be on the mound half an hour after sunrise. Max was of course a complete novice and had been told by Woolley that he would teach him archaeology as they went along. Evidently the two newcomers had made a reasonably good impression. Woolley reported to Hall on 26 October that 'My two young men are shaping well & are quite pleasant fellows & hard-working'. But he was 'thankful not to have Linnell again!'. By that date the expedition team had built a new wing on to the house and had done twelve days' digging in spite of heavy rains. Woolley had taken on 220 men and 'it's a strenuous life'. Legrain had arrived the previous day and it was not long before the three assistants were on easy terms, united no doubt by fear of Katharine, who arrived shortly afterwards. She so disliked Legrain's rather crude conversation that she made sure he did not return the following season.

As the most junior member of the team it fell to Max to perform the more menial tasks of the expedition. His priority was to learn some Arabic: otherwise he could not communicate at all with the workforce which numbered anything between 200 and 250 men. To this end, he bought a grammar book by a well-known Dutch missionary, and, with this for reference and plenty of vernacular practice every day, he soon became sufficiently fluent to make himself understood. This was important when it came to pay day as Max had to interrogate each of the workers as to how many days they had worked and what small finds they had made. It was also quite important for his role as medical adviser, for which he was also completely untrained but, with frequent applications of aspirin and bandages, rather successful. Showing visitors round the site was another of his duties.

One of these visitors was Gertrude Bell, whom Max described as a 'tigress' when she came to supervise the division of the spoils of a season's digging at Ur for her own Museum in Baghdad. At the end of their first season in the spring of 1926, he and Algy Whitburn went to visit her in Baghdad to pay their respects. It was the last time he was to see her; that July she died of an overdose of sleeping pills, whether accidentally taken or deliberately no one knew. Max was a great admirer of her stamina, energy and learning, and of her creation of the Antiquities Museum in Baghdad, and later on he was to be personally grateful to her for the foundation of the British School of Archaeology in Iraq, in which he was to play so great a part.

Following Woolley's instructions, Max began keeping field notes, which he wrote in pencil in a small, neat hand. The first few entries look rather unsure, smudged as they are with much rubbing out of the finer detail and the measurements. But pretty soon the book comes to look much more professional, with Max seeming more like an archaeologist. By February 1926, he was recording confidently '17.55 m Virgin soil Alluvial greenish sand, not salt, stratified with fine layers of dry sand at irregular intervals'. He was also describing objects and attempting to draw them more precisely, though drawing was never his best skill. A 'Section Through the Mound Looking NW' showed that he was beginning to grasp the bigger picture. Woolley had assigned to him the south-west face of the ziggurat for his first project. At the end of his field notes, Max recorded in detail the contents of boxes (e.g. Box 4 contained 4 skulls in 4 separate compartments) with notes on where found, at what level, plus notes on what laboratory techniques had been used or would be needed, as well as cleaning methods and best ways of photographing the objects. This was invaluable information when the objects arrived at the British Museum in the early summer as he would have to unpack them and write the catalogue entries for them, and that needed to be precise.

That fourth season Woolley was concentrating on the building in which some of the fragments of the great stela of Ur-Nammu had been discovered the previous year. These were two temples dedicated to the Moon Goddess, Ningal. One to the north-west of the so-called fortress had suffered greatly, but the other, to the south-east, was better preserved. It had a central brick-paved courtyard in which there had once stood a stela commemorating the victories of the great Babylonian law-giving king Hammurabi (1792–1750 BC). It also had a kitchen which, according to Woolley, 'needed no imagination to see ...

still in use with the Sumerian cooks busy at the well and the stoves'. The kitchen court had a water well, and a bitumen-proofed tank for storing water, a double fireplace, with a circular hearth big enough to take a large cauldron, and a long trough on which pots could be set over the flames. Two chambers leading off the courtyard contained evidence for a large bread-oven, and a double cooking range. Objects found that season included a fine limestone plaque showing scenes of sacrifice in two registers, the top one with a libation to the Moon God being poured, and the lower a libation being poured over the door to a shrine. There was also a rather damaged lunar disk of white alabaster showing another libation scene and an inscription on the back stating that it was presented to the temple of Ningal by the priestess, the daughter of Sargon of Akkad. A white shell plaque showing a plunging bull among tall marsh plants Woolley dated as far back as 3300 BC. There was a throne support consisting of two rather fat rams carved in limestone of the same period, and the first female statue found at Ur, that of a goddess Woolley called Bau. 'A solid and a solemn figure', he wrote, 'she sits upon a throne which is the river, supported by her sacred geese. She wears an elaborately flounced and pleated dress, and her hair is done in the very unbecoming chignon affected by goddesses; her nose ... is missing.'

The most important find was a small head of a goddess, probably Ningal, which Woolley described as 'Sumerian Art of the Third Dynasty of Ur at Its Best': 'this head, instinct with life, the tender modelling of the flesh thrown into relief by the dignified convention of the hair, one feels that the Sumerian at his best could have stood before the sculptors even of Greece and not been utterly ashamed'. The caption to the photograph read 'Hair-waving in 2250 BC'.

It is hard to resist the picture of Katharine Keeling leaning over Woolley's shoulder as he wrote these two rather uncharacteristic descriptions, making as they do personal comments of taste on such feminine matters as hairstyles and dress. Katharine had arrived in the early spring of 1926, and her presence in the excavation house immediately changed the easy camaraderie between the young men. Max described her effect on them in his *Memoirs*; he said that living in the same house with her was rather like walking on a tightrope. She could be bewitching company, well-read, fascinating and fascinated with everything going on, but could turn in a moment to silence, sulky sensitivity and making everyone feel thoroughly awkward and guilty for upsetting her. Agatha's 1936 novel *Murder in Mesopotamia*, based on her memories of Ur, gives a much unkinder character sketch of Katharine as Mrs Leidner, the archaeologist's frail wife, who is brutally murdered early on in the book. Agatha made few allowances for Katharine: her unsettled childhood, how difficult it must have been being German in England at that time, the tragic outcome of her first marriage, or indeed her fragile health (she suffered from agonizing headaches). Until Agatha came to Ur, Max was rather under Katharine's spell, and quite prepared to massage her aching head and apply to her forehead the leeches that were supposed to help her. He also admired her fund-raising talents and her skill as an artist. She once made a bronze head of Hamoudi that was much admired.

Katharine's presence at Ur was now causing enough talk for Dr Byron Gordon from the University Museum of Pennsylvania to write to Woolley on the inadvisability of having volunteer assistants at all, male or female. That August Woolley was forced to address the problem. He told Gordon that Katharine's unpaid contribution was invaluable as she had drawn the finds for the catalogue. His assistant, Max Mallowan, had written the catalogue entries, but he could not draw. If Mrs Keeling was not able to come back for the following season, he would be forced to make Mallowan take drawing lessons, which even Mrs Mallowan, 'who takes a keen interest in her son's work', thought would be hopeless. And in any event, Mrs Keeling also showed round visitors, kept the house decent and comfortable and had a 'good moral effect on the younger fellows in the camp and keeps them up to standard'. If he had not considered it before, Woolley must now have started thinking about marriage so as to make Katharine's presence at Ur perfectly proper.

Also that summer, the summer of the General Strike, Woolley gave six talks on the wireless and embarked on a speaking tour about 'Abraham's City'. Max worked at the British Museum, cataloguing the finds they had brought back from his first season. At the end of October he travelled out to Beirut, where he met the new epigraphist, Father Burrows, and Woolley, before travelling on alone in advance of them to Ur.

Max kept a closely written account of his second season at Ur, starting on 2 October 1926 in Oxford, where he had a last afternoon of golf and lunch with his parents, and sighed outside St Hilda's over Maimie, 'the new love that has come into my life'. The following day he left from Victoria on the first leg of his journey to Paris, in a philosophical mood: 'thought of future success and resolve to do my best under conditions not always easy ... there is work to be achieved and achievement is buoyed up by love'. Max stayed in Paris with his grandmother and his uncle Lucien at 16 avenue de Villars, but did not sleep well. He spent the next day making his travelling arrangements and buying presents for Hamoudi, Yahia, Ibrahim and Isa, 'sundry decorative articles'. He had a long walk in the Bois before taking the night sleeper to Berne.

The following day in Berne was a sad one for Max, for it was to be the last time he was to see his friend Esme Howard. He discovered on his arrival that Esme had been moved to a clinic at Neuchâtel so he climbed on a train and was met at the station by Sir Esme's majordomo Furavente, who warned Max of the change in his friend, but

> I was not prepared for the shock I received on seeing him. Lady Isabella looked tired and worn with watching but full of the indomitable courage of his family ... I felt my heart ready to burst when I saw poor Esme, my dearest friend lying on his side on the bed, limp and reft of all his former strength, reduced utterly to a human skeleton. I had not thought it possible that life should continue in a frame so shattered. We spoke in low tones to one another, Esme tells me dear fellow that when he received my telegram he had wept for joy and I told him of my delight at seeing him again if only for a few hours. We soon reached the point which I fancy touched us both most dearly. 'You will take communion Max', he said, 'won't you? I have suffered for you so' and he wept for weakness. I was filled with a sad tenderness and promised faithfully that I would commune for him as soon as I reached Beirut. I could see at once that I had given him a great joy, he took me by the hand and I saw that a cloud had been lifted from him. Then he said, 'And you are convinced, aren't you'. I answered, 'Yes', for how had I the heart

to answer no, there was nothing that I could have refused him at that moment. But afterwards when I considered my resolve I began to feel my conviction was sincere.

Max went for a walk with Sir Esme in the woods, and at teatime returned to Esme's room and they talked some more, Esme asking Max to bring him coins and antiquities from Mesopotamia.

He told me that now I was to pray for him at Beirut he felt his cure was sure ... I felt there was much to say but could not say it but here was between us that intense mental harmony that made expression needless. At 6.30 p.m. it was time to go ... As I drove down to Neuchâtel I have rarely felt so utterly miserable ... and I prayed frequently for better things for Esme.

Deeply sad, Max travelled on to Venice and found a room in a pension near St Mark's Square. It was impossible not to be overwhelmed with the beauty of it. 'I resolved ... that if ever I am so fortunate I shall spend my honeymoon here! Entered a church in the afternoon and prayed for Esme the first occasion on which I can remember entering a church with the deliberate intention of praying, of my own accord.'

From Venice he had a race to get to Trieste, having missed the train he intended to take by oversleeping, so exhausted was he by the emotions of the past two days. He was the last passenger aboard the boat, and the gangway was pulled up immediately afterwards. He shuddered to think of what would have happened had he missed the boat 'for I had only £15 left in my pocket and my place had been booked on the desert convoy of October 20th to travel over to Baghdad with Woolley, Father Burrows and Mrs K.' Max's fellow passengers were J. W. Crowfoot ('a pompous old fool from the Sudan, a retired civil servant on his way to ask for a post at the British School of Archaeology in Jerusalem, a good classical scholar who declares himself a great friend of Woolley' – he did in fact become Director of the School); General Daily and his wife ('typical of the Englishwoman connected with colonies which is not saying much', travelling to take up a military post in Baghdad); and a coffee-grower from Guatemala whom Max dismissed at first as 'a thorough Philistine and hopelessly uncultured' but then as the voyage wore on found himself rather liking. The older man took him under his wing one evening to enquire about his sex life, professing himself 'astonished ... that I had never consorted with a woman'. Shortly after this conversation, after Max had returned from a day ashore at Haifa (becoming badly sunburnt as he climbed Mount Carmel without his hat), they had another conversation about sex, the Guatemalan informing Max that 'he had resolved to adopt the same way of life at all events for a few months, or failing that he might after all return to marry the Swiss maiden whom he had led astray. I told him if he did so, to send me a postcard.'

On 15 October he reached Beirut and called on Father Burrows, who had arrived that day from Crete. 'Told him I wanted to take first communion if possible by 17th. Had a long talk on R. Catholicism and found him a delightful person.' After more talks with Burrows, Max attended Mass sitting in a little side chapel in the Jesuit College in Beirut that Sunday. 'Prayed fervently for Esme and felt happier for his sake.' On 20 October, he made his first communion and was 'truly thankful for the light that has come upon me. Had a sumptuous breakfast with Father Burrows in the College afterwards and felt a sense of peace and happiness, especially for the sake of my dear Esme and mother ... Afterwards read in the library an exceedingly interesting article by De Morgan on the pottery from Susa.'

The following day, Woolley and Katharine arrived 'looking very tired' and shortly after lunch they set off for Baghdad in a convoy of three Cadillacs. Woolley pointed out landmarks of archaeological interest and also a cave which he had used as a post office during the War. They arrived at Tripoli soon after 8 p.m., and had a 'quite a good dinner' in the station rest house where they also stayed the night, Max sharing a large room with Woolley and Burrows. On they went the next day, to Homs, Palmyra and Rutba, and finally arrived at the Maude Hotel in Baghdad, where they were given 'a hearty greeting'. Max was exhausted and he fell thankfully into bed only to find that he was sharing his room with two large hornets.

The next day Hamoudi appeared and was given his instructions. He was to set off for Ur that evening, and Max and Burrows the following day. 'Given many commissions by W. and various instructions repainting of the house etc. I shall have 600 parcels it seems.' Max went to

Ctesiphon, 'all the aesthetic pleasure without the intellectual exercise of disentangling a jumble of ruins', dined with friends of the Woolleys, where there was interesting conversation and lots to drink, and boarded the night train. It was slow, it was hot and he was pestered once more by hornets. It was a relief to smell the pure fresh air of the desert and to be back at the expedition house.

There was always much to do on the domestic front at the start of a new season, and this year Max had been instructed to enlarge the window in the cuneiform room and to distemper Woolley's study. About three hundred men then turned up, all wanting to be employed on the dig. This year there was the excitement of some old expedition boxes turning up from Nippur; they had once belonged to the 1896 expedition run by Hilprecht and they had been at Hillah in storage for the past thirty years. They seemed to contain a large number of 'weird books, but several valuable ones of Rawlinson and Layard'. For a spot of light relief, Max went outside and drew the Arabic alphabet in the sand for Hamoudi. Then he tried his hand at carpentry, making a cupboard for Woolley's clothes, with five shelves and a hinged door. The newly engaged expedition cook took to the bottle and on Woolley's orders was clapped into jail. Max went to Mass for the first time at Ur. He slept outside as much as possible as it was still so hot, though the early mornings were cold. The autumn rains began on 7 November; shortly afterwards the expedition house roof began to leak and Katharine became rattled because water was pouring into her room. The rains became heavier, and the leaks worsened. 'Woolley's bedroom was like a swimming bath and all Mrs K's dresses were soaked in slimy mud, on her eiderdown a pool of water ... poor W lost heart and was really depressed for on top of his troubles he has bad neuralgia. Mrs K very sporting and cheerful this time.' Max had tried to get to the top of the ziggurat and in places had sunk into earth up to the top of his gumboots. Fortunately the rain stopped about ten days later and the dig started to dry out remarkably quickly.

When it was too wet to work on the dig, Max occupied himself with 'Assyrian', learning cuneiform under the aegis of Burrows, and writing letters. His mother had been to see Esme and he wrote a long letter to her, and one to Maimie, enclosing some photographs. He also wrote a long letter to Esme, which he never read, having died nine days before it reached him, on 28 November in Hampstead. His mother broke the news to Max in a letter he read at Ur station when collecting the mail on 17 December. Max felt shocked but accepting. 'Never before had I believed so firmly in a life to come as I did when I knew that he had passed from this world. As I went back to Ur, I seemed to speak with his spirit on the desert wind ... I shall always keep Esme's letter which speaks of my entry into the Catholic church as a birthday gift ... Went to talk things over with Hamoudi, that tower of philosophy.' Max also told Burrows, who reminded him that suffering was all part of the experience of being a Catholic. For the next two days Max thought incessantly of Esme. He went to confession, and he prayed for him. He turned up on the dig late, and received a mild ticking off from Woolley. Luckily it was practically Christmas, which meant two days off. On 27 December, he was not up on the dig till 7 a.m. and was again reprimanded by Woolley, who said that 'getting up so late was not playing the game. I quite agreed.' It was time to put his intense grieving aside and get on with his work. From then on he was on the site at sunrise.

The work that season (1926–7) would have been enough to distract anyone. It was the start of a quite extraordinary two years which were to make headline news worldwide. The season started quietly enough, with Woolley deciding to leave the Temple of the Moon God and excavate a number of private houses which he knew existed below a great mound close to the *temenos* wall. In the upper levels of the mound, they came across many destroyed remains of houses dating to the time of Nebuchadnezzar and to the Kassite kings of Babylon (c. 1370–1155 BC). Excavating further to a depth of some 5–6 m, they discovered some much better-preserved domestic buildings, which they were able to date accurately because the contents contained some written tablets, and built into some walls were bricks stamped with royal names. The houses had been built about 2100 BC and had been in occupation until about 1900 BC when Ur had been sacked by the Babylonians. This proved, said Woolley, that these houses dated from the time of Abraham himself, and from their ruins he was able to obtain a clear picture of life in his time.

The picture that emerged was remarkably similar to present-day well-built houses in narrow streets in any modern town in Iraq. The façade was generally of mud-brick, with the interior walls burnt brick below and crude mud-brick above, but all the walls plastered and whitewashed. The houses tended to conform to one plan, the main feature being the central courtyard on to which opened all the downstairs rooms. There was evidence for staircases leading to an upper storey, the first flight being solidly built of brick, and the higher flight of wood resting on beams. Nothing was left of any upper storey, but it must have been a wooden gallery built around the central court-yard. A drawing was published of how just such a house would have looked.

In his second season, Max was considered by Woolley to have made sufficient progress to be given his own part of the site to excavate. This was the vast palace adjacent to the temple. Together he and Algy Whitburn plotted the area and drew a plan.

The season was as usual well covered by *The Illustrated London News*. On 19 February 1927, two excellent official RAF aerial pho-tographs were published showing a general view of the excavations. Woolley's orderly trenches were clearly visible, and the newly exposed ziggurat. On 12 March and 23 April, photographs of objects found were published. These included objects two thousand years older than Tutankhamun and 'rival even his treasure in artistic merit and in skill and craftsmanship'. This was a brave try: the tomb of the boy king was still, five years after its discovery, continuing to yield objects of exquisite workmanship with which there was really no comparison. But Woolley hoped that with a combination of Abraham, the Old Testament and sheer age, he could eclipse Egypt for a time.

As Woolley had discovered, the sacred *temenos* had been extended at its south-eastern end in the time of Nebuchadnezzar, and his new enclosure wall had penetrated a burial ground of a much earlier period. It was here that Woolley had made a deep trench. He came across a cemetery which was buried in the rubbish heaps of earlier generations. The graves themselves were rectangular in shape, built of stone rubble, sometimes vaulted and occasionally domed. Many had been robbed in antiquity. First they saw scattered in the soil beads and pendants of polished carnelian, lapis lazuli and gold, exquisitely worked, then nearby 'a silver baldric to which was attached a golden "vanity-case" enriched with filigree work and containing intact its tiny tweezers, spoon and stiletto, all of gold hung on a silver ring, and a dagger which was the season's crowning reward'.

The dagger was indeed superlatively fine, with its gold sheath with applied decoration and its hilt of a particularly dark blue lapis lazuli studded with gold beads. Its blade was made of burnished gold. 'It is in perfect condition and to see it gradually emerging from the heavy, clinging soil was well worth a year's labour. Produced at any date, it would have been a marvel of design and workmanship.' A fine photograph accompanied the description, but that November it merited a full-page coloured illustration entitled 'The Gem of the "Dagger Grave" at Ur'.

Not surprisingly, this was a season when there were many visitors to show around, not only the devout from home who had come to see first-hand the home of Abraham but also people from as far away at Japan and Chile, and even the King of the Belgians, who took breakfast with them all at the excavation house. Max was now considered sufficiently trustworthy to pack up antiquities at the end of the season, and to travel with them in an open carriage by train to Basra and to see them safely on to the ship for their long voyage to London. He would be there to receive them when they arrived, and his work in London consisted in unpacking them, cataloguing them and putting on display as many of them as possible. Max went home slowly via Egypt, where in March he and Algy Whitburn travelled to Luxor to see Tutankhamun's tomb. Max spent the summer holidays in France, at Dinard, where he did some gambling at the casino and went to several light operas. He also worked hard on his cuneiform and sketched some pots with Phoenician inscriptions in the Louvre. Meanwhile Woolley and Katharine had married and gone on honeymoon to Cairo, a peculiar choice in the circumstances. Max had personally delivered a wedding present from him and his mother to them in Dorset.

At the end of September Max left Dinard and set off again for Ur. He travelled to Paris and spent the day making travel arrangements at Cook's ('most irritating of all agents'). Once more he went to Venice which 'seemed on my second visit even more wonderful than the first'. He went by boat to Alexandria and from there took a quick trip to Cairo to see the objects from Tutankhamun's tomb. They had just been put on display: 'gloated over the marvels of Tutankhamun, the king's throne, unique of its kind, must always stand out for its combination of sumptuous wealth and sensuous beauty'. He saw the coffins, the gold mask, the jewellery, the two gold daggers 'of surpassing excellence', then dragged himself away to visit the predynastic room and make comparisons with alabaster vases from Saqqara of Dynasties I–IV, and black-and-red predynastic vases with pottery from Mesopotamia.

Max travelled on by train across the desert, crossing the Jordan river twice, and reached Damascus where he met the Woolleys. They travelled together to Baghdad in a Nairn six-wheeler which could take sixteen passengers. It was exhausting and extremely hot: 'Mrs W was feverish and almost delirious.' On arrival in Baghdad they met the faithful Hamoudi, ordered stores and visited the newly opened museum, 'which was surprisingly well laid-out, well lit, and the objects were reasonably well displayed'. They also called on the Minister of Education.

Max then travelled on alone to Ur. It was about 42°C in the carriage, but became a little cooler as the evening progressed. About half an hour before they arrived at Ur, Max caught sight of the great ziggurat in the moonlight. The entire staff of the expedition house had turned up at the station at 1 a.m. to meet him. The next few days were spent turning the house out, meeting the Woolleys, unpacking, painting the study and the dining room and dealing with one mishap: 'cleared up pottery room and in error threw away CLW's senna pods, a mistake fortunately not irreparable as we were able to go out and collect them from the mound upon which Isa had cast them in the desert!'. Then there was carpentry, at which he was becoming quite expert, shelves for Katharine, a frame for a mosquito net for Woolley, and pigeon holes and cupboards for the pottery room.

There unfortunately Max's diary of his Ur seasons ends. They were so busy that year that he had hardly time to make any entries. The last short one covers the three weeks from the beginning of the start of the digging, and is written in a hand which conveys the impression that the writer was much too exhausted to have any time to write up his diary.

Work began where it had stopped the previous spring, on the so-called Dagger Grave. New treasures emerged immediately, hundreds of gold beads and pendants. Then in December, at last the major find that Woolley anticipated so keenly: 'A Wonderful Discovery in a Royal Grave at Ur, Rivalling the Gold Mask of Tutankhamun, and Some 2000 Years Earlier', ran the headline. 'A great and unhoped-for discovery – that of a royal grave ... has just been announced.'

The most wonderful discovery was in fact the gold wig of Meskalamdug, illustrated in all its glory on the front cover of *The Illustrated London News* on 27 December 1927. Meskalamdug was the owner of the magnificent dagger found at the end of the preceding season. He was clearly royal and had been buried with some ceremony. 'In the coffin itself ... were placed the more personal possessions of the dead prince ... perhaps the most remarkable object that has yet been found in the land of Sumer a great wig of hammered and engraved gold. It is life-size, meant to be worn ... and was perhaps a helmet, perhaps a ceremonial headdress', wrote Woolley. The article had two further pages of illustrations showing other objects found in the tomb. The second most beautiful object was a gold fluted bowl with lapis-lazuli handles. There were also two drinking-bowls inscribed with the name of their owner.

Woolley's first report made no mention of the number of human sacrifices that attended these rich burials. He had certainly made the gruesome discovery, but for the time being he kept silent, no doubt wondering how best to deal with the matter. Meanwhile, he published two photographs showing how delicate techniques were needed if artefacts were to survive excavation: a gold-mounted wooden harp lying in the soil covered with muslin. Wax had been poured over its lapis-lazuli inlay to keep it in place.

That winter there were plenty of reports of what was happening at Ur. In January *The Illustrated London News* published photographs of objects found so far in the 1927–8 season (Woolley's sixth) in a grave equally rich as Meskalamdug's and 'even more remarkable'. There were gold vessels, a set of gold ceremonial tools and the harp that had been so carefully lifted at the end of the previous season, in all its delicate and fragile beauty. 'The upright of the harp is capped and bound with gold, and the twelve keys are of copper with gilt heads; the sounding-box is adorned with mosaics, and has in front a series of shell plaques engraved with mythological scenes.' There was also a sledge, even more ornate. Three golden lions' heads with engraved manes of

49

lapis lazuli and shell decorated the body of the chariot on each side. This tomb belonged to a royal personage called Abargi, identified by his cylinder seal.

In March that year, Woolley decided he had to reveal the dreadful secret of the human sacrifices: 'New Light on Art and Architecture in an Age of Human Sacrifice'. The two royal graves in the royal cemetery at Ur discovered so far were full of skeletons: the bodies of six soldiers killed in their positions, still guarding the tomb in death, the grooms at the head of the oxen that drew the four-wheeled wagons, the drivers across the seats of those wagons, another fifty bodies in a narrow space, men and women, servants and ladies-in-waiting. It was 'literally a shambles'. Not lingering over this, Woolley passed immediately on to his greatest find, the tomb of the consort of Abargi, Queen Pu-abi (known at first as Queen Shub-ad), found intact and full of treasure. The queen herself lay on a wooden bier, at either end of which crouched the body of an attendant. But what immediately caught the eyes of the excavators was everywhere the gleam of gold. The queen's headdress consisted of coil after coil of broad gold ribbon, and across her forehead lay a band of lapis and carnelian beads from which were suspended heavy gold rings. She also wore one wreath of big gold leaves (which Woolley described as mulberry leaves) and another with smaller gold leaves, like willow leaves, with large gold flowers in between, each one with petals inlaid with lapis lazuli and white shell. She wore enormous gold earrings and a golden hair ornament like an outsize comb. Her cloak was fastened on the left shoulder with three gold pins with lapis lazuli heads and by the fastening lay gold amulets. Beside the bier lay a second crown, as well as three gold bowls, rings, earrings and quantities of beads, a harp, a gaming-board: in all about 250 objects.

That June, the revelations at Ur were complete. 'Wholesale Human Sacrifice at Ur – Unrecorded Barbarities Practised at Royal Burials' was the title to an article which was illustrated with a double-page reconstruction by A. Forestier of the scene in the shaft of Abargi's grave 'just before the sacrifice took place, based upon the actual plan of the grave, with the exact position of every body marked'. The artist had taken his view from the corner of the rectangular pit. Following on, the next page was wholly devoted to a drawing of the same scene after slaughter, 'the grisly sequel'. Then came two full-page coloured illustrations of a golden bull's head with hair and beard of lapis lazuli, part of the decoration of the harp and the famous so-called Royal Standard of Ur, with its extraordinary inlay work in shell, lapis lazuli and pink limestone. It was, as Woolley said, 'unparalleled as a work of art and as an historic document invaluable'.

The gradual excavation of the Royal Tombs (some two thousand graves in all) involved heavy physical labour. The technique of plotting them, recording the evidence in a long cross-section through one end of the cemetery and disentangling the complex stratification all called for a high level of ingenuity, imagination and knowledge. In the late 1920s a prismatic compass was used in conjunction with frequent cross-checks and levels by using poles set up on fixed bases in the cemetery corners. The careful analysis of these readings helped to determine the chronological sequence. (Some dates had later to be adjusted by comparison with readings from other excavations.)

On 23 June, the British Museum put the Royal Standard and the other latest objects from Ur on display. The wonderful headdress of Pu-abi was displayed on a head made by Katharine. She skilfully modelled the features in wax over the cast of a nearly contemporary skull found elsewhere in the grave and it made a compelling image, especially after a wig of glossy black hair was placed over it and the massive gold headdress attached. It was photographed and used as the cover for *The Illustrated London News* on 20 June. On 11 August, it was published again in colour, the work of Mrs Woolley, 'the wife of the famous archaeologist', a description which no doubt gave them both much pleasure. Recognition had been slow in coming but now the man and the place were linked: he was indeed Woolley of Ur.

CHAPTER THREE

The Lure of the Past
Came Up to Grab Me

Woolley's seventh season (and Max's fourth), 1928–9, saw the culmination of the glorious discoveries from the royal cemetery. It was almost too much for Woolley, as he reported to Hall on 26 December: 'We are doing marvellously well: I'm sick to death of getting out gold head-dresses.' On 26 January 1929, Woolley sent his first report of the season to *The Illustrated London News*, 'Sumerian Art and Human Sacrifice'. There seemed to be no end to the gruesome discoveries. In a so-called 'Death Pit', about 8 m square, they found the remains of no fewer than 74 people, mainly women, 'victims in the wholesale sacrifice which celebrated the funeral of the king'. The article was illustrated by a drawing showing the exact position of the skeletons.

The occupants of this tomb had been even more richly adorned than the women of Pu-abi's, so that the ground was thickly covered with gold ribbons, gold leaves from their wreaths, beads of gold, lapis lazuli and carnelian and the inlaid flowers of the tall hair-combs. Woolley could only speculate at what the sight must have been when all the glitter lay not on brown earth and among crumbling bones but upon living bodies lying on white and red draperies in all their riches.

There were also some magnificent objects in the Death Pit: four harps piled together, and in another corner two statues of rams, 'perhaps the most remarkable things that our work at Ur has yet produced'. Of the four harps, one in particular was outstanding. Its sounding-box was decorated with inlay, the uprights covered with mosaic and gold, and its top beam with silver. From its front projected a massive golden bull's head. Below the head were shell plaques engraved with mythological scenes, the engraved lines picked out in red and black.

The rams are one of the most familiar images from Mesopotamia. They were made of gold, lapis lazuli and white shell over a wooden core. The core had decayed over the millennia and the bodies of the rams had been crushed by the weight of the soil over them so that before their full splendour could be seen they had to be carefully restored. The rams stood upon their hind legs, and their forelegs were caught in a thicket of golden stems and flowers, through which peered the ram's head. The eyes, horns and shoulder-locks were of bright blue lapis lazuli, the head and legs were of gold and the fleece made from shell, each lock carved separately and inlaid. The bellies were of silver. Woolley showed these treasures as he had found them, lying in the earth. Not until late summer was he able to publish coloured photographs of the restored harp and one of the rams, looking almost new and to be seen on display in the British Museum.

At an early stage during these exciting discoveries at Ur, Woolley's now quite experienced assistant had succumbed to appendicitis, and, after an operation, went home to his mother in England to recuperate. Not only did Max miss most of the season, but also he missed the visit of the celebrated crime novelist Agatha Christie, which took place in November 1928.

Agatha related in her autobiography (published in 1977 but mostly written much earlier) how it was that she found herself in Baghdad that winter. Her first marriage had ended that April in a painful divorce, her daughter Rosalind was away at boarding school in Bexhill and she herself badly wanted to get away from everything on her own for a short time, to recover from the battering to her self-esteem and to try to find some peace of mind in the sunshine. She had decided on the West Indies, and had even booked her tickets. Two days before she was due to leave, she went to a dinner party and met a young naval officer and his wife who had just come back from a posting to Baghdad, and the conversation was all about the place. Agatha had been keeping up with all Woolley's 'marvellous finds' at Ur and 'had always been faintly attracted to archaeology, though knowing nothing about it'. When she discovered that the only way to go to Baghdad was by train ('Trains have always been one of my favourite things'), and not just any old train but the fabled Orient Express, she felt Fate had taken firm control of her future life. She cancelled her tickets for the West Indies and booked to go to Baghdad instead.

Agatha was then thirty-nine (she was born in 1890) and the author of several successful crime novels, the best known of which were *The Mysterious Affair at Styles*, *The Secret Adversary* and *The Secret of Chimneys*. Hercule Poirot, her famous Belgian detective with the improbable moustache, had already made his appearance in four of her books, and she was currently working on *The Seven Dials Mystery*. She was tall and fair, and rather large, with a reserved manner which was the result of shyness rather than unfriendliness. But she was still attractive enough to be romantically propositioned aboard the Orient Express on her journey to Baghdad, and in Istanbul, where she was taken sightseeing by another admirer

Once in Baghdad, she found to her dismay that she had been absorbed at once into the British expatriate community. She felt she could play tennis and attend tea parties just as well at home, so, in a bid to escape, expressed an immediate desire to go to Ur. Arrangements were made with the Woolleys, who treated her with great kindness, and went to some trouble to make her feel welcome. Agatha discovered later that this was because Katharine had read and very much admired her book *The Murder of Roger Ackroyd* and had made everyone in the expedition house read it too.

Leonard Woolley himself showed Agatha round the site, as did Father Burrows, the Jesuit priest and epigraphist who had replaced Leon Legrain that season. Although the two women were so very different, and Katharine was frequently to irritate Agatha beyond belief, Agatha became very fond of Katherine and described her as 'one of my greatest friends'. They remained in regular contact until Katharine's death and, if Katharine realized that she was later on the inspiration for the nervous Mrs Leidner in *Murder in Mesopotamia*, she did not bear a grudge.

Agatha, as she said,

fell in love with Ur, with its beauty in the evenings, the ziggurat standing up, faintly shadowed, and that wide sea of sand with its lovely pale colours of apricot, rose, blue and mauve, changing every minute. I enjoyed the workmen, the foremen, the little basket-boys, the pick-men – the whole technique and life. The lure of the past came up to grab me. To see a dagger slowly appearing, with its gold glint, through the sand was romantic. The carefulness of lifting pots and objects from the soil filled me with a longing to be an archaeologist myself.

Somehow in Mesopotamia, Agatha did find peace: 'I did feel from that moment onwards a great sensation of comfort and truer knowledge of serenity than I had ever obtained before.'

The Woolleys had made it clear that they would very much welcome another visit the following year, and had even suggested that they might all travel part of the way home together. Agatha readily agreed to the plan before journeying home in time for the Christmas holidays with Rosalind.

In Max's absence someone else must have taken on the task of packing up the antiquities and arranging for the shipment of their share of the spoils of the season. The Woolleys probably oversaw some of it before travelling home. In May 1929, they stayed for a time with Agatha at her house in Chelsea, 22 Cresswell Place. Agatha had bought the mews house on her return from Baghdad at the end of 1928 and she was highly delighted with it, as it was like a country cottage in the middle of London. Indeed, when she bought it, it still had its original stables on the ground floor, with loose boxes and mangers for its first equine inhabitants. With the help of sympathetic builders, it had been transformed into a fashionable pied-à-terre for a celebrated lady crime novelist, straight out of one of her own novels, complete with an all-green bathroom with a frieze of dancing dolphins.

Leonard Woolley was an easy guest; he spent much of his time at the British Museum and writing in his room. Katharine needed more of her hostess's attention and Agatha made the most of her opportunity to observe Katharine's mercurial nature. At the end of their visit, Woolley himself showed Agatha round the Ur exhibition at the British Museum where no doubt she saw the recently restored ram in his thicket. She did not apparently meet Woolley's assistant, hard at work in the British Museum laboratories (which one lunchtime he inadvertently set on fire after an object from which he was cleaning the paraffin wax spontaneously burst into flames because of the hot sunshine coming through the glass roof. Max returned just in time to extinguish the flames). Both Woolleys firmly reiterated their invitation that she should join them at Ur at the very end of the 1929–30 season, see the latest finds and then travel back home with them, through Syria and Greece, with a special trip to Delphi, which Agatha had always wanted to see.

Apart from working at the British Museum, Max was writing his first proper excavation report, to be published in the *National Geographic Magazine* the following January (1930). It runs to 35 pages and was accompanied by 44 photographs and one map, covering all aspects of the work till the end of the 1929 season, tactfully stressing that this was a dual American–British expedition and that it was their joint and enlightened efforts that had led to such a successful outcome under the 'brilliant direction' of Leonard Woolley. Woolley himself had written a preliminary report on Ur for the magazine published in August 1928, and it was doubtless at his suggestion that Max had written his own account. The writing bears many of the hallmarks of Woolley's own style, starting in a theatrical way which invites the reader to imagine that he or she is standing on abandoned dust heaps with the only living creatures jackals, prowling the ruins in search of food when, suddenly, at dusk

> at the still hour when the East begins to revive after the exhaustion of a boiling day ... instead of dry sand and the refuse of bricks and pots, the desert transforms itself into a network of canals. We find ourselves at the quayside ... In the dimness of evening the black forms of great barges, moored to the quays by stout creaking hawsers ... On the banks we perceive the figures of burly bargemen ... clothed in sheepskin skirts ... we hear oaths uttered in a broad-sounding, uncouth tongue. It is Sumerian ...

One of Woolley's talents or weaknesses, depending on the point of view of his audience, was his ability to bring history to a sort of recognizable modern life, or to over-simplify the facts for the sake of coherence. Although Woolley's influence here is apparent, Max's article was very readable, clear and, with its many picturesque photographs of local scenes (Arab sheikhs on horseback in the desert, waterwheels on the Tigris, Kurdish ferrymen and so on), very likely to appeal to readers of the *National Geographic Magazine*. Doubtless it was a useful exercise for the author, who learnt early on in his career that archaeologists must keep proper records: for themselves, for their academic colleagues and for a wider general public, on whose support they depend.

In the autumn the Woolleys went back to Ur. It was Woolley's eighth season and Max's fifth and the one in which they dug to the lowest level yet at the site. The excavations reached a depth of 18 m, thus taking them back to remote antiquity, or, as Woolley put it 'beyond calculable dates'. They found a fresh series of graves which illustrated for Woolley the very beginning of history: shallow trenches beneath a clearly defined stratification of changing types of bricks and pottery. They went down to virgin soil, 'the clay in which the reeds of the marsh first found root'. The graves must have belonged to the first people who occupied Ur, about 4500–4000 BC.

The bodies lay on their backs rigidly extended with their hands crossed over the pelvis. The bottoms of the grave trenches were paved with large fragments of pottery which proved to be Ubaid ware, buff-coloured clay often turning green when fired, and decorated with a design in dark brown or black paint, thin-walled and inclined to be brittle. Among the objects found were strange, rather disturbing bird-headed clay figurines of women with abnormally broad shoulders bearing tattoo marks, but with narrow hips and pronounced pubic triangles. Some had their arms bent with their hands resting on their waists and some held a baby to their breasts. Some were green clay with black markings and others white clay with wigs of black bitumen and blobs of red paint on the cheeks. They clearly had some religious significance, and Woolley described them as 'the earliest sculptures of Mesopotamia'. They were shown on the cover of *The Illustrated London News* on 1 March 1930.

Agatha probably saw the objects themselves when she travelled out to Baghdad that March, arriving at Ur in the middle of a violent sand-storm which lasted five miserable days. There were some familiar faces apart from Leonard and Katharine's – Algy Whitburn and Father

Burrows – but one new one, that of Max Mallowan. 'He was a thin, dark, young man, and very quiet – he seldom spoke, but was perceptive to everything that was required of him.' He for his part found her 'immediately a most agreeable person'.

In her imperious way, Katharine decreed that Max must look after Agatha, something the latter felt was a terrible imposition on a young man 'who was probably yearning for freedom and for some fun in Baghdad' after the hard work of the season. But Katharine's word was law. As Algy Whitburn said to Agatha, 'if Katharine has made up her mind, then that's settled, you see'. As indeed it was. But not only was Max ready to obey Katharine's instructions, he was actually only too happy to do so.

Agatha was thirty-nine, Max not yet twenty-six. She was well established in her profession, he had yet to prove himself. But, despite the obvious disparities, they had much in common, not least of which was an ability to extract fun out of even the most unlikely circumstances. Put to the test, they both emerged with unimpaired good humour and to Max, whose experience with women so far had been with his mother and with Katharine Woolley, Agatha's refusal to fuss and ability to take things as they came was a revelation. He had never met a woman like her before.

It suited the Woolleys to have Agatha taken round the nearby sites, so they could pack up at Ur without distractions, so an interesting itinerary was planned. Agatha embarked on this with some trepidation, rather in awe of the self-possessed young archaeologist at her side. They went to Nippur, to Nejef and Kerbala.

At Nippur, Max set a gruelling pace. Agatha stumbled about the excavations becoming more and more enamoured of archaeology (and her relentless and knowledgeable guide) as the visit progressed. A terrible evening with an English couple, the Ditchburns (he was the political officer at Diwaniyah and loathed all archaeologists), united them still further as the only sane people in a world of eccentrics. The next day they left at 5 a.m. to visit Nejef and Kerbala and spent a night in a police station in adjoining cells. There their friendship crossed a new boundary.

In the days of my Victorian upbringing I should have thought it most strange that I should awaken a young man whom I hardly knew and ask him to be kind enough to escort me to the lavatory … I woke Max, he summoned a policeman, the policeman fetched a lantern, and we three tramped along long corridors and finally arrived at a remarkably evil-smelling room containing a hole in the floor. Max and the policeman waited politely outside the door to light me back to my couch.

After another early start the next morning, Max and Agatha set off for the Arab city of Ukhaidir, where there was a fine Crusader castle. All the way there they sang songs, nursery rhymes and any others they both knew. They walked round the turreted top of the castle gazing down at the dizzy drop, Agatha clutching on to Max for safety. After lunch they started back to Baghdad, and in the boiling hot afternoon came upon a desert lake, clear and sparkling. Agatha had always loved bathing and Max readily agreed to a stop. It was then that Agatha realized that she did not have her bathing-dress. 'Haven't you got anything that would – well – *do*?' asked Max delicately. Agatha stripped modestly to her pink silk vest and put on an extra pair of knickers and, shapely in the sunshine, took to the water, where Max in shorts and vest joined her. 'It was heaven – the world seemed perfect', wrote Agatha.

Max's ever-growing admiration for his companion reached new heights when they discovered that, during their bathe, their car had sunk into the sand and was quite impossible to move. Unperturbed by this and by the information that it might take as long as a week for anyone to come by and rescue them, Agatha left Max and the driver to do what they could, and went calmly to sleep in the shade. How unlike his mother, how impossible to imagine Katharine behaving like that! It was at that moment that the happy experiences of the past three days crystallized into certainty. Agatha was wonderful; she was unique.

They were fortunately rescued later that afternoon and continued their journey to Baghdad, stopping at likely tells (the settlement mounds that suddenly loom out of the flat plains of Mesopotamia) and picking up stray pieces of pottery. The Woolleys were already at the Maude Hotel when they arrived and not best pleased with them, though Katharine confined her displeasure to Max. She was probably aware of the new relationship between her two protégés, and this could have annoyed her still further, for several reasons.

The four of them set off for Mosul two days later, on the first stage of their journey home. After Mosul, they travelled slowly northwards across country, stopping at various sites along the Euphrates. Branching off, they stayed first at Tell Afar then with an Arab sheikh whom Woolley knew. They were given an extremely warm welcome and a massive dinner, and then shown to their night's accommodation. This consisted of two tumble-down rooms in a mud-brick house whose roof was leaking copiously on to three of the four iron bedsteads. Katharine naturally chose the one dry bed, which left Max and Agatha to share the other room and to become soaking wet during an uncomfortable night. So it was a great relief to reach Aleppo, where they stayed at Baron's Hotel (T. E. Lawrence's 'beautiful hotel'), famous throughout the Middle East for the luxury of its European-style plumbing and its modern cocktail bar. After the privations of the previous days, Agatha had one thing on her mind: to put the plumbing to the test and sink into a long, hot bath. Unfortunately Katharine had exactly the same idea. Agatha found a bathroom and started grappling with the taps to no avail. She summoned Max to help. He took over and said he would call her when her bath was ready. She went back to her room and waited, and waited. Eventually she emerged into the corridor in her dressing-gown clutching her sponge-bag and went back to the bathroom. The door was locked. Max appeared. 'Where's my bath?' asked Agatha. Max looked straight at Agatha and told her firmly that Katharine wanted a hot bath and was having one. Agatha was outraged, though she said nothing. But she resolved to remove Max from Katharine as soon as possible. The incident still rankled nearly half a century later when Agatha wrote her autobiography.

The following day Katharine complained of a sickening headache and took to her room, irritably asking them all to leave her alone. Agatha took her at her word and she and Max went on a happy expedition to a crusader castle at Kalat Siman. It was blissful: the scenery, the hills covered with anemones, the flocks of sheep, the black goats dotted about, the picnic lunch, jokes, laughter and more singing. They returned to Aleppo to find Katharine in a rage. 'To think that you and Max *could* go off in that heartless way ... perhaps it's not so bad of *you* ... but Max – that Max who knows me so well, who knows that I have needed *anything* – could go off like that.' Katharine's hold over Max was terminally weakened and from then on Max gradually came to see Katharine in the light of Agatha's assessment of her character.

They travelled from Aleppo to Athens by boat, stopping off at various ports on the way. Max and Agatha went ashore as often as possible. On one particularly significant day on the beach at a place called Mersin, Max picked her an enormous bunch of golden marigolds, which she made into a chain and hung around her neck. This was a memory both of them always cherished. When they arrived in Athens they had fallen into the habit of spending all their time together and they were both rather dreading the impending separation. Max was to join some friends and have a holiday before going home and Agatha was going to Delphi with the Woolleys.

But Fate had other plans. On arriving at their hotel, Agatha was handed her post, which mainly consisted of a great many telegrams which bore the frightening news that her daughter Rosalind was seriously ill with pneumonia. By that time she was in fact on the slow road to recovery, but she had been very dangerously ill and in those pre-penicillin days people quite often died from pneumonia. Agatha had to get home as quickly as possible.

Quiet and practical, Max went at once to the travel agent to book her on to the next departure of the Orient Express. Meanwhile Agatha wandered round in a daze, and stepped into a hole on the pavement, badly twisting her ankle so that she could barely walk. Max returned from the travel agent, took one look at her and disappeared again. He came back a little later with crêpe bandages and sticking-plaster, and the news that he had booked himself too on to the Orient Express and would travel home with her and help her on the train.

It was useless to protest: 'But you're going up to the temple of Bassae', meeting friends, having a holiday. Max knew he would be needed and he had made up his mind. The following evening they boarded the train, and, as it travelled inexorably back to Paris, Max told Agatha about his family, his parents Marguerite and Frederick, and his two younger brothers, Cecil and Philip. The time passed very pleasantly. At Milan, Agatha's ankle was sufficiently strong for them to wander along the platform to buy oranges, having been assured that the train stopped for twenty minutes. After five, it steamed off with all their luggage, passports and papers, leaving them with just the clothes they were wearing, and the bag of oranges. Just as in a scene from a film that might well have been written by Agatha Christie herself, they hired a car to chase the train, which at that part of its journey went rather slowly as it had to negotiate many tunnels. The passengers in the train entered enthusiastically into the chase, waving and gesticulating encouragingly to the passengers in the car whenever they were close enough. Eventually at Domodossola they caught up with the train and were hauled back into it just before it roared off again. They were exhausted, exhilarated and completely broke as the hire of the car had used up all their money. At Paris, Max's mother was waiting for them, and Agatha later said that it was a wonder that Marguerite did not take instantly against her since, as soon as she had been introduced, Agatha borrowed every last franc Marguerite had on her, so that she could continue her journey to London.

The madcap race across northern Italy, the long chats and companionable silences on more peaceable parts of the four-day journey, the easy ways into which they had fallen with Max handing Agatha along to the restaurant car, or else bringing her meals to her compartment, had cemented a friendship, and at least on Max's side it had blossomed into love. He apparently made up his mind then that Agatha was the wife he was looking for, although he confined his declarations at that stage to telling her she had a noble face, a compliment which Agatha found surprising. She described herself as good-tempered, exuberant, scatty, forgetful, shy, affectionate, completely lacking in self-confidence, moderately unselfish, but noble! She would have to try to live up to it. Max described the faces he loved in just such terms, as relating to ancient sculpture.

After the separation in Paris, Max went off on holiday with his mother, and Agatha continued her journey home. As soon as she arrived in Cresswell Place, she picked up the telephone and rang her sister and found that Rosalind was much better, and definitely out of danger. She went immediately to Cheshire where she found her lively daughter unusually quiet and listless, and looking distinctly frail. As soon as she could, she took her down to her own childhood home,

Ashfield in Torquay, where the sea breezes soon put some colour into her cheeks.

All that spring and early summer, Agatha contemplated the adventures of the past few weeks. She realized how much she had changed since her divorce from Archie. From being a cherished child, a carefully chaperoned young lady, she had become a protected wife, never really on her own and having to make her own decisions. Now she had become an independent woman, relying on no one, someone who was making her own living through writing, meeting new people on her own terms. When an old admirer made her a proposal of marriage that summer, she turned him down. It was not only that she was still scared of marriage, but more that she realized that she was quite happy as she was.

She was however frequently thinking of Max. They had parted so hurriedly in Paris that there had not been time to make any definite arrangements to meet again. When Max returned from France and had started work in the British Museum, he wrote to Agatha politely suggesting that, if she were to find herself in London, she might like to come and see the Ur objects on display. She in turn wrote back to say that she would like that very much, but was doubtful when she would be in London. Then Fate stepped in again. Agatha's publishers wrote to say that her American publishers wanted to meet her, so Agatha decided to go to London on the overnight train. She wrote to Max and asked him to breakfast in Cresswell Place. He came and at first it was awkward. 'I was delighted at the thought of seeing him again but strangely enough, the moment he arrived I was stricken with shyness ... He too ... was shy.' Agatha took refuge in the kitchen – she was a good cook – and, by the time they had eaten bacon and eggs, they were on their old friendly terms again. Agatha asked him if he would like to come down to Devon, and they arranged that he would come for a weekend in April.

The weekend came, and Max and Agatha met at Paddington to travel down to Torquay together. They were met at the station by Rosalind and plunged straight into a domestic drama: Agatha's favourite dog had bitten her housekeeper's small boy on the nose. Once that had been resolved, and the various parties pacified, a picnic on the moors was suggested. Naturally it poured with rain and, sitting in Agatha's open-top Morris Cowley, Max had water pouring down his neck. He showed every sign of enjoying himself enormously. They returned to Ashfield and had hot baths and a huge tea. Max played games with Rosalind. On the Sunday they went for a long walk, in more pouring rain. 'I was very happy being with Max again. I realised how close our companionship had been; how we seemed to under-stand each other almost before we spoke. Nevertheless it was a shock to me ... after Max and I had said goodnight and I had gone to bed, as I was lying there reading, there was a tap at the door.' Max came in and sat down on the end of her bed. He looked thoughtfully at her and said that he wanted to marry her.

According to Agatha, a long and 'ridiculous' discussion then took place. She protested that they were such good friends, and anyway she was far too old for him. He countered by saying that he had always wanted to marry someone older than himself. Then there was the problem that he was a Catholic, and she was a divorced woman, a problem which was indeed insoluble. But even as she made these objections, Agatha was thinking that 'nothing in the world would be as delightful as being married to him'. They talked for two hours, Max gently wearing down the obstacles, but after Agatha had driven him to the station the next morning she returned to Ashfield miserably undecided. She asked Rosalind if she had liked him: 'Oh yes.'

The next few weeks were miserable ones for Agatha. Since he says nothing at all in his letters or memoirs about his feelings at the time, Max was presumably unshaken in his belief that the marriage would take place and continued serenely with his work at the British Museum. Agatha agonized, thinking about Archie her former husband and how very badly he had hurt her, realizing that 'the only person who can really hurt you in life is a husband. Nobody else is close enough. On nobody else are you so dependent for the everyday companionship, affection and all that makes up marriage.' She pondered long and hard upon the sort of person she was, and the sort of person Max was. She listed the things she liked best in life: sunshine, apples, almost any kind of music, trains, puzzles, anything to do with numbers, the sea, bathing, silence, sleeping, dreaming, eating, the smell of coffee and of lilies of the valley, most dogs and the theatre. The two virtues she admired most were loyalty and courage. What she hated were crowds, being jammed up against people, particularly at cocktail parties, which she hated in themselves, loud voices, noise, smoking, alcohol, marmalade, oysters, grey skies and most birds. Max shared many of these loves and hates; they really had much in common after all. And even though he really ought to marry a younger woman, what young woman would take such an interest in his work, and follow him round archaeological sites and listen to him expounding his ideas? It took a mature woman to appreciate that side of him.

Agatha went to Cheshire to consult her sister and brother-in-law. Her sister was totally aghast at the idea. The age difference! James, her brother-in-law, was more rational but asked her to reflect carefully on whether she had not fallen in love with a way of life, pottering through the past, romantic as it was. Then she spoke to Leonard and Katharine. Leonard was pleased, and immediately said so. Katharine was more cautious. She thought they should marry, but not for two years as it would be bad for Max to have everything he wanted all at once. 'I think it would be better to make him wait', she said. Agatha reflected sadly that in two years she would be even older and rejected the suggestion.

Eventually she spoke to Rosalind. Her reaction was so favourable, based as it was on three very good reasons why Agatha should marry Max, that she sensibly saw the whole thing in perspective. Rosalind's reasons were: first, Max would be useful in the boat she was hoping to acquire; second, he was good at tennis and could be her partner; third, Peter (the dog) liked him, this being the most important reason of all.

By the end of May, Agatha's letters to Max were full of their future together and they became privately engaged, with only their families and the Woolleys in on the secret. Agatha had loathed publicity about her private life ever since she had unaccountably disappeared for eleven days at the end of her marriage to Archie, when the press had had a field day. They decided to marry in Scotland in September so that they could have a honeymoon before Max had to be back in Ur. It was agreed that Agatha, Rosalind and Carlotta Fisher 'Carlo', once Rosalind's governess but now Agatha's secretary, would go on a month-long holiday in Skye and there the banns would be called. It was most unlikely that anyone would take any notice of them at all.

It was not easy, however. Rodney Kannreuther, Max's Oxford

contemporary, rang to suggest that as many of the old Ship Street set as possible should go to the New College commem. ball in June. 'Yes', said Max full of enthusiasm, 'you get up a party and I'll bring Agatha Christie.' Much laughter from Rodney. 'You do that, old man.' Rodney took an instant liking to Agatha when he met her at the ball. She was 'terrific fun', large but very pretty. Agatha must have been putting on a brave front. She was horrified by the sheer youth of Max's friends at the ball, realizing that they were the same age as her nephew, Jack. In fact Jack himself had been one of Max's contemporaries at New College. But Max remained unperturbable, and his unshaken belief that they were meant for each other reassured her in this dark moment. And James Watts, Agatha's brother-in-law, added his words of encouragement: 'you have always shown good sense, and I think he is the sort of young man who might go far.'

Those weeks in Skye waiting to marry Max were a mixture of fun and fear. Agatha went for long walks with Rosalind, Carlo and Carlo's sister, Mary. They went to church and listened to the banns being read. Rosalind thought Agatha had better be prepared for the worst. 'You know, when you are married to Max, you will have to sleep in the same bed as him … I thought you might not have thought of it.'

Meanwhile her bridegroom was working till 5 a.m. some nights trying desperately to finish off the drawings and catalogue entries for the last season's digging. He was also helping Woolley with his register of the small finds made at Ur that he was preparing for his annual report of the Ur excavations in the *Antiquaries Journal*. Agatha suspected that Katharine was behind keeping Max so busy, being cross that neither Agatha nor Max had heeded her advice to wait for two years. She herself was fairly annoyed with Woolley, who had made it his business (though again Agatha was sure Katharine was behind it) to come and see her in Cresswell Place to tell Agatha that there would be no room for her at Ur. Agatha accepted that. But when it was suggested that it would be better if she did not even come to Baghdad, her usual mild composure deserted her, and she told Woolley quite firmly that she could travel wherever she liked in the Middle East and it was not up to the Woolleys to dictate where she could go. This ultimatum from Woolley was the last straw for Max. 'I am not going to be parted from you for another six months the season after this. Len will have had plenty of time to find a successor by then.' He was ready to be persuaded when Reginald Campbell Thompson approached him with a view to coming to Nineveh for the 1932–3 season, especially as it seemed likely that his wife would be welcome to accompany him.

The wedding itself, on 11 September 1930 at St Columba's Church in Edinburgh, was a low-key affair held far away from the press hounds that Agatha so dreaded. Not even Rosalind attended the ceremony, no photographs were taken, not even one glass of champagne drunk. Immediately the ceremony was over, Max, who had only come up on the overnight train, departed once more for the station and travelled back to London for three last days' work on Ur. He had been given strict instructions by Woolley that the following season began on 15 October 'and that no excuse whatsoever would be accepted if I were late'. He would be expected to start work on extending the expedition house with several additional rooms, details of which would be given to him by Woolley when they all arrived in Baghdad.

For the moment, however, all that could be put aside. If Agatha felt the marriage ceremony itself had been lacking in romance, her honeymoon more than made up for it. 'I am sure nobody enjoyed a honeymoon better than we did', she wrote. Max had planned the whole thing himself, as a surprise. The first surprise was the usually thrifty Max sweeping her off in a hired Daimler to Dover from where they crossed the channel and travelled to Venice. On to Dubrovnik, Split, to Patras by a tiny cargo boat which produced the most wonderful meals. At the various little harbours at which it called, they wandered ashore and walked in olive groves, or sat in flowery fields, hurrying back to the boat when they heard the funnel sound. 'How lovely it was … feeling so completely peaceful and happy together … Paradise on earth.'

From Patras they took a little train to Olympia. It was as soul-stirring as Agatha had hoped. Then on to Andritsena by mule, an easy ride of perhaps ten hours, said Max. In fact it took fourteen and was hideously uncomfortable, and poor Agatha suffered so badly that it took her the next two days to recover. Being the sort of person she was, however, she confined her displeasure to a few cross words on the subject of husbands who failed to calculate how far it was and how long it would take – a lifelong failing of Max, who always liked to think he could get somewhere miles away in an impossibly short time. Agatha assumed that the episode had been 'an early foretaste of the trials to which an archaeologist's wife was likely to be submitted' and readily forgave him, even to the extent of travelling on another mule to the temple of Bassae. On to Mycenae, Epidaurus, Nauplia and finally Delphi, the highlight of a blissful itinerary. Max was of course the perfect companion, erudite, knowledgeable, able to explain things to her and bring the past alive. They kept a joint diary of their travels. Her entries are all about food and people, funny incidents and sweeping descriptions of scenery. His are shorter, factual and confined mainly to remarks about the ancient sites they had seen.

The honeymoon ended in Athens, where it had been agreed they would have to part. Max had his assignation at Ur with the Woolleys, and Agatha was to travel home on the Orient Express to her old life, her writing and her daughter. What should have been a wonderful last few days was memorable for all the wrong reasons. Agatha contracted a most virulent form of food poisoning which gave her a temperature of 40°C and reduced her in a short space of time to skin and bone. The Greek doctor who attended her told her that his last patient with the same sickness had died after four days, but Agatha did not tell Max this. He was quite worried enough. He knew he had to keep his promise to Leonard Woolley and be back at Ur by 15 October, but he also knew he could not leave Agatha so desperately sick in a foreign country all by herself. Both Agatha and Max knew the Woolleys well enough to doubt whether they would ever be forgiven if Max was not there on time, and Agatha knew she would be the one who was blamed for his defection. In her unselfish way, she convinced Max that she was feeling a little better, that she would lie peacefully in bed and try to eat the plain boiled macaroni which was all she was allowed, and that when she felt strong enough she would totter to the station and travel home.

So Max went off to Baghdad, where he found to his utter fury that the Woolleys had put off their arrival, so he need not have left Agatha after all. He went straight to Ur and began work on the expedition house without the precise instructions he had been told would be ready. He built the new rooms to his own specification, taking revenge in making the new bathroom for Katharine as small as possible (it had to be rebuilt later) and, on a happier note, making the chimneypiece in the new living room just like the one at Cresswell Place.

Agatha heroically managed to board the Orient Express a few days later and, feeling terribly fragile, travelled home and collapsed thankfully into her own bed where she stayed for nearly a month until she recovered her strength and her spirits.

The whole episode had confirmed them both in their resolve that this season would be Max's last one with Leonard Woolley and at Ur.

CHAPTER FOUR

The Dangerous Chasm

'I missed Agatha sorely during that first season of our marriage', wrote Max in his *Memoirs*. They wrote to each other every two to three days. His letters are precise and give the impression of coming from an indulgent schoolmaster rather than a new husband. He sent her reading lists; one of his early suggestions was that she should read Herodotus. Hers on the other hand were full of doings, excitements and new ideas.

As soon as Agatha arrived home she bought another London house, numbers 47 and 48 Campden Street in Kensington, which had been knocked into one house with a pleasant roof garden. It was a much easier journey to the British Museum for Max when he was at home, so she thought they would live there and let Cresswell Place. Having another house naturally necessitated the purchase of much new furniture, and china dinner services, all of which she much enjoyed. She was also trying, in a way that must have touched his heart, to acquire skills suitable for an archaeologist's wife. To this end, she took drawing lessons and tried making pottery, the latter pursuit rather unsuccessfully.

She also had the threads of her old life to pick up. First of all Rosalind, whom she took to Switzerland over the Christmas holidays. Agatha was working on her current book, *The Sittaford Mystery,* and was also engaged in a somewhat chaotic crime serial for the BBC which was being organized by Dorothy Sayers and included five other well-known crime writers, each of whom was to write a different episode. Though Agatha greatly appreciated being included in such eminent company, and enjoyed the incidental correspondence between them as they struggled to make the plot hang together ('something has gone wrong with the alibi and … the 9.48 may have to get in late'), she decided not to become involved in the next serial proposed by the BBC. She much preferred to work alone.

Meanwhile Max had also been hard at work, as Woolley's reports from Ur in *The Illustrated London News* showed. In January, there was a report of 'A Startling Discovery: Royal Tombs Over 4000 Years Old'. These were the tombs of the great rulers of the Third Dynasty of Ur. At the end of the 1929–30 season Woolley's team had exposed part of a wall-front whose bricks were stamped with the names of Amar-Sin (2046–2038 BC), the grandson of Ur-Nammu (2112–2095 BC), the first king of the Third Dynasty. Now they found that the building was just an annexe of a much larger one erected by Shulgi, the latter's father. They had cleared this and found it exhausting work because they had to dig through the massive mud-brick walls which Nebuchadnezzar had built around the *temenos*. Digging below Shulgi's building, they found a huge brick-lined pit more than 6 m deep. 'In a recess on one side is a bricked-up door through which steps led down to the pit's bottom ... What may be below and behind it all we have yet to learn.' The work had been particularly arduous because of the need to shore up the vaults with timbering. Once that had been done, they were going to excavate beneath the pit, where more steps ran steeply down on either side and passed under corbelled vaults over 8 m high, with 'tottering brickwork' which also needed to be propped up with heavy timbering. At the foot of the stairs were arched doors leading to the tombs themselves, one of them more than 17 m long. All had been plundered in antiquity by the Elamites who had brought the Third Dynasty of Ur to its disastrous end, in 2004 BC. Half the workforce had been clearing the underground tombs while the other half were digging out private houses in the residential quarter to the south-east of the city. In one corner of a private house where the street ran past they came across a little chapel dedicated to a goddess whose function seemed to have been the protection of travellers.

In March 1931, Agatha set off once again to Ur, to be reunited with Max who had been involved in overseeing the excavation of the great pit, and to see for herself all the things about which he had written. She was graciously received by Katharine and Leonard, who had accepted, though reluctantly, that this was to be Max's last season at Ur. Woolley had advised Max against accepting Reginald Campbell Thompson's invitation to go to Nineveh, but Max had made up his mind. After his experience of the deep sounding at Ur, Max was keen to make another possibly even deeper sounding at Nineveh, as suggested by Campbell Thompson.

At the end of that season he took stock of what he had learned from Leonard Woolley. When he had arrived at Ur in October 1925, he had known absolutely nothing about archaeology, and not much more about Mesopotamian history. Woolley had taught him about both. Woolley was a brilliant archaeologist. As the leader of the expedition he had set a fine example by his application. Out in all weathers, and never slacking during the working day, he even worked far into the night, writing. Woolley kept up-to-date records of the day's work in his field notes, including careful descriptions of find spots, and made sketches of objects where appropriate and arranged to have them photographed. This daily record before the start of the next day's digging was a vital stage in the process of reaching tentative conclusions about an object, conclusions that might well have to be reassessed in the light of the recovery of more evidence. He wrote articles for both popular and learned journals, and he wrote letters. He usually had a book in progress, destined either for the general public or for his academic colleagues. Although he could be harsh (he did not hesitate to tell either his assistants or the local workforce when they were doing things badly) he never lost his temper, and he was perfectly willing to admit when he made mistakes himself. He engendered team spirit and communal pride in the work being done. His English was 'a model of lucidity' and he had brought Mesopotamia to public awareness almost on his own. His twice or thrice yearly reports to *The Illustrated London News* had captured the interest of a much wider public than had hitherto been aware of the existence of the ancient civilization that had flourished there. Ur was a place about which people had heard. And, because he had made it interesting and popular, he had continued to receive the support of the University Museum of Pennsylvania and the British Museum.

The Woolleys and the Mallowans parted company amicably, and Max and Agatha departed for Persia, which Agatha had been intent on visiting since January when she had gone to Burlington House to see the International Exhibition of Persian Art. It had been opened jointly by King George V and the Shah of Persia and exhibited examples of Persian art both ancient and modern, including textiles, ceramics, gold and silver, bronzes, sculpture and painting, arms and armour and architectural decoration. It also showed valuable items loaned personally by the Shah and by the Gulistan Museum in Tehran. These particular items were protected by a new-fangled invisible ray, which, if it was interrupted, set off a strident klaxon horn 'which can be heard throughout the building and leads to the closing of all doors'. It had all been most inspiring and Agatha had begged Max to take her to Persia on the way home.

They travelled first to Tehran and then on to Shiraz, from where they drove to Isfahan over a rough track through the desert. They stayed at a primitive rest-house and Agatha fell in love: 'Never have I seen anything like its glorious colours, of rose, blue and gold – the flowers, birds, arabesques, lovely fairy-tale buildings.' Isfahan was to Agatha, as for many others, the most beautiful city in the world.

They had planned then to travel to Russia, even though everyone they consulted advised them against it. Undeterred, they stocked up on food, including two vast tins of caviare which was the easiest thing to buy, hired a car and drove down to the Caspian Sea at Resht. They then boarded a Russian boat to Baku, where they were met by an Intourist guide who ignored all their ideas about what they might like to see and took them on a tour of building sites instead. The next day they took a train to Batum, a three-day journey when their food parcel came into its own. As is so often the way, they ate everything they liked on the first two days, and by the third were left with a jar of pineapple marmalade. But they ate it anyway. At least hot tea was always available; they just had to ask the engine-driver to fill their teapot with boiling water.

On their arrival at Batum they had to ask themselves why they had come. There seemed to be no hotel that would take them, no sign of their luggage, which had been carried off into the night by a porter, and, worst of all, no sight of the French boat they were supposed to be taking back to Istanbul, and on which they had booked tickets. Eventually and rather to their surprise, their luggage reappeared and they found their boat, and had a very pleasant trip down the Black Sea, enlivened for Agatha by the presence of ten adorable little brown bears, so small that they looked like teddy bears. Rugged French sailors fed them with babies' feeding bottles.

That summer the British Museum put on a small exhibition of finds from Nineveh. This was at the suggestion of Sidney Smith, who had written to Reginald Campbell Thompson in the late spring to tell him that, as Woolley was not putting on his usual Ur exhibition that summer, this was an opportunity Campbell Thompson might like to seize. Campbell Thompson knew the value of publicity and corresponded enthusiastically with Smith about the exhibition, one highlight of which was to be the great stela of Ashurnasirpal which Layard had found in the Ishtar temple. Doubtless Max took Agatha to see the exhibition before they went to spend the weekend with Reginald Campbell Thompson and his wife. Agatha said that this was so that she could be vetted, and apparently she was set various tests, most of which she managed to pass quite creditably. Reginald Campbell Thompson, known to everyone as C.T., was an easy-going, hearty man with a pleasant open face, rather bald but with a fine moustache. Barbara his wife was a 'delightful, kindly and altogether unselfish character'. Agatha became very fond of them both.

The tests she was set were first a vigorous country walk over rough country. Absolutely no complaints were to be made whatever the weather and however long the walk took. She must not mind if the walk meant scrambling through hedges or cutting a path through impenetrable woods. Fortunately a childhood spent near Dartmoor meant she was well prepared for that. Next came a trip to the cinema, to which C.T. was passionately devoted. No inane remarks must be made. She managed that one too. Then there was fussiness about food, which C.T. could not abide. Agatha could eat more or less anything. Max had apparently to be adept at riding, as it seemed his predecessor at Nineveh had lost his authority with the workforce by falling off his horse. Max assured C.T. that he was perfectly competent though he had in fact been on a horse only twice, and the second time it had run away with him. He did not tell C.T. this. Max fully intended to enrol at a riding-stable and take a few lessons, but, whether he did or not, he was certainly not prepared for the horrid little mount that C.T. had bought for him in the market at Mosul. It was typical of Max, however, that somehow he managed to stay on it, even though it frequently tried to rid itself of its inexperienced rider by bucking.

Another of C.T.'s traits of character was extreme parsimony, although he could be surprisingly generous on occasions, as for example when he distributed sweets to the entire workforce. Generally, however, he disapproved of extravagance in any form and was horribly shocked when Agatha arrived at Nineveh by her purchase of a table to write on, having dismissed the orange-crate that C.T. thought suitable for the purpose. Although she bought the writing table herself, with her own money, 'it took him quite a fortnight to forgive me'. He did, however, admire her work and took a great interest in the current book, *Lord Edgware Dies*, even to the extent of naming a skeleton found on the mound Lord Edgware.

The Mallowans arrived separately at Nineveh in the autumn of 1931. Max arrived first in September and was instantly captivated. 'No greater contrast to Babylonia can be imagined than the land of Assyria which lies several hundred miles to the north ... To discover how far the inhabitants differed from the scholarly, religious and placid peoples of Babylonia was indeed a challenge ... After the windswept dusty plains of Babylonia the green downland of Assyria was a paradise.' He shared a house with C.T. and Barbara. It stood at the foot of one of the great mounds of Nineveh, Nebi Yunus, from where it took twenty minutes to reach the top of the other mound, Kuyunjik, on horseback. The house itself was sparsely furnished, mainly with orange-crates, but the Campbell Thompsons were generous hosts and kept a good table. Max and, when she arrived, Agatha had an upstairs room furnished with two camp beds.

Agatha arrived in October, having spent a few weeks in Rhodes, where she rested, wrote and bathed in the sea. Then she took a small boat to Alexandretta in Syria, from where she was to hire a car and a driver to take her to Aleppo. From there she was to take the train to Nisibin, then hire another car and driver to take her to Mosul, an eight-hour journey, at the end of which she would find Max waiting for her. Unfortunately her plans were thrown completely off course by very rough sea on the way to Alexandretta which meant not only that Agatha was violently ill but that the boat could not put in there, but had to go on to the harbour at Beirut instead. Agatha found herself in a fragile state undertaking a sixteen-hour journey to Aleppo on a train which had no lavatory. 'I was fortunately gifted in that direction.' She continued next day by the Orient Express to Tell Kochek, where she hoped to change trains for Mosul. More bad luck attended her progress: the line had been washed away in two places. She was forced to spend two utterly boring days in a rest-house while the line was mended. Eventually, several days late, she arrived at Mosul to find Max waiting quite happily. 'Weren't you terribly worried?' she asked. 'Oh no', said Max, 'it often happens.'

Agatha loved Nineveh, the expedition house and the way of life. The two husbands woke at 5 a.m. and immediately went up on the flat roof of the house to check the weather. If it was dry enough to work that day, they signalled to the night-watchman on top of the mound with a lantern. He then marshalled the workforce ready for the day. C.T. and Max then departed on horseback. At 8 a.m., Barbara and Agatha set off on foot and walked to the top with breakfast: bread, hard-boiled eggs and tea. After they had eaten, the two wives went back down again, but returned at lunchtime with another picnic. When Agatha first arrived it was pleasantly warm, but as the season progressed they had to wrap up warmly. That winter of 1931 was a cold one and they were glad that the house had a fireplace in the dining room. There were occasional days when Max was able to take Agatha to see the surrounding countryside, which was beautiful. On one of these expeditions, they went to look for the great mound of Nimrud which, when they did find it, was inspiring: 'big stone Assyrian heads poked out of the soil. In one place there was the enormous wing of a great genie ... I remember Max saying, "This is where I would like to dig, but it would have to be on a very big scale ... this is the mound I would choose, out of all the world".'

This was to be C.T.'s last season at Nineveh, the ancient royal capital of the great Assyrian kings on the east bank of the Tigris. Its two high mounds, Kuyunjik and Nebi Yunus, had been occupied from the seventh millennium BC till the early Middle Ages. The city was known chiefly because of the magnificent building programmes of those mighty kings with their extraordinary, tongue-rolling names: Shalmaneser I, Sennacherib (who had moved his capital there from Khorsabad and built the so-called South-west Palace, an armoury on Nebi Yunus and around the city an imposing double wall 12 km long, with fifteen gates), Esarhaddon and his son Ashurbanipal (who also built palaces on the mound of Nebi Yunus). Ashurbanipal's was the so-called North Palace, with its most magnificent reliefs and its library, which produced nearly twenty-five thousand cuneiform tablets.

Nineveh had been comprehensively sacked by the Babylonians and the Medes in 612 BC. Its modern excavation had been started by the Frenchman Paul-Emile Botta in 1842. He was followed by Austen Henry Layard between 1846 and 1851, when Hormuzd Rassam had taken over. He in turn was followed by W. K. Loftus and by George Smith, and in the early twentieth century by L. W. King. Campbell Thompson had been there since the 1927–8 season with R. W. Hutchinson as his assistant.

They had begun work by digging and clearing the Nabu temple, but just when they were about to leave they came upon traces of a palace of Ashurnasirpal (883–859 BC) 'and this was the bait that drew us back again in 1929'. That season, they were a party of four, made up by Barbara Campbell Thompson and Miss Campbell Shaw. They were funded by various bodies, including the Gertrude Bell bequest and Sir Charles Hyde, who had agreed to finance two further seasons. That season too ended on a tantalizing note as they came across 'a solid mass some 6 feet thick lying about 7 feet below the surface made of good Assyrian unburnt bricks. Only the edge was showing when we closed down for the season, and speculation ran high whether it could be the great temple of Ishtar.' That season C.T. was again accompanied by Barbara, and by a new assistant, R. W. Hamilton, and a friend of Barbara, Miss Hallett.

Immediately they began work in October 1930, they came across confirmation that the tantalizing find was indeed the temple of Ishtar: remains of a pavement of fine inscribed burnt bricks which recorded Ashurnasirpal's rebuilding programme. The temple had once covered an area of some 76 m by 43 m but had been laid waste in the destruction of 612 BC. In its ruins they made several small finds but from much earlier periods, mainly metalwork and pottery. The principal treasure they found was a life-size bronze head dating to the time of Sargon of Akkad (2334–2279 BC) and a large and nearly complete stone cylinder of Shamshi-Adad I (1813–1781 BC) inscribed with cuneiform. There were also innumerable fragments of tablets dating from the time of Tiglath-Pileser I (1114–1076 BC) to the time of the destruction, including 'a good piece of syllabary or sign-list with linguistic values'. For an epigraphist it was a most satisfactory season with numerous other inscriptions on stone and brick, on cylinder seals, and figurines.

Max was far less interested in inscriptions than in pottery and particularly in how pottery could give clues to chronology. Agatha said that at that time prehistory was all the rage in the archaeological world. Max had been at the forefront of trying to establish an early chronology with his involvement in the excavation of the deep pit at Ur. It was on the strength of this that C.T. had been eager to have him at Nineveh. Max almost immediately began work on the new deep pit. C.T. gave a full account of the work in his report to *The Illustrated London News* in July 1932. Unlike Woolley, C.T. was always ready to give personal credit to his assistants, whom he identified by name, and it must have given Max great pleasure to see credit given to his work.

'Our big pit', wrote C.T., 'dug to virgin soil under Mr Mallowan's care, occupied about half our workmen some two-and-a-half months, and it was with a feeling of infinite relief that we saw the last basketful of earth thrown back into it, and the dangerous chasm filled up, without accident to man or boy ... a formidable task successfully completed thanks to the Arab workman's fearless head for heights.' Poor C.T. had no head for heights at all and it was thought to be greatly to his credit that he made an almost daily trip to the bottom of the fearsome pit for inspection. Max positively enjoyed this dangerous pursuit, as did the workmen who blithely leapt over the corners at the top, with a drop of some 30 m beneath them.

The purpose of the pit was to try to establish a chronology by digging from the surface of the mound right down to virgin soil at the bottom. No one quite knew how deep they would have to go on digging to reach it. They began by selecting a spot at the highest point of the mound. There they measured out an area some 25 m by 17 m. The first part of the digging was easy and they soon reached the bottom of the Assyrian levels, some 4.5 m below the top surface. Below that lay débris that was all prehistoric, and they soon reached a level they could date fairly certainly about 3000 BC. The pit reached 10 m from the top, then 15 m, and eventually 20 m. As it became deeper, the sides began to slope inwards in an alarming way and C.T. started thinking they should abandon the whole project. But potsherds were appearing in ever increasing quantities, and Max was determined to continue, though even he described the operation as 'truly frightening'. They had cut the first 10–15 m obliquely so that they would be safe if the top should collapse, but the sides had now begun to look very unstable. When they did eventually arrive at virgin soil, after seven weeks' digging, 30 m below the surface, the area of the pit was only 4 m by 4 m. They cut steps in the side so that a basket of earth could be handed up to a workman who could then attach it to a chain so it could be pulled up to the top to be emptied. Then the basket was hurled down again so that the process could happen all over again.

The virgin soil, which was a hard reddish marl, was the starting point for the classification of the prehistoric strata into five distinct periods. They called these periods Ninevite I–V, with Ninevite I at the bottom, dated to 6000 BC, and Ninevite V at the top (below the Assyrian levels), to 3000 BC. Each of the five periods was characterized by pottery specimens, and in the level Ninevite V by the débris of mud-brick houses.

Very careful examination of the pottery samples in each different period was then made, with comparisons drawn with similar specimens from other Mesopotamian sites. It became clear that these parallels were not only local sites in northern Mesopotamia but, most vitally, sites in southern Mesopotamia.

The Ninevite V period produced remarkable painted pottery of a type not seen in the north before: large footed vases and big jars with geometric and animal designs executed in black or violet paint. They were clearly related to the Jemdet Nasr pottery of the south. At the same level, Sumerian cylinder seals provided proof of those close links. It was clear that there had been a sizeable settlement at this period.

The deep stratum of Ninevite IV produced a certain red ware, 'sealing-wax red', very fine in character, and very similar to pottery found at Ur. There was also a more plum-coloured ware, which was like that dating to the Uruk and Jemdet Nasr periods.

Ninevite III was another wide band of accumulated débris, some 7 m in depth, which produced a series of grey ware, some of it burnished, and made by hand, not on the wheel. It was partly contemporary with a southern period known as Ubaid, with which Max was also quite familiar, after his time at Ur. This dated to between 3500 and 4000 BC. If proof were needed of the southern connection here, he found it in the discovery of clay sickles of a type he immediately recognized as belonging to the Ubaid period.

Ninevite II could be divided into three phases. The earliest produced painted pottery with simple geometric designs, which were sometimes incised. The middle phase, called Samarra after a type-site some 150 km north of Baghdad on the Tigris, produced pottery characterized by decoration in horizontal bands with precise geometric designs between them. And above that was Halaf ware, so called because it exactly matched designs even then being found by Baron Max von Oppenheim at Tell Halaf on the Upper Habur river in Syria. This pottery was particularly eye-catching and unmistakable, being brilliantly coloured and decorated, the designs predominantly geometric. It was probably made as early as 5000 BC, i.e. before the Ubaid period.

Below that, Ninevite I, was débris lying over the virgin soil, dating to 6000 BC. Its pottery remains were coarse, both plain and incised ware.

Reginald Campbell Thompson wrote a full report of his work at Nineveh (1927–31) in the first volume of *Iraq*, the journal of the newly formed British School of Archaeology in Iraq, founded in memory of Gertrude Bell and partly funded by a legacy she had left for the purpose. The full report of Max's pit was published in *Annals of Archaeology and Anthropology* published by Liverpool University Press in 1933 (volume XX) and it aroused much interest.

Entitled 'British Museum Excavations at Nineveh 1931–2', the report written by Sidney Smith gave a brief account of Dr Campbell Thompson's work in the test-pits and a full publication of the inscriptions he had found before moving on with enthusiasm to the deep sounding. Mr Mallowan, it said, had given 'an admirably full and clear description and discussion of the pre-Assyrian strata', but, although his exposition of the pottery stratification and associated objects solved some questions, it also raised new ones. The material, being new and fragmentary, was not easy to interpret, and it might be necessary to take the level of Ninevite V down to a later date in view of Professor E. A. Speiser's current excavations at the nearby site of Tepe Gawra. This small but important historic site some 24 km north-east of Mosul on the Tigris, occupied continuously from about 6000 BC into the Middle Bronze Age (*c.* 1800 BC), was excavated in the 1930s by a team from the University Museum of Pennsylvania under the directorship of Ephraim Speiser. It became a key site for the stratigraphy of northern Mesopotamia. The report ended on a heartening note.

'Mr Mallowan is to be congratulated on his most instructive work.'

The deep sounding established Max as a serious contender in the field of Mesopotamian archaeology. At the end of his season's report, published in *The Illustrated London News* on 16 July 1932, Reginald Campbell Thompson was also able to give advance notice of Max's intention to take his research further. 'Mr Mallowan, attracted by the great interest of these finds, is proposing to lead an expedition to a neighbouring site on behalf of the British Museum next season, if only his funds are sufficiently augmented.'

Max knew this was to be C.T.'s final season at Nineveh, and there was no question of returning the following year. There were no more funds forthcoming from his generous sponsors. He knew that, by comparison with Woolley, C.T. was an epigraphist, and not really an archaeologist. He had no clear plan of campaign: 'the mound of Kuyunjik was not a tidy one'. Work had been done in a rather disorganized way, taking each day as it came. Consequently plotting the site had been more or less impossible and in many ways excavating with C.T. had been more of a 'glorified tablet-hunt'. C.T. was more interested in recovering tablets than buildings, and his methods were frequently haphazard. Even his end-of-season reports had a certain breeziness. One, for *The Illustrated London News,* began, 'From Nineveh always something fresh …'. The two men parted as very good friends, however, and remained so for the rest of their lives. Max was C.T.'s executor when he died. Max respected him as man of ideas, of wide enthusiasms, and one with an enviable grasp of cuneiform. He had also realized a belated admiration for C.T.'s extreme carefulness with his sponsors' money. C.T. did not squander money on inessentials and he felt honour-bound to account to his sponsors for every last penny. According to Max, who always relished a good story, even if it acquired a bit extra in the telling, when C.T. made a full account of his expenses to his sponsors at the end of the Nineveh excavations, he dutifully refunded the exact balance outstanding, in stamps, to his chief benefactor, the millionaire newspaper and racehorse owner Sir Charles Hyde. It amounted to 11d.

Reginald Campbell Thompson was somewhat of a poet; he wrote verse in idle moments and, after the excavation season with the Mallowans had ended, he wrote a play in verse, *Digger's Fancy (A*

Melodrama), which he dedicated to them 'in token of the last season at Nineveh'. The characters of Ann (a botanist) and Alan (an anthropologist) are loosely based on Agatha and Max. Agatha would probably have been amused at her description as she enters the stage, in a car driven by an Armenian: 'young, and with those good looks which scholarship gives, when properly bridled and now allowed to run rampant'. The following speech by Alan gives a flavour of the piece, though it is extremely doubtful that Max ever indulged in such hyperbole:

> Give me a north Iraqi mound in spring,
> Its tumbled rampart clipping emerald fields,
> The winter dead, and summer's heat forgot,
> Unfathom'd deeps of gentian for sky...

As for Agatha, her first experience as an archaeologist's wife living on a dig and sharing in the everyday events had been extremely satisfactory. 'I had liked Mosul; I had become deeply attached to both C.T. and Barbara; I had completed the final demise of Lord Edgware, and had tracked down his murderer successfully.'

She left Nineveh in high spirits, only to find herself embroiled in events aboard the Orient Express which must have sown the seed for her subsequent novel set on that romantic but unreliable train. Although actual murder did not take place, everything else that could have gone wrong did, and it was with some relief that Agatha stumbled into the haven of Campden Street, two days late, exhausted, filthy and greatly relieved to be home.

Max had learnt much during that short season. Not only had he helped to establish a pottery sequence that revealed a great deal of the prehistory of Mesopotamia but also he had discovered that he had a wife who was equal to the demands of expedition life. Better still, she seemed to enjoy it, had been a thoroughly good sport when life was less than luxurious or even comfortable, facing rough patches with unruffled good humour. He had also learnt that there were at least two different ways of running a dig. And he now had his own ideas about both where and how he might proceed. Where was destined by what he had been doing so far, and how by his experience of two such very different chiefs.

A New and Enthralling Chapter

M ax's selection of the mound of Tepe Rashwa next to the modern village of Arpachiyah, just to the east of the Tigris and north-west of Nineveh, was by no means haphazard. While engaged on the digging of the deep pit at Nineveh, workmen had brought him samples of pottery from that nearby 'pimple'. These pottery samples were similar to the Halaf ware found in Ninevite II. They were much more accessible, being near the surface of the mound. That had been the great problem at Nineveh: illuminating though the pottery sequence displayed in the strata of the great pit was, it had become a thoroughly dangerous exercise to remove it from the soil.

C. T. was not encouraging, despite the fact that he was one of the few Assyriologists to have visited the site. In 1928 he had noticed hundreds of fragments of finely painted pottery on the slopes of the mound. Unlike Max, however, he had very little interest in prehistory and he advised against the venture. But Max was determined. Marriage had given him self-confidence, and being married to Agatha not only brought him personal happiness but had also increased his standing in his own world. Although she was not then the national treasure she was to become, her name was a household one and doubtless being married to the famous crime novelist enhanced Max's reputation. Her being nearly fifteen years older than he was meant he had automatically entered a world of people older than himself. It was hard to remember that it was only seven years since Max had first travelled to Ur, very much the junior assistant, to be corrected at every turn by Woolley, and ready to spend his summers helping his chief with the publication of his finds without much personal credit. Now the Woolleys were social companions of the Mallowans, the two

husbands exchanging learned views almost as if they were contemporaries. Mrs Smith, the wife of the Keeper of the Department of
Egyptian and Assyrian Antiquities at the British Museum, who was
very much Max's superior, was a fan of Agatha and wrote to congratulate her on her latest book. It was partly because of Agatha but also
because Max himself had proved to be competent, especially after the
deep sounding at Nineveh, that people were prepared to back him.
Max felt quite convinced that he was ready for a dig of his own 'and
the prospect of having a first independent command wholly free of
servitude to others ... was bliss, for I have never shirked responsibility'.
Agatha was more anxious, knowing that his career would stand or fall
by the outcome of this first independent dig.

That summer of 1932 was spent mainly at the British Museum,
sorting out the antiquities that had arrived from Nineveh. In May,
Sidney Smith reported to Reginald Campbell Thompson that the
boxes had all arrived and were being unpacked by Max, 'who is engaged
(by arrangement with you) in studying the prehistoric material and the
pottery ... Mallowan tells me that he has arranged the antiquities in
such a way that you can get anything you want from the boxes without
difficulty'. Max was also busy fund-raising for his proposed expedition
to Arpachiyah. He spoke first to the Director of the British Museum,
Sir George Hill, who consulted with his Trustees. They were apparently happy to sponsor him but only in a small way. He had more luck
with Sir Edgar Bonham Carter, the Chairman of the British School
of Archaeology in Iraq, which put up £600. By the end of August, Max
was able to report to Sidney Smith that 'I have heard today that the
Trustees of the Percy Sladen Memorial Fund have unanimously made
the grant of £400 for which I applied on the 4th June, as a contribution
towards the funds required for excavating Tell Arpachiyah. The total
funds now amount to £1100 and I think that with this backing it should
now be less difficult to find the remainder.'

To this end, Max prepared an impressive-looking brochure entitled
'The Gertrude Bell Memorial Expedition to Arpachiyah near Nineveh'.
There were various headings 'Backing of Expedition' mentioned the
British School of Archaeology in Iraq, the Linnaean Society and
Sir Charles Marston JP. 'Patrons' added to those who had already
contributed Major General Sir Percy Cox (Gertrude Bell's chief in

Baghdad), Sir Frederick Kenyon (a former Director of the British Museum) and Sir Arnold Wilson (Sir Percy Cox's successor in Baghdad). The 'Staff of Expedition' were M. E. L. Mallowan, Director, and J. Cruickshank Rose, Architect. Then the brochure described 'The Site', a prehistoric settlement about 320 km north of Baghdad, near Nineveh, the only known site in Mesopotamia which exhibited remains of the fifth millennium BC on the surface over a wide area. The 'Purpose of the Expedition' was to discover a lost civilization, the oldest in the neighbourhood of the Upper Tigris. Arpachiyah was an unknown quantity, and it was only first-hand information on the spot that could solve the problems connected with it. 'Surface Indications' were a very fine series of painted pottery fragments, specimens of eggshell ware with decoration in lustrous red and black paint on an apricot slip, with an elaborate variety of designs unsurpassed in technique by any other school of painted pottery in Mesopotamia. 'Classes of Possible Finds' included a town plan (if forthcoming to be the earliest known), houses, burials and implements. 'Historical Connections' pointed out that one day's spade work at Arpachiyah was the equivalent of two months' work at Nineveh. All the surface indications offered great expectations of finding evidence which would throw fresh light on Nineveh and the other great northern sites. 'The Period' was at least as early as the archaic levels at Ur, Kish and Uruk and the so-called Pre-Flood pottery, that is, before 4000 BC, and before the art of writing had reached north Mesopotamia. The brochure ended with the reminder that the expedition was undertaken as a tribute to Gertrude Bell, explorer and archaeologist, the first woman to realize by her life work the intimate relationship between the study of the ancient history of the Middle East and the conditions of the present day. 'Only by an understanding of the past can we grapple with the problems of the present.'

The brochure apparently brought in the rest of the money Max needed. He saw Sidney Smith at the Museum in early September to report progress, and spent most of the rest of the year in Devonshire. These were sad days for Max and Agatha since it was some time that summer that she lost the baby she was expecting, and was advised that it would be unwise for her to try again.

By the New Year of 1933, everything was set up for the expedition.

Sidney Smith wrote to Max to ask him to transfer the account of the expedition to the Ottoman Bank in Mosul, but Max had already made arrangements with the Eastern Bank. He did, however, agree to transfer the money sponsored by the British School, the Percy Sladen Memorial Fund and Sir Charles Marston to the Ottoman Bank, amounting to almost half of the expedition funds. There was, he said, 'an advantage in having two banks in Mosul as it means that we have two sources from which to draw small change for paying the men'. Max and Agatha also had enormous fun in the Army & Navy Stores and Woolworth's shopping for the necessities of expedition life; a huge long list submitted to his sponsors included, among other things, four bottles of quinine tablets, toast racks, eating utensils, sieves, bed linen, damask napkins and a set of gimlets.

The Mallowans set off for the Near East at the end of January. They travelled by train to Trieste and then took a boat to Jaffa, an unpleasant voyage on rough seas. When they reached Syria, it was to find violent rain storms in progress. It took them 54 hours to travel from Damascus to Baghdad. At one stage they were bogged down for seven hours until two cars belonging to the Iraq Petroleum Company (often the saviours of archaeological expeditions) towed them across a *wadi*. During this operation four of their suitcases were entirely submerged in muddy water. 'Fortunately', wrote Max to Sidney Smith, 'none of the expedition material was harmed – we had nursed the expedition camera like a baby throughout.' It is questionable whether Agatha felt quite the same way about his priorities, as she then spent an unpleasant hour or so wringing out her clothes in the Maude Hotel at Baghdad, a somewhat primitive establishment at the best of times. The only real casualty was a case of mathematical instruments, for which Max put in an insurance claim for £8 16s od, which also covered the cost of laundry and dry cleaning.

The Director of Antiquities for Iraq at the time was Dr Julius Jordan, a German scholar whom they later came to despise because of his political views. At the time, however, relations were cordial, and Jordan was 'most friendly and did all he could to assist us. He appeared confident that he could secure us a permit for the season without much difficulty.' In return, Max promised to let him have preliminary reports of the work in progress, week by week, for the first month. It was after the Mallowans returned to Baghdad following their Arpachiyah season that their attitude towards him changed. At a tea party at which Julius Jordan was entertaining them with a piano recital of pieces by Beethoven, Agatha found herself gazing at his fine head and thinking what a splendid chap he was. Then someone mentioned the Jews, whereupon his expression changed. 'They are a danger', he said. 'They should be exterminated. Nothing else will really do but that.' His excuse that German Jews were perhaps different from other Jews made absolutely no difference to Agatha, who realized she was in the presence of her first Nazi, something she had read about but not taken particularly seriously in England. It sent shivers down her spine.

Having obtained from Jordan their permit to dig, and having acquired for £75 a splendid lorry capable of carrying a load of a ton and a half, the Mallowans set off in it for Mosul where they stayed at the station hotel efficiently run by a Syrian Christian with the unlikely name of Satan. There seemed to be innumerable, insuperable problems, not least of which was the weather. Continuous torrential rain had made the streets and roads beyond the town impassable. They needed to find out who owned the site of Arpachiyah so they could obtain his consent to their excavation. Fortunately one of C. T.'s former servants, Majid Shaiya, was working at the Ottoman Bank and he managed to ascertain that there were fourteen, or even, in Agatha's account, nineteen different mortgagees. They had to obtain the consent of each one of them. With the help of Majid Shaiya, they were eventually corralled and brought to the Ottoman Bank where they all marked their consent to the contract. The Mallowans paid over a small sum of £7 for the annual rental, with an option to renew for a further two years, and no obligation to refill where they had excavated, and the mortgagees agreed to pay them a huge sum of money in return if they 'molested' them in any way, by hampering them in their digging. This added enormous prestige to the owners of the mound, who apparently boasted about the huge sum involved as it seemed to suggest hidden riches beyond compare.

Max kept Sidney Smith up to date with progress, writing from Mosul on 6 February 1933,

I thought you might be glad to have some unofficial news of the progress, or non-progress of the expedition … In a day or two Rose and I hope to do the preliminary contour survey of the whole site and to fix the position of the Tell on the map. The Air Force have also consented to make us an air mosaic of the site over a strip two miles wide running the whole way from Arpachiyah to Nineveh … I very much doubt whether we shall actually be able to stick a spade into the ground before February 15th … we have to get our mapping done first. They have had a very wet January and bitter cold as well as rain in December – I think we were wise not to come out earlier. I am hoping the unprecedented early rains will mean a dry March. We ought to be able to work up till the middle of May.

Next the Mallowans concentrated their efforts on finding a suitable house and decided to rent again the same one at the foot of Nebi Yunus that they had shared with the Campbell Thompsons the previous year. Then at the last minute they decided it was not quite big enough so they moved to one very close by which they rented for £4 per month. It too had glorious views of the mound of Kuyunjik and a pretty garden filled with rose bushes. In addition to its extra rooms and several large store rooms, however, it had a useful and spacious flat roof, on which they could spread out pottery fragments. Once installed, they wasted no time in acquiring a cook, a house-boy and a large fierce guard dog, which then amazed them by producing six fine puppies; one of them, called Swiss Miss, became a particular favourite. This house too was rather short of furniture (the Campbell Thompsons had been quite happy to make do with orange-crates) so the Mallowans hired carpenters and other workmen to transform the bare rooms. It took them only ten days and cost amazingly little. In the so-called Antiquities Room, the carpenters fashioned a series of pigeon-holes carefully designed for the storage of stratified pottery as it emerged from the site, a construction which was the envy of all who saw it, particularly Henry Frankfort when he came over from the site of Tell Asmar where he was then digging. The landlord of this house was a man in his nineties who said he remembered the legendary George Smith when he was looking for tablets during 1873 and 1874.

They also needed another vehicle and were soon the possessors of a fine lorry and an Irish driver whose name was Gallagher. He had stayed on in Mosul after the First World War, and was quite a character. He took on responsibility for the puppies, and drilled them in military fashion so that they marched up to the house for their meals and to have their fleas removed each day. He was an avid reader and fell on the books that Agatha's sister Madge sent her out from England each week.

Max and John Rose began work in February 1933. They had no difficulty recruiting labour, offering a shilling a day to the men, most of whom came from the village of Arpachiyah itself. 'It was pleasant to be able at last to order the men to dig exactly where one wished without further consultation', wrote Max. He also instituted the use of the spade to shovel away earth, as opposed to a triangular hoe-like instrument used by Campbell Thompson. For the first fortnight, the results were very disappointing, only mud-brick remains of the poorest type appeared. Both men wondered if they had made a bad mistake. 'We, who had come from a site as rich as Ur were perhaps rather easily discouraged.' But then things changed.

At the top of the mound the miserable mud-brick remains began to yield potsherds of the Ubaid period. These overlay Halaf remains, just as they had hoped. Then, over on the west side of the settlement, they found a cemetery also of the Ubaid period with graves richly supplied with pottery, with some particularly fine specimens. They bore tiny and intricate designs, most pleasing to the eye. Larger bowls were decorated with broad sweeping bands on the inside, 'a strange and rather attractive design' which was unfamiliar to them. There were 45 Ubaid graves in all, and not one overlay another, so that it was likely that they had all been dug and their owners placed in them at the same period. Small objects which also emerged included mainly beads and amulets, but there were some interesting incised beads, and terracotta stamps, which Max believed might have been used to stamp cloth. There was also a metal object: an open-cast flat copper axe of a rare type previously found at Susa in Iran.

Below the top four levels of Ubaid houses on the top of the mound, they found a series of eleven much earlier settlements, most of which belonged to the Halaf period. At a deep level, which they dated to about 5000 BC, they found some remarkable domed buildings, ten in all. One in particular to the northern end was enormous: its round room measured 9 m across and was some 10 m in height. It was approached by a long ante-room about 30 m in length. In seven of these ten domed buildings, the foundations were intact, and Max wondered why, in a country where stone was so scarce, later builders had not removed earlier foundations for re-use. He came to the conclusion that the buildings must have been preserved as an act of piety, so the round constructions probably had a religious significance, an opinion enhanced by finding graves laid directly up against the walls. The graves contained extensive deposits of painted pottery.

John Rose made some fine reconstruction drawings of these buildings, which showed a clear resemblance to modern beehive buildings in northern Syria. Many of the buildings contained figurines of women, some with pendulous breasts, some nude, some wearing elaborate costumes but with exposed breasts, which caused Max to think that the buildings were probably dedicated to some sort of fertility goddess. The figurines were probably not meant to represent the goddess, but were dedicated to her by women who were or hoped to become mothers. He noticed that none of the figurines had a realistic head, and wondered whether some sort of taboo was operating in the representation of a lifelike human countenance.

Other finds included models of horned heads of bulls, two wonderful bull amulets, and stone bowls decorated with bulls' heads. There were many knives and scrapers, some quite sharp enough to be used as razors, made of obsidian, the black and semi-translucent volcanic glass, and one particularly fine obsidian vase, and a girdle of alternate obsidian beads and cowrie shells, which indicated a trade with areas towards the Indian Ocean. There were numerous clay models of animals: cattle, oxen, sheep, some birds. There was a steatite duck and a painted terracotta hedgehog, as well as little steatite double-axes. There was a limestone mace head, a basalt axe and some pumice. But, most important, there was a beautiful series of Halaf ware ranging through a long sequence of occupation spanning several centuries. It overlaid the Samarra ware and early Ninevite underneath the eleventh level at the bottom.

The most exciting part of their excavation was in the middle of the mound itself, however: a potters' workshop containing more than 150 objects belonging to the potters and stone-workers. The building had been sacked and burnt by an invader, presumably an Ubaid raider who subsequently settled down and built his house on the ruins of the old workshop. The roof had collapsed during the sacking but this had pre-served the contents of the workshop. Max described the pottery found here as 'unsurpassed': gorgeously decorated plates and bowls, the design almost exclusively geometric. What made it so remarkable was its beautiful finish, the purity of the clay and the high glaze of the paint. Some of the most attractive pieces were apricot colour with decoration in a lustrous black, brown or red. Many of these pieces of pottery were drawn by John Rose, and published in volume II of *Iraq*, making it a collectors' item. To Agatha, the discovery of the potters' workshop came as a great relief as it had been 'an anxious time for us'. She wrote of that exciting time:

> we were so frantically busy we didn't know how to cope. Vessel after vessel came up. They were smashed by the fall of the roof – but they were there, and could nearly all be reconstructed ... One enormous burnished dish, in a lovely deep red with a petalled rosette centre and beautiful designs all round it, very geometrical, was in 76 pieces. Every piece was there and reassembled ... I was bursting with happiness.

The flat roof of the Mallowans' house must have begun to look like a giant jigsaw puzzle with pieces of pottery laid out and all three of them trying to match fragment to fragment. The previous autumn Agatha had been learning to draw to scale. She had enrolled in a local secondary school in Devonshire and been taught by a charming man who had showed her how to measure and calculate. Now she had ample opportunity to put this skill to good use. Max spent his days out on the mound and John Rose spent his drawing the finer pieces, both fragments and when reconstructed. One evening he staggered down to dinner saying he thought he was going blind. 'My eyes feel queer and I am so dizzy I can hardly walk. I have been drawing without ceasing at top speed since eight o'clock this morning.'

Max also had to find time to report back to London, both to Sidney

Smith in the Department and to one of his sponsors, Sir Charles Marston. He was also keeping copious daily field notes, with pencil sketches of objects, and detailed records in little black notebooks, one always to hand. He was also writing a report for *The Illustrated London News*, having learnt by example particularly from Woolley but also from Campbell Thompson that this was the best way to bring a site to the notice of the general public while keeping sponsors happy. Max's report on Arpachiyah was published on 13 May under the title 'New Light on a Lost Civilization, Relics of the 5th Millennium BC'. Having introduced the staff of the expedition, and its sponsors, the article mentioned Agatha for the first time by name: 'As at Nineveh, Mr Mallowan has been accompanied at Tell Arpachiyah by Mrs Mallowan (Agatha Christie, the novelist).'

The article, which covered one full page, and carried seven illustrations (of figurines, amulets, pottery and a skeleton lying in a grave), told of the latest remains lying immediately below the surface, and how they corresponded to similar pottery found in southern Mesopotamia. The pottery of the earliest period was closely related to material found at the site of Tell Halaf, which itself had been widely reported in earlier editions of the magazine.

Max also sent weekly reports to Julius Jordan in Baghdad, the first one on 12 February enclosing a map of the tell with form lines and spot levels, and a map on the scale of 1 in 2500 divided into 100-m squares. On 1 March, Jordan wrote to Max to tell him that he was 'highly enjoyed at the interesting and important results' and asking whether, in view of such a good start, Max might like to have his permit extended for another year, till March 1934. Max was enthusiastic, and Jordan duly arranged for this to be done.

Agatha too had been busily writing. It was at Arpachiyah that she wrote possibly her best known book of all: *Murder on the Orient Express*, which was published in 1933 and dedicated to Max. The book drew freely on Agatha's own experiences aboard the train and employed her favourite device, a group of disparate personalities in a closed-off situation, so that it had to be one of the group, and not an outside agent, who had committed the murder. The fun for the reader was to weigh up the reasons for which any one of those personalities might have been driven to kill, and of course each one of them was discovered to have a perfectly irresistible motive. The plot was cleverly linked with the real-life kidnap and murder of the Lindbergh baby in the mid-1920s. The book was made into an immensely successful film in 1974.

The Mallowans decided to celebrate the end of their first season by arranging a cross-country race, open to all those who had taken part in the work. Agatha christened them AAAA, the Arpachiyah Amateur Athletic Association. The AAAA racers were required to run from the Nergal Gate at Nineveh to Arpachiyah itself. This was a distance of some 5 km and involved a complicated river crossing, as the Tigris was in full spate at the time. Various large rewards were offered to the competitors: a cow and a calf for the winner, a sheep and a lamb for the runner-up, a goat and a kid for the man in third place, and so on, with every competitor given as much halva as he could carry away at the end. Although the men were somewhat bemused by the whole concept, the lure of the prizes was enough for them to take part, despite the fact that the pontoon bridge at Mosul was broken and they had to swim across the Tigris. On the day there was much excitement, a large crowd of cheering witnesses and heavy betting on the likely winners. After the race, the prizes were ceremoniously handed out. The Mallowans were sent off from Arpachiyah with much local goodwill. Fifteen years later, they went back on a visit and were amazed and gratified that they were recognized at once. Former basket-boys and pot-boys rushed out to greet them and hastened to introduce their wives and describe their children. They received the warmest of welcomes. It left Agatha feeling humbled: she would always love that part of the world and treasure the memories of that very happy time in her life.

Max had made careful arrangements for the transport of his sponsors' share of the antiquities at the end of the season. They were carefully packed into six cases which were collected by The Mesopotamia Persia Corporation (telegraphic address, and known by everyone as, Mespers) to be delivered to the Iraq Museum in Baghdad during the morning of 20 May. Max and Agatha were planning to arrive in the evening of the same day. The next morning at 7 a.m. Max went round to the Museum to help unpack the cases so that the Antiquities Department could check everything was in order before issuing the necessary export licences. This process apparently all happened quite amicably, despite the heat (42° in the shade), so Max was a little annoyed to receive a communication from Jordan on 26 May that the Minister of Education was demanding personally to see all the antiquities allotted to the expedition. Meanwhile the local *Al Ahali* newspaper was rousing nationalistic fervour about the removal of any antiquities at all from Iraq. It was becoming increasingly clear that digging in Iraq in the future would be severely limited. The situation with Max's cases became more protracted, with Jordan writing to Max in London in early August to tell him that his cases were still sitting in the courtyard of the Iraq Museum. The Director of the British Museum, Sir George Hill, took up the matter with the Foreign Office, a personal appeal was made to King Faisal, all to no avail. At the end of September, Max received a telegram from Jordan saying 'PLEASE POSTPONE DEPARTURE ARPACHIYAH EXPEDITION UNTIL FURTHER INFORMATION'. It was clear, as Max put it, that the Iraqi government was 'not in an amicable mood'. In mid-October, his cases did finally arrive at the British Museum, but on the 26th Max wrote a cool letter to Jordan saying, 'I regret that at present it is most unlikely that the Arpachiyah expedition will take the field next season. I find that no scientific body or individual subscriber is prepared to assist in financing an expedition without full knowledge of the conditions likely to govern excavators.' Max started thinking seriously about moving north-eastwards into Syria, where other prehistoric mounds looked tempting. The country was under French mandate and the authorities positively welcomed archaeologists.

None the less, in retrospect, Agatha wrote proudly that they came home 'flushed with triumph'. When Max, writing in his *Memoirs* in 1977, looked back to 1933, he said, 'Since Arpachiyah, I have led many other expeditions or have been closely connected with them in the Orient over a period of 50 years, but this, my first independent dig in which Agatha and John Rose alone took a main share, stands out as the happiest and most rewarding: it opened a new and enthralling chapter and will forever stand as a milestone on the long road of prehistory.'

As usual, the Mallowans spent as many of the summer months as possible at Ashfield with Rosalind, and bathed in the sea as often as possible. Max worked hard at writing up his season's work and on an exhibition of his finds at the British Museum. Unfortunately the exhibition was being hampered by the difficulties in Iraq. In early October, Sidney Smith had forwarded to Max a letter from Julius Jordan which warned that the Antiquities Law passed in Baghdad in 1924 in the days of Gertrude Bell was definitely to be altered in November so that the conditions governing the export of antiquities thereafter were to be severely curtailed. Max wrote to Wilson, the Administrative Inspector for Mosul and Erbil, on 16 November, full of regret, asking him to make arrangements for the excavations to be filled in, saying that he would pay the local sheikh an appropriate sum for doing it.

Max's 178-page report in volume II part I of *Iraq* was dated June 1934 but, trained by Woolley to get things down while they were still fresh in the mind, he began work immediately that summer of 1933. It was an immense labour, beautifully illustrated, much of it in colour, by John Rose, and covered all aspects of the dig, the sponsors, the staff and the workforce. It began with a topographical introduction, a precise location and measurement of the mound, an archaeological introduction, an historical introduction ('At Arpachiyah lived a peaceful community of peasants and potters ...') before moving on to the detailed archaeological and historical information that his academic readers would want to have.

Much of the report was written in Devon, and the rest in London, where Agatha had just purchased yet another London house, at 58 Sheffield Terrace, w8, soon to be called Green Lodge. The first time Agatha saw the house she said she 'wanted to live there as badly as I had ever wanted to live in any house. It was perfect.' Apart from a large room for Max's library, with plenty of space for large tables for all his papers and pottery samples, it had enough room for Agatha to have her own workroom and sitting room. This was the first time she had had such a room, and although Max and Rosalind as well as the faithful Carlo were all a little surprised, they all agreed that it was about time. Agatha had firm ideas about what she wanted in her room: a grand piano, a large stout table with a good upright chair for writing, a comfortable sofa and armchair, and absolutely no telephone. Into this fastness she barricaded herself, much enjoying her new-found privacy, and a family rule was made that she was not be disturbed when writing, under any circumstances, except perhaps if the house were on fire. 'I don't know why I never had anything of the kind again', she wrote a little sadly. 'I suppose I got used to using the dining-room table or the corner of the washstand once more.'

Max too enjoyed setting up his new study. He wanted a new chimney, and as Agatha said, after his experiences of building in mud-brick in the Near East, rather fancied himself at the job. Needless to say, his London builder was scathing, and told him such a fireplace would never work. Max insisted he proceed exactly to plan, and the chimney was a great success, much to the builder's disappointment. It must have been a fine sight with its great inscribed Assyrian brick inset over the mantelpiece. Unfortunately it, and indeed most of the rest of the house, was to be the casualty of enemy action during the War.

In December 1933, Max and Agatha went with Rosalind to Egypt. To Agatha, it was an inspiration as they cruised gently down the Nile to Aswan aboard the SS *Karnak*, to disembark at the Cataract Hotel with its atmospheric terrace looking straight down to the first cataract where a myriad of little feluccas bobbed about in the bright sunshine, sails flapping in the breeze. From the terrace where large and delicious English teas could be taken, or cocktails sipped while watching the sudden and dramatic sunsets which occur so near the equator, they could see across to the island of Elephantine. There was plenty to do: boat trips to nearby sites including the island of Philae, walking in the famous gardens, indulging in sand baths to ward off rheumatism, donkey and camel rides, or even just meditating on all that vast antiquity. They made the excursion to Abu Simbel, perhaps on the luxurious motor-boat *Dixie* at a cost each of £35 Egyptian. Agatha's fertile brain was teeming with plots. It was always said that *Death on the Nile* (published in 1936) was planned on the Cataract Hotel terrace. One of the characters in it had been inspired by a female battleaxe they had encountered aboard the SS *Karnak*.

Back in London, plans for Max's exhibition of Arpachiyah finds were being finalized. On 23 February, he wrote to Sidney Smith about the lay-out of the exhibition, which he thought quite unsatisfactory, in particular the placing of a certain screen. As he said, the British School in Iraq

is sending out three hundred invitations to the opening of the show and the principal supporters of the expedition hope to be present. I think if I may say so, that the separation of our screen

ABOVE: Max and his younger brother, Cecil (© John Mallowan)

ABOVE: Max's mother with his youngest brother, Philip (© John Mallowan)

The three brothers in June 1926 at Bossington: Philip, Cecil and Max (© John Mallowan)

ABOVE: The station at Ur Junction

BELOW: The ziggurat with workmen at Ur

The dining room at the expedition house, Ur: (left to right) Woolley, Max, Katharine Keeling, Harding and Legrain (© John Mallowan)

Katharine Keeling and Leonard Woolley on the ziggurat at Ur (© John Mallowan)

At Eridu: Gertrude Bell, Legrain, Max and Whitburn (© John Mallowan)

Outside the expedition house, Ur: (left to right) Katharine Keeling, Hamoudi and Max (© John Mallowan)

BELOW: Max at Hezekiah's tower, Jerusalem, 1926 (© John Mallowan)

ABOVE: Christmas Day picnic expedition, 1926: (left to right) Whitburn, Legrain, Woolley, Ammran, Hamoudi, Saad and Yahia (© John Mallowan)

(© Rosalind Hicks)

Agatha and Max
at the time of
their marriage in
September 1930

(© John Mallowan)

LEFT: At Ur, 1931: Max,
Agatha and Leonard Woolley
(© John Mallowan)

BELOW: Max and Agatha at
Chagar Bazar, 1935

BELOW: Arpachiyah, 1934, end of season
photograph with Max, Agatha and Robin
Macartney in the front row

ABOVE: Agatha beside a
road in Syria, about 1936

BELOW: Baron's Hotel, Aleppo

Agatha at Chagar Bazar, 1937

Max in RAF uniform, 1942
(© John Mallowan)

ABOVE: Agatha and Max in Venice in the 1950s
(© Rosalind Hicks)

ABOVE: In later life, about 1970
(© Topham Picturepoint, Edenbridge)

Max, about 1973
(© John Mallowan)

Agatha and Max (upper right) at the bicentenary dinner
at the British Museum, 1953

from the cases will spoil the continuity of the exhibition, and as much of the explanation of the significance of the finds must be placed on the screen, it is really important that everything be kept together ... Please do not think that I do not appreciate the care and consideration that you have continually shown us. We are fortunate in obtaining three admirable cases for our exhibits, and if you could possibly see your way to shifting the screen nearer, nothing could be more desired. Is it not a pity to spoil the ship for a ha'p'worth of tar?

This placatory ending did nothing to avert an irritated response from Smith. 'I saw no way to satisfy your wishes ... as I had no labour to spare and cannot agree to your own suggested arrangement of the room, until I consulted the Keeper of Greek and Roman Antiquities who has very kindly arranged ... to move the boundary stones. It may therefore be possible for you to have your way.'

The exhibition opened on 7 March in the so-called Nineveh Gallery and included specimens of painted pottery, stone bowls and jewellery, as well as a full series of maps, drawings and photographs. Some items were on loan from the Iraq Museum. Max took pains to acknowledge this, and to make proper arrangements for their return.

Max was already planning his next campaign, and on 9 April wrote to Sir George Hill and Sir Edgar Bonham Carter to ask them to give their patronage and financial support to a second expedition in the autumn. 'The proposed campaign would have two main objects: 1. The completion of the excavations at Arpachiyah 2. A surface exploration of mounds in the Jebel Sinjar, west of Mosul, together with soundings, where possible; an examination of mounds on the Upper Tigris and Euphrates, both in Syria and Iraq; a visit to the site of Harran in Turkey.' Having added to his two categories at some length, he concluded, 'In view of the fact that the expedition will not have to purchase equipment or household effects, and can complete the excavations at Arpachiyah by employing 100 men (instead of the 180 of last season) I estimate that we may by strict economy carry out the above programme, for a minimum sum of £1000, though this does not provide for the salary of director or architect.' He was obviously still hoping even at this stage to return to Iraq just for a few days.

As Max's fund-raising activities continued, necessitating spending more and more of their time in London, Max and Agatha began to long for a country house where they could spend weekends when Ashfield was too far away. Faced with where to start looking, they sensibly narrowed their search to just two areas near enough to London to make a weekend house practicable: somewhere near Stockbridge in Hampshire, near Bossington where Max had spent so many childhood idylls with his mother's friend Molly Mansel-Jones, or alternatively somewhere near Oxford. His time at Oxford had been one of Max's happiest ones; he knew the surrounding countryside well, and loved the Thames and its villages and small country towns. They thought the stretch between Henley and Oxford would suit them well. They began looking at both these areas and spent many weekends dashing off to look at likely properties. A week before they left for Syria, they finally found what they were looking for: an advertisement in *The Times* showed a small Queen Anne house in a little village called Winterbrook, then as now almost part of Wallingford. They immediately went to look at it and took an instant decision to buy it. Even though the house itself was rather close to the road, it had behind it a pretty garden and then a meadow which swept right down to the Thames so that they had their own river frontage. The house had five bedrooms, three sitting rooms and a good kitchen. In the garden was a large cedar of Lebanon, and Agatha immediately resolved to rearrange the garden: this fine tree would be the centre of a newly laid lawn, so that they and their guests could wander out with coffee cups after lunch, or with the tea things and sit under its spreading branches. The house was, according to Agatha, 'remarkably cheap', so they snapped up this apparent bargain and shortly afterwards set off to Syria, not to see it again for nine months, and wondering meanwhile if perhaps they had been rather precipitate.

In November, they travelled to Beirut and stayed at a modest small hotel called the Bassoul which had a particularly pleasant terrace overlooking the waterfront. From here they made contact with the Director of the Service des Antiquités, Henri Seyrig. Max had definitely abandoned his original intention to spend a last few weeks at Arpachiyah, and had decided to concentrate solely on Syria.

A light-hearted but evocative account of this archaeological season and the others leading up to the Second World War was made by Agatha in her book *Come, Tell Me How You Live,* written in Hampstead during the War as a comforting reminder of those happy and carefree days. It was published in 1946.

Henri Seyrig was also the Director of the French Institute, and was much respected. He made a point of visiting every dig during the season and was considered to be very fair when it came to the division of finds at the end. He was also extremely welcoming and helpful: the Mallowans soon became very friendly with him and his vivacious wife, Miette, so much so that they spent much of their stay in Beirut at the Seyrigs' flat.

The most pressing item on the agenda was for Max to decide exactly where he wanted to dig. He was determined that it should be in a part of Syria closely related to Iraq, thus helping him to widen his experiences so far on a familiar sort of territory. Having decided that, it was easy to see that the Habur valley in the north-eastern part of the country would be a good starting point. This was pretty much uncharted ground, though Max von Oppenheim had excavated at Tell Halaf near the headwaters of the Habur river from 1899. He had retired from the site in 1929. Max was still fascinated by the prehistoric period, and thought he had a real opportunity to expand general knowledge about this era in this part of Syria so near to the Iraq border. He was also very keen to find, if possible, written historical information on cuneiform tablets, something that had eluded him so far. He was helped in his decision by Sidney Smith.

Once Max had decided on the area and sought the necessary licence to dig, the next task was to find a stout vehicle capable of coping with the very rough ground that the expedition team would have to travel over while conducting their survey. There was not much choice but they finally decided to buy a four-cylinder Ford with a sturdy engine. A local workshop was asked to build up the chassis. After they had done so, the vehicle began to look distinctly top-heavy, and, as it had also been painted a distinctive lavender blue, it reminded them of their own dear queen at home, and they promptly christened it Queen Mary. Queen Mary was like a small lorry, and had the great advantage of being visible from miles away, a comforting sight when stuck in the desert. They also bought four tents, two for themselves and Robin Macartney (the architect on this expedition), one to be used as a kitchen and the last as a lavatory.

At 5 a.m. one morning, they were awakened by the arrival of Hamoudi and two of his sons. Tea was ordered and the four men got down to business, Agatha sleepily wondering whether perhaps this could not have been done at a more reasonable hour. Every now and again Hamoudi addressed remarks to her in Arabic. Max translated them, and also Agatha's replies to the three men sitting on her bedroom floor. It was impossible to mind about anything: 'All three of them beam with happiness, and I realise anew what very delightful people they are.' Apart from Hamoudi and his sons, they engaged a cook and a driver, both of whom turned out to be rather inept at their assumed professions. They also hired an extra vehicle, a Citroën, and its driver, a man called Aristide.

Thus equipped with staff, transport and stores, not to mention the requisite licence, they set off for Homs, where they stayed in a fine hotel chosen by Hamoudi, where unfortunately the plumbing did not seem to be connected. They then went to Palmyra. Agatha had not seen it before and was entranced by 'its slender creamy beauty rising up fantastically in the middle of hot sand'. There was more trouble with the plumbing at the Hotel Zenobia. They then drove along the extremes of their new territory, pitching camp near Hasuka at the junction of the Upper and Lower Haburs at the top of the *wadi* Waj. This was not a pleasant place to camp, as it was both windy and dusty and had absolutely no plumbing of any kind. Even the lure of a nearby post office could not persuade them to stay and they moved a few kilometres south to a place called Meyadin where they camped in the courtyard of a great *khan* or caravanserai. Agatha sat on a large chair and watched the men pitching the tents in a strong desert wind.

It was Max's policy to use young newly qualified architects on his digs, paying for their services himself and training them in archaeology and the ways of the Middle East. His architect this season was Robin Macartney, who had been recommended to Max by Aurel Stein, who had written to him from Gloucestershire on 14 September 1934 about

the son of my old and much cherished friend Sir George Macartney the late Consul General for Chinese Turkestan. I understand from the latter that the young man is anxious to be allowed to join you as architectural assistant on the expedition to some sites in Northern Syria ... I have known Robin since he was a small boy in Kashgar ... His career at school in Jersey has been brilliant ... As far as his personality goes I feel sure that he would make a very energetic and keen assistant in the field.

Aurel Stein had failed to mention the most obvious characteristic of the young man: his extreme silence, which to Agatha at least was quite unnerving. Her attempts at conversation were met with a monosyllabic responses and, being shy herself, reduced her to 'nervous idiocy', even though she realized that he was probably even more shy than she was. Max on the other hand found his silence excellent and told Agatha that she could have no idea what it was like to be stuck in the desert with someone who never stopped talking. This awkward situation was resolved that first night at Meyadin in the howling wind and rain when the main pole in the big expedition tent snapped, and Robin went down face first into thick slimy mud. Getting up, he let forth a string of thundering oaths that reduced the whole party to laughter, and afterwards, all shyness gone, the three of them became firm friends and had no difficulty in living together in the sort of basic circumstances that many would find quite trying. Robin, or Mac as they began calling him, designed two book jackets for Agatha, now collectors' items. Agatha drew freely on his background and childhood in her 1951 crime thriller *They Came to Baghdad*.

At Meyadin, the expedition was well placed for conducting the first part of the survey, which was to examine mounds to either side of the lower Habur between Haseke and Circesium, where the river joined the Euphrates. Unfortunately their survey failed to find any early settlements, and Agatha soon discovered that the word 'Roman', uttered in a tone of disgust, meant an instant dismissal of the mound in question and a hurried departure to the next one.

They then turned their attention to the tributaries of the river to the east, where they found a number of 'formidable' mounds 'riddled with Assyrian potsherds'. The Assyrian potsherds marked them as riverside forts built to protect trade routes. The most important of them was Tell Ajaja, which had once been a provincial capital of Assyria, called

Shadi-kanni, and had been partially excavated by Layard in about 1850 during a three-week period. Reminders of Layard's *Nineveh and Babylon* lay before their eyes: in a tunnel overlooking the river they saw an inscribed, winged human-headed bull which he had used as an illustration. In medieval times the former fort had become a flourishing city called Arban. Max was tempted by Tell Ajaja but there was nothing prehistoric about it, nothing to reinforce those links with the earliest periods of Mesopotamian culture that was his mission, and with reluctance he decided to move on.

They next pitched camp at Haseke, 'an unattractive place' according to Agatha but another one which had the advantage of a post office. Haseke was ideally suited for a survey of the upper Habur. Using Tell Halaf as a 'beacon of light urging us onwards to discover more', they worked their way gradually up the right bank of the river to the tell itself, then back to Haseke along the left bank. They lingered over various mounds, and examined innumerable potsherds but the outcome was again disappointing. Prehistoric remains were not evident, and they had to conclude that the lower two-thirds of the upper Habur was of no interest to their present survey, perhaps because climatic conditions in antiquity did not appeal to the pottery-makers of the time.

Agatha was enjoying every moment of the survey, despite having been quite seriously ill earlier on with a violent stomach upset. The autumn days were some of the most perfect she had known, she wrote.

> We get up early, soon after sunrise, drink hot tea, and eat eggs and start off. It is cold then, and I wear two jerseys and a big woolly coat. The light is lovely – a very faint soft rose softens the browns and greys. From the top of a mound one looks out over an apparently deserted world. Mounds rise everywhere – one can see perhaps sixty if one counts. Sixty ancient settlements ... where nowadays only the tribesmen move with their brown tents, was once a busy part of the world. Here, some five thousand years ago, was *the* busy part of the world. Here were the beginnings of civilization, and here, picked up by me, this broken fragment of a clay pot, hand-made, with a design of dots and cross-hatching in black paint, is the forerunner of the Woolworth cup out of which this very morning I have drunk my tea.

It was then only left to them to examine the last piece of the Habur jigsaw, a triangle of land bordered to the west by the upper Habur from Ras al-Ain to Haseke, to the east by a small river called the Jagjagha, and to the north by a railway line which was also the boundary between Syria and Turkey. The whole area was criss-crossed by innumerable *wadis*. The *wadis* were the source of much drama, as both Queen Mary and the hired Citroën taxi were for ever becoming stuck in the thick mud that lay at the bottom of them, a situation which became worse as the winter rains began. Agatha described with feeling the practical solution: the stout planks of wood (carried at all times) which had to be wedged under the back wheels, one man behind the steering wheel in the stranded vehicle while the others took their positions behind ready to heave and shove. Sometimes the only answer was to fasten a tow-rope to the bonnet and invite another unstuck vehicle to pull as well. Frequently the tow-rope snapped and the whole process had to begin again. Luckily for her, women 'toil not in the East (an excellent idea!)' and her role in the proceedings was limited to sitting on the bank and uttering cries of encouragement and helpful advice.

This last area of investigation, described by Max as 'an archaeological paradise', contained hundreds of promising mounds, the majority of which produced remains of agricultural settlements which flourished in the fifth millennium BC. Time was short, so they had to content themselves with making only brief soundings at two of the most likely: Tell Ailun and Tell Hamdun. They looked longingly at others before deciding finally on the site of Chagar Bazar. A trial sounding here yielded rich evidence of Halaf ware overlaid by remains of the second millennium BC. It was, said Max, 'the most tempting, rewarding and practical prospect'. From a more prosaic point of view, it was near the town of Kamechlie some 40 km to the north, where they would find everything they needed: a shopping centre, a bank and a post office.

They made their way to Amuda where there was an unappetising hotel which they rejected altogether as a base for operations, and instead, thanks to Hamoudi, found a house belonging to an Armenian French-speaking priest, who could let them have it for rent the following season. For the time being, he promised to clear out one big room so that they could store their equipment immediately. The road from Amuda joined the main road from Kamechlie to Chagar Bazar so it was convenient. Triumphant, they returned to Haseke to pack up, and travelled back again to Amuda, where Queen Mary and the taxi were parked in the courtyard of the house of the Armenian priest, who had been as good as his word and cleared out a room for them. They were still using their tents: the worsening weather made it rather a trial, especially for Agatha, but she continued to be a good sport about the hardships and to look on the whole enterprise with interest and enthusiasm, huddling in her coat in the cold wind while Max and Mac made their last few soundings under overcast skies. After one particularly trying day as Agatha slithered across the mud to her tent, Hamoudi said to Max, 'It is good to have the Khatun with us. All things make her laugh!'

Final arrangements were made at Chagar Bazar for the start of the spring season next year. The local sheikh who apparently owned the land was approached and it was decided that a fine new excavation house would be built, to become his when the excavations were over. Compensation and obligations on both sides had been agreed and ratified by the French colonial officer. The Armenian priest agreed to let them his house till theirs was ready – though this was complicated by the discovery that it was in fact occupied by six different families, all of whom eventually agreed to move out – and to leave the house spotless and covered with a new coat of whitewash.

Agatha climbed to the top of the tell and looked at the line of hills to the north, and over the fertile land to the south. She imagined it covered with green and starred with wild flowers in the spring, and thought how peaceful and remote it was, so far from people and civilization. She thought she could be very happy coming back the following year.

In the meantime, however, she decided to take a train back to Aleppo, leaving Max and Mac to pack up and drive the 300 km distance in Queen Mary. The fleshpots made an immediate appeal: 'Shops! My hair shampooed! Friends to see!' The Hotel Baron had become her home from home. The two men arrived exhausted and covered with mud, and the Mallowans took a fond farewell of Mac, who was going to Palestine. They themselves set off once again for the reliable warm sunshine of Egypt.

A Fine Leader

Max's official report to his sponsors on his season at Arpachiyah was read by Sidney Smith over Christmas 1934, and he wrote Max an encouraging letter, saying he had read it through several times 'and congratulate you very warmly on it. A very excellent piece of hard, really hard, work ... Chagar Bazar seems the very site we have been looking for; it should enormously strengthen our collections, particularly in the various classes of objects lumped together as "Hittite".'

Max replied from Cairo on 14 January 1935: 'I thank you ... for your kind words about our survey; your encouragement has given me good heart for fresh efforts.' Smith had made the suggestion that he should send a young member of his Department, Richard Barnett, to help Max with his excavations at Chagar Bazar: 'He should be most useful to you for his knowledge is wide and various, he has been trained at Athens in digging, it will be most valuable experience for him.' Max said he was delighted with the proposition.

> I shall welcome him both personally and as a colleague, and of course his help will be invaluable to us. If you can get the travelling and maintenance allowance granted by the Treasury that will be most satisfactory, and as to payment of his keep, cost of living is as you know not high in these parts and I will be satisfied with whatever sum you are able to raise. In any case I regard the offer of Barnett's services as a most generous contribution.

Richard Barnett was some five years younger than Max. He had been a scholar at Corpus Christi, Cambridge, where he had gained a double first in Classics. He had then excavated at Athens for two seasons, as

Sidney Smith had told Max, and had also worked at Perachora, near Corinth, with Humfry Payne in 1931 and 1932. In June that year he was appointed as Assistant Keeper in Smith's Department of Egyptian and Assyrian Antiquities at the British Museum, where his father had had a most distinguished career in the Department of Oriental Printed Books and Manuscripts. Barnett's duties in the Department were to sort and classify the large number of ivories found by Layard and Loftus at Nimrud during the nineteenth century.

Max told Smith that their intention was to reach their rented house at Amuda on 15 March.

As we have first to make the house comfortable, install our furniture, make arrangements with our workmen and make our contract with the landowner, I suggest that Barnett had better join us not earlier than the 24th or 25th of March. This will ensure six weeks with us on the dig (I anticipate that our funds will not hold out beyond 15th of May) and this will also give us time to make things comfortable for him. There is no difficulty about reaching us. Barnett has only to take the Taurus Express to Kamechlie where we will send our car to meet him (forty minutes' drive from our house in Amuda). If Barnett requires any further information, I will be very glad to write to him on any matter of enquiry. I strongly advise both inoculation against typhoid, and vaccination, together with an official certificate of vaccination. If Barnett can bring his own blankets and sheets, this will be very useful.

He added that he was hoping to find some of 'those dreadful Hittite sculptures' at Chagar Bazar (such as Leonard Woolley was recovering at Alalakh), and that he was waiting for page proofs for his Arpachiyah season to arrive.

From Cairo, the Mallowans went to Malta, where they spent a happy week finding 'the ancient remains and the Museum extraordinarily interesting'. They then went to Tunis, from where they travelled to Algiers, then to Sicily, finally reaching Beirut on 9 March. They found Mac waiting for them on the quayside, grinning from ear to ear. 'This is a reunion with friends', wrote Agatha.

On 10 March, Max wrote to Smith at the British Museum:

> I am sending you a line to let you know that I am back in Syria
> and leave tomorrow for Aleppo where I make my final arrange-
> ments before starting for Amuda – this includes getting all our
> furniture out of Mosul as we have much household apparatus in
> store ... I have seen Seyrig and all is in order and I will sign the
> concession tomorrow ... I am employing Hamoudi during the
> first week: he will be useful in getting the men down to it at the
> start – afterwards I will carry on with his two sons. Macartney is
> very fit and has put in 5 weeks ... in Palestine where he should
> have gained some valuable experience ... Seyrig is going to do
> our division in the field, personally ... I think the stage is now
> well set for excavating Chagar Bazar. I shall expect the worse
> and hope for the best.

In Aleppo they repossessed Queen Mary (instantly renamed Blue
Mary because she had been repainted a particularly lurid colour) and
acquired a new driver, a tall Armenian who apparently knew something
about mechanics. Mac and Hamoudi then set out in Blue Mary and
Max and Agatha travelled by train to Kamechlie, from where they
travelled by road to Amuda. It was immediately clear that all was not
well: Hamoudi was distracted and Mac had a stoical air that was
distinctly worrying. It seemed that the six families, who were supposed
to have moved out of the large mud-brick house the archaeologists had
arranged to lease from the Armenian priest, were still very much in
residence and vociferous about their right to stay. It took the combined
efforts of an irate Max and Hamoudi to evict them and then to do what
they could to make the place habitable. Agatha for once lost her
amused tolerance when she found that the one habitable room was
literally crawling with mice. As she said, 'I have never been one with
an exaggerated distaste for mice. An odd mouse or so in a bedroom has
left me unmoved ... But our first night at Amuda is an experience I
shall never forget.' As soon as the lights had been turned out, hundreds
of mice emerged from the holes in the walls and the floor and ran
everywhere. She tried to remain calm but when one ran across her
face, she knew it was hopeless and became hysterical. She would go

to Kamechlie at first light, she would take the first train to Aleppo, and the very next one straight back to England!

This was enough for Max, who summoned Hamoudi; the two men moved the camp beds out into the courtyard where eventually Agatha calmed down and went to sleep. An anxious Max was all solicitude the next morning and Agatha agreed to stay. The mouseholes were plugged and a large and vicious cat purchased. Eventually the house was free of vermin (except fleas) and they were able to turn their minds to less basic matters, such as its furnishings.

Max demanded tables and Agatha a chest-of-drawers and a towel-horse. A mud-brick lavatory was designed for Agatha by Mac, as his first professional commission. 'It will not, I fear, look well in Mac's memoirs when he comes to write them.' Eventually all was organized and they were able to start the work for which they had come.

Max left early, before 6 a.m., every day for the mound, and on most days Agatha went with him. Sometimes she stayed at the house and mended pottery or labelled finds. Occasionally she even did a little writing. She loved her days on the mound, especially when the weather was good. It was cold until the sun was well up, but then she was able to bask in the warmth and admire the beautiful countryside and the spring flowers that were just beginning to emerge everywhere: tiny blue lupins, wild tulips, marigolds and broom, as well as a scarlet ranunculus. Breakfast, consisting of hard-boiled eggs and flaps of Arab bread, with hot tea drunk from enamel mugs, took place at 8.30 a.m. after which everyone went back to work. Agatha saw her role as that of 'master-spy'. Looking impeccably English in her tailored coat and skirt, a large hat pinned to her head, and holding her handbag, she wandered about observing what was happening, absolutely nothing escaping her sharp eye. Leaning on her shooting-stick, she kept an eye on the basket-boys, children who were employed to remove baskets of earth from the place of excavation and take it to a dump where it would be thoroughly investigated in case it contained any small objects of value or interest. Some of them took an unnecessarily long time in sifting through their baskets of earth, and others abandoned pretence altogether and went happily to sleep on the job. It was Agatha's mission to report back to Max and Hamoudi which were good at their job and which particularly lazy.

Lunch took place at 12.30 p.m.: a picnic prepared by Dimitri the new cook and brought to the site by Michel, the new driver. Sometimes afterwards they went to inspect the site of the new excavation house, designed by Mac and to be built of mud-brick, to the south-east of the mound. The dig ended at about 4 p.m. with men who had found anything potentially valuable bringing it to Max so as to be suitably rewarded. The *bakshish* payable to each man was recorded in a little book held by Michel, and at the end of each week the man's wages plus his accumulated tips were paid over. Max tried hard to be fair, and if really good finds were made and handed over – for example a cylinder seal – he made sure the finder was properly rewarded. On the other hand, he occasionally awarded small sums for worthless items as a means of encouragement.

It was about 5 p.m. when everyone went home, the men running headlong down the mound and the expedition team walking down more sedately to Mary parked below. Then it was time for dinner, cooked by Dimitri, and well-earned rest in the priest's just-about-habitable house. They were all longing for their own to be built.

At the end of March, Richard Barnett arrived and immediately made an impact with his boundless enthusiasm. Max found his energy quite overwhelming and continued to spend much of the day alone drawing. Agatha too needed to be on her own to write, but she tried to be friendly towards the newcomer. It was clear however from her account in *Come, Tell Me How You Live* that she found him bumptious and took a somewhat malicious delight in his problems with his special pyjama suits into which he once managed to zip up a mouse. Fortunately Barnett spent most of his time out on the mound where he was able to make a useful contribution to the work in progress.

In his unpublished memoir written some fifty years later, Barnett implied that Max was anti-Semitic, which he found strange as he thought Max himself had some Jewish blood. His evidence for this was Max's paternal descent from Jewish Austrian Czech stock and the fact that there had once been a large Jewish department store with the name of Mallowan in Prague. Max never referred to this. Agatha often made rather derogatory references to Jews in her books, as did many people of her age and class in conversation at the time. The horrors of the Second World War cured most of them of this unthinking prejudice.

With the help of 140 workmen, a mixture of Arabs and Kurds with some Yesidis – who, said Max, worshipped Satan in a mild kind of a way – and a few Turks who had crossed the border, they were trying to obtain a broad idea of what lay within the great mound. They began by selecting a plot some 20 m by 25 m, not on the highest point but some 7.5 m below it, at a point where there was a certain amount of exposure. At the end of six weeks they had dug a deep chasm some 15 m deep, which descended to bare soil.

Max was really the instigator of this way of tackling prehistoric sites, a method with which he felt confident especially when it yielded the results he was anticipating. As Max reported to Smith at the end of the season:

> We have just stopped the excavations after completing a deep cut down to virgin soil, and a fairly extensive top dig of private houses of our latest period (I) which have produced some interesting plans, but no further dating evidence ... Period I as far as I can see corresponds to upper half of first millennium BC ... We have quite an attractive collection of small objects – of which I am sending a selection of photographs next week. Next season the way is prepared for an extensive dig in the second level and a larger scale investigation of all the levels down to Period V (corresponding to Ninevite V) that is if and when funds are forthcoming ... We all stop here till May 14th though my wife leaves a few days earlier. Seyrig comes in person for the division on May 4th. We have nothing spectacular but we do not return empty-handed ... Barnett is flourishing – it has been very pleasant to have an extra hand with his experience especially during a first season ... We have now obtained a good footing in the Habur ... We are building a house entirely of mud-brick, vaulted and domed ... at Chagar Bazar itself ... we thus have a pied-à-terre and will no longer have to pay an extortionate rent for a house full of fleas in Amuda.

Barnett for his part was also enthusiastic about his first season at Chagar Bazar, writing to Smith at the end of April to report that they had just finished the deep sondage.

It produced the same sequences as Arpachiyah ... About half way down, there was a most interesting and rich burial containing incised black pottery of Ninevite V type, with jewellery exactly paralleled from Sumerian finds. We have now started opening up the top level of the central ridge of the Tell and a complex of well-built walls of the first millennium BC (apparently) being dug out, possibly private houses, in which there is a good chance of interesting finds, as the walls are preserved to a good height. Mallowan is amazingly resourceful and a fine leader and gets over all the obstacles that are for ever cropping up without worrying, a real gift.

Unfortunately this mutual respect did not last. In later years, when Barnett became the first Keeper of the newly independent Department of Western Asiatic Antiquities at the British Museum, there was a barely veiled animosity between the two men.

Max wrote a full report of his first season at Chagar Bazar (March to May 1935) for the Department and his sponsors which described the deep excavation on the north-west side of the mound through 16 m of débris to virgin soil, and how that had revealed fifteen building levels, explaining how he had tried to date each one by reference to pottery samples. He described the more extensive excavation made at the highest level of the mound on the main ridge, and how it had revealed good buildings of mud-brick. Lastly he reported the making of a number of trial trenches at the foot of the mound on the south side. He produced an efficient-looking 'Table Showing the Levels as Illustrated by the Deep Sondage at Chagar Bazar and the Correspondences on Other Sites'. From the table it was plain to see that more than half the accumulated débris of Chagar Bazar belonged to the prehistoric Tell Halaf period. This corresponded with the time of the site's greatest prosperity and expansion.

An article for the more general reader was written for *The Illustrated London News* and published on 23 November 1935 under the title 'Tapping a New Archaeological Source in N. Syria'. In it Max described art relics dating from about 4000 BC to 1500 BC, including a fine black soapstone cylinder seal decorated with four bird-headed figures engaged in a ritual dance, and so-called Mother Goddess figurines of terracotta and sun-dried clay with details of their distinctive costumes – turbans, striped jackets and trousers – painted on them. The article contained some excellent photographs of these finds and also two excellent ones of the deep shaft, showing steps skilfully cut into the sides so that the workmen could get up and down with their baskets. Two further full pages of pottery samples were published, one of prehistoric pots and the other of wheel-made pots from upper and later levels of the Chagar Bazar mound. In a season which had seen reports from Henri Frankfort at Khafaje and Tell Asmar (with beautiful coloured illustrations of five-thousand year-old pottery), Gordon Loud at Khorsabad, Thorkild Jacobsen at Ischali, André Parrot at Mari and a team sponsored by the Wellcome Trust directed by J. L. Starkey at Lachish, it was important to make sure Chagar Bazar was not forgotten.

The Mallowans returned home feeling 'well satisfied' with their first season. They were already looking forward to their second, to be in the spring of 1936, not least because they would be living in their new house with its handsome dome. The finds arrived in London at the beginning of September and they spent a busy and happy time moving into Winterbrook House. Max's first letter from the new house was dated 25 October 1935, and he was to live there (except when in London or in Devon) for the rest of his life.

One of his first tasks in his new study was to write the excavation report on his first season at Chagar Bazar for *Iraq*. It was published in volume III in 1936 and consisted of three parts, an 'Introduction and Archaeological Survey', the 'Excavations' themselves and 'Details', comprehensive descriptions of the objects illustrated. The long article included maps, plans and several plates, as well as a great many beautifully drawn pottery samples.

Their second season at Chagar Bazar began in March 1936 in the middle of spring rains which that year were prolonged and made them even more grateful to be in their splendid new house. Agatha thought it had a 'holy appearance' because of the great white dome. It did in fact look a little like a monastery. Inside, the dome gave them just the sort of airy spaciousness they craved, and had the advantage of keeping the house cool on hot days. There was a different team that year. Mac, who must have missed the opportunity to live in his fine new creation, had gone back to Palestine to dig, but hoped to join them at the end of the season, in late April. His replacement was called Louis Osman. He had acquired the nickname of Bumps because on the train journey to Nisibin, after pulling up the blind, he made a quite understandable but perhaps unfortunate remark on the curious number of bumps all over the landscape. He was a good-humoured young man, happy to be teased, which was just as well. The Mallowans had decided to acquire the services of another archaeologist, albeit an amateur, in the shape of Colonal A. H. Burn, formerly of the Indian Army. It had been decided in London that, as Chagar Bazar was so near the promising mound of Tell Brak, at some times during the season Max would go over to Tell Brak to make some trial soundings there, and be able to leave the Colonel in charge of the work at Chagar Bazar. The Colonel's former life was still quite ingrained; he had a neat and well-ordered way of doing things, and an almost military way of drilling the workforce and making them line up properly on pay-day. They rather enjoyed this. In the expedition house, he spent much time tidying up round the others, and on one occasion put five Camembert cheeses (which Max had unrealistically thought might last them for most of the season) in the back of a cupboard which had then been filled with large pieces of pottery. It took them several days to find out where the terrible smell was coming from.

In the new expedition house, Agatha flourished and became quite inspired with her house-keeping talents. She left a vivid picture of her difficulties in this regard in *Come, Tell Me How You Live* with its stories of pristine kitchen tea-towels being whisked off outside to clean car radiators, of the breakfast dishes being dried with a dirty sheet, of the incomprehension that met her requirements of proper table laying, and most of all her culinary aspirations. It would not have occurred to a woman of her upbringing that it would have been far simpler to eat what was eaten locally (except of course for Turkish delight and glacé fruits). It was important that standards should be maintained, and that meant English breakfasts, picnic lunches, a proper English tea, with cake and sandwiches, and the sort of four-course dinner that people in England sat down to as a regular evening ritual. The problems were first the cook's lack of experience either of cooking or eating this sort of food, and second the lack of suitable ingredients. Agatha loved eating, and she had made Max interested in his food too, so this was a serious matter. A typical dinner might be hors d'oeuvre (egg mayonnaise, sardines, a cold bean salad and anchovies), a main course of perhaps lamb stuffed with rice, and then pudding, perhaps tinned pears, and cheese or perhaps a savoury at the end. Agatha travelled east with a great many tins, mainly of fruit, but she also brought dried goods that kept well in the heat. Luckily both fresh fruit and vegetables were readily available in local markets, as well as honey. Cream could be made from buffalo-milk. With this commissariat, she could order (and supervise) quite elaborate dishes, such as lemon curd, chocolate éclairs and vanilla soufflés, and she left an amusing account of her visits to the kitchen. The expedition house at Chagar Bazar was run in rather the same way as Ashfield, or Winterbrook House, with some eccentric local features.

The sheikh with whom they had made their contract was a frequent visitor to the new house, which he already regarded proudly as his own. On one visit he saw that Agatha was engrossed in the *Times* crossword. 'Does she also write?' he demanded, and, on being told by Max that she did, he nodded appreciatively and asked if this very learned lady would not also give medicine to women. Agatha's protests that she knew nothing of medical practice fell on deaf ears and before long she was acting as chief medical adviser, for which she soon acquired an enviable reputation, which she felt was distinctly unmerited. Among her patients, 'The commonest gesture is an expressive rubbing of the abdomen. This has one of two meanings – (a) acute indigestion; (b) complaint of sterility. Bicarbonate of soda does excellent work in the first case and has attained a somewhat surprising reputation in the second.' The following season she was informed that this amazing drug was responsible for the birth of two strong twin boys.

Work started immediately on the mound, and they were rewarded almost immediately. Some 7 m from the first trial trench dug eighteen months earlier, a new excavation uncovered a mud-brick building with a small chamber at its extreme end, which contained 70 cuneiform tablets. They were illuminating documents, mostly written in a single year when Shamshi-Adad (1813–1781 BC), an Amorite, was king of Assyria, and his son Yasmah-Addu, a rather feckless character addicted to horse-racing and women, was the governor of the district, based at Mari. On one occasion he arrived at Chagar Bazar with three thousand men and a large number of horses and oxen, all needing to be fed. The tablets gave a picture of a busy and thriving agricultural community engaged in the traditional pursuits of sheep-rearing and cultivation of barley, from which both bread and beer were made. The population of the city consisted of rural types: farmers, shepherds, cattle men, fullers, weavers, gardeners, with of course priests and scribes in attendance. It was clear that trade was widespread; trading posts on both the Tigris and the Euphrates were mentioned. Their language was Akkadian, though personal names showed that the inhabitants included some Amorites and Hurrians and others with west Semitic names. The tablets also gave vital chronological orientation and established the dating of the painted Habur ware, for they lay over fragmentary sherds of it. The tablets were deciphered at the British Museum by Cyril Gadd and published in *Iraq*, volume VII, in 1940.

The discovery of the tablets was a triumph indeed, and Max now felt he could move on to Tell Brak himself, leaving Colonel Burn in charge at Chagar Bazar. The Mallowans had first visited Tell Brak two years earlier, and Max was well aware that tackling this mighty mound was a formidable task. For a start, it really was immense, the largest mound in the district at its most extended, with dimensions of some 800 m by 600 m. At its highest point it was 40 m above the level of the plain, some 10 m higher than the Kuyunjik mound at Nineveh. It literally loomed over the surrounding countryside. The mound was at its highest and steepest on its north-western flank, which appeared to be mainly a residential quarter. The south-eastern flank seemed to have been reserved for public buildings and temples, and was apparently abandoned in about 2000 BC. The occupation of the north-western flank probably continued for a further six hundred years, by which time Max concluded that simple daily life would have been quite an effort for its occupants with a strenuous climb to the top, and no water except what they carried up themselves.

Sad though it was not to be at the expedition house at Chagar Bazar for the whole season, it was not practical for Max and Agatha to commute from it to Tell Brak every day. So they took lodgings in the high tower of a nearby *khan*. Unwanted livestock seemed to be a feature of every lodging they ever took in the East, and here at Brak it was bats. They spent a large part of every night trying to beat them down from the rafters and eject them from the windows. Otherwise the *khan* made an excellent expedition centre, as it had at least ten rooms, servants' quarters and a kitchen, and, best of all, an enormous courtyard into which they could drive Mary to unload. They very soon arranged to have a huge double door made for the arched entrance to the courtyard, a door that could be barred and bolted so that they had complete security for themselves and their finds. When they finally left Tell Brak in late 1938, they piled all their furniture and equipment into one of the empty rooms. They never saw it again.

Every two days, Max and Agatha swapped places with Bumps and the Colonel. On one of their drives across country to the Tell, Max and Agatha in Mary came across a couple of their workmen with a dog on a length of string. They stopped to give them a lift, whereupon they left the dog behind. Agatha, who had taken a fancy to it, decided to pick it up and take it with them. It was a pathetic object with ribs sticking through its skin. On arrival at Brak, Agatha commanded that it should be fed, and inevitably the dog, christened Hiyou by Bumps, became very much part of the team, a worthy successor to Swiss Miss in the history of archaeological dogs.

Wisely they confined their efforts on the mound to making a preliminary survey of it, and starting to trace the ground plan of a large structure which lay to the south of the south-east flank of the mound. Although the structure proved to be extremely large, the plotting was done in a fortnight, because it was easily accessible. The structure had four courtyards, one of which was 40 m square, and around it were placed several other large rooms. The building had only a single entrance, once flanked with towers. The outer walls were 10 m thick and even the inner partition walls were solid. This was exciting stuff: they now knew exactly where to start at the beginning of the 1937 spring season. At the end of April Mac arrived from Palestine and added immensely to the proceedings, no doubt playing his part in the plotting of the large structure. When the season ended, the finds were divided into two lots as equal as possible, and Seyrig's colleague at the Service des Antiquités, Maurice Dunand (the excavator Byblos), arrived at Chagar Bazar (at 2 a.m., having gone to Brak by mistake and had trouble finding the way in the dark to Chagar Bazar) to decide which of the two lots the Service would take. He and his wife then settled down to an enormous four-course dinner, after which the division was made amicably enough. Then the usual packing of the expedition's share for shipment to the British Museum took place, after which the expedition broke up. Warm farewells were taken of the staff and a more calculated one of the sheikh, who subtly indicated that a gold watch was a pleasant thing to have, though two might be better, if one wanted to lend one to a friend.

Max and Agatha started their journey home on a track through a 'complete wilderness' which led eventually to the city of Raqqa on the Euphrates. Max was jubilant as he would be able to inspect the Balikh valley on the way. 'Whacking great Tells all along it', he told Agatha jubilantly; clearly Chagar Bazar and Brak had not been enough for one season. An eventful day driving across completely uncharted territory gave Agatha the most hideous headache, but, being the sort of person she was, she sank into her camp bed at a primitive house at Raqqa that evening, drank a cup of tea, took four aspirin and went to sleep, waking up the next morning full of vigour, ferociously hungry and not bearing a single grudge. They crossed the Euphrates on a perilous ferry, and Agatha began to think longingly of a trip to a hairdresser, a manicure, a proper bath with taps, bath salts, electric light ... Max began to describe a certain Tell that had caught his fancy the day before, but Agatha had had enough: 'I'm tired of Tells', she announced. 'You can't be!' said Max with horror, but even he was prepared to admit that it was a pity that there was not a way of travelling straight from Chagar Bazar to the Savoy. For the time being, however, the Hotel Baron would have to do.

Max reported to Sidney Smith from there on 4 June that they had just completed a successful season and that a full report had been sent to the Director of the British Museum. 'I contemplated sending a mid-season report but with soundings and the work on Chagar my hands were so full that I postponed it from day to day. We had an enjoyable time and Burn was a great stand-by. I am delighted to have had him with us.' He expected to be back in London about 20 June.

The rest of the year was spent in their usual fashion, partly at Ashfield, partly at Winterbrook House but mostly in London. Their five cases of antiquities did not arrive until mid-October, delayed by 'administrative error' according to Seyrig. Max arranged to be at the

British Museum to unpack them, and he asked Sidney Smith to look at the tablets. He was pleased to know that Smith had identified some non-Semitic and Hurrian names, but disappointed that none of the tablets revealed the ancient name of Chagar Bazar. He spent most of his time writing up the past season's work and planning the next one, to begin the following spring. His report of his second season was published in *The Illustrated London News* on 27 March 1937, and in *Iraq*, volume IV part II, in the autumn of 1937.

Meanwhile Agatha was hard at work on *Murder in Mesopotamia*. The plot had been suggested to her by their old friend Algy Whitburn, who had been with Max in his very first season at Ur. Agatha's usual method of working was to start with notes and a draft plot written in her large black writing on whatever was to hand, and for this book she had written down 'Woolleys, C.T.s, Father Burrows' and made a sketch of an expedition house, which was based on the Chagar Bazar house. She had made a tentative timetable of everyone's movements at the time of the murder.

The book owes all its impact to Agatha's experiences in Iraq and Syria, and certainly would never have been written if she had not met and married Max. The narrator of the story, Nurse Leatheran, is an outsider with all the outsider's slightly irritating reaction to an arcane subject which she does not comprehend, which echoed Agatha's own reaction to life on an archaeological expedition but in a much more naive way. This was a device for introducing Mesopotamian history to an audience for whom it would have been completely unfamiliar. On the other hand, the 'house-party' contrivance was one with which readers of crime thrillers were familiar; it was the best way to contain in one place a group of people who all had a very good reason for wanting one of their number out of the way. The book had its own merits of course but its main interest for Max and Agatha's own circle was on exactly whom each of the characters was based.

The most obvious association was that between the (soon to be murdered) heroine Louise Leidner and Katharine Woolley. Although Katharine was German and dark-haired, and Louise American and very fair, the character of the two was well beyond coincidence. Both Katharine and her fictional counterpart had a special sort of charm that inspired men and for the most part irritated women. Both suffered ill-health and mood swings, causing distress to others. Dr Leidner too owed much to Leonard Woolley, absorbed in his subject but constantly worried about his wife, whom he adored, however trying she could be. Father Lavigny in the book doubtless owes much to Father Burrows. The other characters are less easy to attribute to living counterparts, with one exception, though they probably owed a variety of characteristics to characters whom Agatha had encountered on her travels in the East. Was there a touch of Bumps in the bumptious and garrulous Coleman? Did Dr Mercato remind people of Reginald Campbell Thompson (apart from the drug habit of course)? The one exception was David Emmott, the silent young assistant at the Tell Yarimjah dig. There are several reminders of the young Max in the quiet, self-possessed, capable and reliable young man whom Louise Leidner liked so much, who seemed to get his own way without really trying, who possessed an even gaze before which other eyes fell. There were some private jokes for Max to enjoy: 'I had taken rather a fancy to Mr Emmott'. The book was dedicated to 'My many archaeological friends in Iraq and Syria' and had a jacket drawn by Robin Macartney.

The Mallowans were back in Syria for their third season in the early spring of 1937. This had again been sponsored by the British Museum and the British School of Archaeology in Iraq, but they had also received generous support both from the Ashmolean Museum in Oxford and the Museum of Archaeology and Ethnology in Cambridge. They had with them Colonel Burn once more and two architects, Mac and Bumps.

Their first task was to complete the excavation of Chagar Bazar, but they were anxious to move on to Brak as soon as possible. The work at Brak that season was mainly on 'A Gigantic Palace of 2500 BC in a Remote Stronghold of Sumerian Culture', as Max described it to readers of *The Illustrated London News* in his record of the work published in January 1938. This was the palace they had plotted so easily at the end of the previous season, and now they began to make sense of it, digging more deeply in some areas. Even so, at the end of the season, there was still more than half of the palace as well as newly discovered subterranean chambers in the south-west corner of it to be excavated the following season. 'From that distant stronghold of Sumerian civilization, firmly established in remotest Syria during the third millennium BC, we may confidently expect to learn much of vital importance for an understanding of the course of history in Western Asia', wrote Max.

Apart from the palace, they started to excavate a religious structure they called the Eye Temple (because of the many hundreds of eye-idols found in it). This structure they provisionally dated between 3900 and 3500 BC. They found that it consisted of five temples superimposed upon one another, but decided to concentrate mainly on the second of these, which they dated to the end of the Uruk period, about 3300 BC. The floors of the second Eye Temple were made of mud overlaid with bitumen and reed, and its walls of white washed mudbrick which had once been panelled with copper sheets hammered from the back with eye representations. The most important room was the main sanctuary which was 18 m long by 6 m wide, with two entrances in its short north wall. At the opposite end to this, they made one of their principal finds: a white-washed clay altar 1 m high with a frieze of exquisite workmanship mostly still in place. Of the three panels which had once adorned it, two were practically intact.

The panels were 1 m long and 12 cm wide and were carved in fretted bands of blue limestone, white marble and green corrugated shale. Each one was surrounded by gold foil casing. The entire frieze had been backed by wood and attached to the altar by means of copper fastenings and gold-headed silver nails. This was a tremendously exciting find, easily surpassing anything they had found in Syria so far.

Other good finds that season were a ritual vessel in the shape of a trough decorated with raised snakes and scorpions in relief, and the most extraordinary 'face-vase', a vessel some 13 cm high, made first on the wheel and then modelled by hand to give it features. Its facial characteristics had then been emphasized by a free hand with the paintbrush. The face had long narrow eyebrows, big circles painted round the eyes, painted ears with curly sidewhiskers in front of them and a circle surrounded the grinning mouth, which had been filled in with curly dots to give the impression of stubble. Painted triangles round the rim were meant to suggest a crown perhaps. It was a very unusual piece and occupied a full page in the report in *The Illustrated London News*.

The season was practically over when Max wrote to Sidney Smith on 24 April, enclosing photographs.

I am sorry to have kept you waiting so long for these poor prints but the fact is that I have till quite recently been somewhat pulled down by a boil and after the day's digging was over, or indeed when I was not actually on the dig had no surplus energy left for photography. I am glad to say that I am now recovered ... Brak is proving very interesting and seems to contain material of many different periods ... I believe that eventually we shall light upon something pretty good and in general all the material from Brak is much superior in quality to the Chagar finds. Of the 'Hurrian' period we have a splendid goblet modelled in the shape of a man's head – with a distinct grin on the face ... There is no lack of small objects.

At the end of the season, on 26 May, and after a satisfactory division of the finds, the Mallowans went to Greece. Max wrote to Smith from Athens on 7 June, sending him some copious general news, 'not a formal report', on the season's excavations and enclosing a second batch of photographs of tablets. He apologized for the quality of these: 'as far as I can see it is not possible to produce a legible photograph of a tablet with a convex face unless one takes six photographs of each individual tablet'. He summed up the season by saying that they had learned much more about the Habur region as a result of their recent work and that Brak had provided them with much material that was not represented at Chagar Bazar, for example cylinder seals, finely worked amulets, a rich collection of metal (including a bronze battleaxe with a ribbed socket and a pin surmounted with an ibex head – both to come to the British Museum), a good collection of painted pottery, good terracotta figurines, and 33 gold objects, mostly beads and earrings. He anticipated that the British Museum's share of these objects would arrive in London some time in August, but meanwhile he and Agatha were about to go to Crete and would be back at the end of the month.

Max spent the summer as usual, writing. He was preparing a full report on his Habur survey during 1936 for *Iraq*. He was keen that Cyril Gadd should finish his work on the tablet find from Chagar Bazar so that it could be completed in the report. He also wrote to Smith on 18 July, saying he had been buried in the country, trying to finish it, and asking for help. 'There are several points on which I would be glad of your advice – particularly with reference to the cuneiform texts and the chronology'. The relationship between the two men had changed. Max's tone had become much less deferential and Smith's much friendlier. In August, Max invited Smith out to lunch so they could discuss the continuance of the work at Brak, and the best way forward.

Following the lunch, Max wrote a draft appeal for funds, which he sent to Smith asking for his comments, erasures and additions. Smith wrote from the British Museum on 17 September in his usual rather detached manner, but Max was not intimidated by it; indeed he appreciated the work Smith had done and instantly removed the 'preliminary palaver'. Smith had said to Max,

> I hardly like to interfere in what is your personal affair but I suggest that as this letter [to his sponsors] is intended for at most half a dozen rich men who have already supported or at least know about your work the rather general paragraphs on pages 1 & 2 are superfluous. The point of your application is really … that the finds at Brak last season make it most desirable that the dig be continued a) because you will be able for the first time to study early Sumerian civilization outside its own territory and b) because you have an early site which reaches down into the dark period about 1700, and the evidence criss-crosses with Woolley's at Atchana. Your further point is that a failure to dig next season may mean less favourable conditions for digging later. If you would amplify this theme and assume more knowledge of your general points and therefore leave them out, I think the letter might carry more weight. In other words be more specific.

Clearly the appeal reached its mark, as four of his former sponsors – the British Museum, the British School of Archaeology in Iraq, the Ashmolean and Sir Charles Marston – continued their support, and a new sponsor, Sir Robert Mond, the great industrialist, added his generosity to what had already been promised.

Max's fourth season in north Syria began on 14 March 1938 and ended on 31 May. He was once again accompanied by Agatha, and assisted by Colonel Burn. He and Burn had come to Brak via Ankara so that they could meet the Director for Antiquities for Anatolia. This was because Max had an idea that he would like to move northwards into Turkey for his next excavation project, possibly in the direction of Lake Van. The meeting had been inconclusive, though the Director for Antiquities had received them with great courtesy and had even come to see them off at the station, which, Max reported to Smith, 'I took to be a compliment!'. Max had three untried new members of staff this season: Guilford Bell (the nephew of a Australian friend of Agatha) as architect, a young man called R. T. Threlfall as general assistant and a Miss R. M. C. Christie.

This last person would have been well known to people who knew the Mallowans: she was Rosalind, Agatha's daughter and Max's stepdaughter. Rosalind had gone to Benenden School in Kent, where she had been head girl, but she had been bombarding Agatha in Syria with letters telling her that she was bored, and begging to be allowed to leave. Agatha had insisted that she stay on long enough to pass her School Certificate, which, despite gloomy predictions by her head-mistress, she had succeeded in doing. She was still very young, however, and Max and Agatha had spent a rather anxious time since then trying to find a place for her to be 'finished' abroad. She had turned into a ravishing beauty but she also had decided views as to her own future, and these did not always coincide with those of her mother and stepfather. A finishing school in Gstaad had proved to be a complete fiasco, so they tried another one at Château d'Oex, after which she went as a paying guest to a pleasant family in Paris so that she could perfect her French. On the way home in 1936, they had collected Rosalind and discovered during a somewhat fraught taxi ride that she did indeed speak fluent French. Next, she had been sent to Germany so that she could perfect her German as well. The last stage in her education was to be a debutante and to be presented at Court. Rosalind was a great success, being beautiful, and according to Agatha it did her a great deal of good as she acquired good manners and self-confidence in the process. Agatha could not present her at Court herself, because she was divorced, so she was presented by Agatha's friends the Mackintoshes, old friends from Torquay. He was the Director of the Science Museum in London.

At the end of her London season Rosalind was free, and looking for something to do. Her mother, horrified, turned down the suggestion that she should become a photographic model and persuaded her to come to Brak for a time instead. Rosalind was good at drawing, though she lacked confidence in her own ability, and Max thought she might like to help with sketching objects. Unfortunately she was a perfectionist and, unless entirely happy with the result of her endeavours, tore it up. This led to some furious quarrels between Max and Rosalind, who were extremely fond of one another. Some of Rosalind's drawings were, however, used in publications about Tell Brak.

Rosalind found herself very impressed with the very different Max she saw on the site: he was up so early, he was so organized, worked rigorously all day long on the mound and seemed to have the workforce completely under his thumb, rather a different Max to the one who enjoyed lazy summer holidays at Ashfield, when his disciplined routine extended only to afternoons writing in his study. In Devon, Max always found time for tennis, swimming and other relaxing occupations.

Max reported to Sidney Smith on 28 March that they were concentrating all the men (about three hundred) on the palace. There had been exceptionally heavy spring rains and the country was green and full of wild flowers. 'We have a wild and woolly set of ruffians on the dig and it takes all the time to keep them in order. We are all very fit.'

Smith replied on 6 April about the proposed Turkish excavation. 'I should much prefer you to examine the Balikh sites.' The letter started, 'My dear Mallowan', and ended with 'Mary' (his wife) joining him in wishing Mrs Mallowan and Burn 'a happy time'. This definitely marked a new stage in the relationship. She had always been Mrs Smith before. Richard Barnett described Max as being Smith's 'blue-eyed boy' during the 1930s.

That season Max and his expedition team excavated at four different buildings, covering a period that extended from 3100 to 1500 BC. They continued their work on the Akkadian palace, which they now knew to have been constructed for Naram-Sin (2254–2218 BC), the fourth king of the Dynasty of Akkad, which had begun in 2334 BC, having discovered at the end of the season mud-bricks stamped with the name of this king. As yet the temple platform at the south-west end of the palace had been only partially excavated, but they hoped to be able to recover the complete ground plan of that building in the course of the next (fifth) season.

They had spent much of the season, and in particular the last four weeks, in clearing the subterranean chambers beneath the temple platform and it had been slow and difficult work done by the light of electric torches and in airless conditions. They had found about forty thousand beads, mainly of faience, but some gold, carnelian, rock crystal and steatite ones, 'a complete menagerie' of amulets, including representations of lions, gazelles, bears, hedgehogs, ibexes, hares, frogs, eagles, ducks, fish, sheep and cows, made from alabaster, lapis lazuli, marble, steatite, limestone, carnelian, shell, bone and faience, and a hoard of alabaster idols, about whose exact significance they were unclear, though they had eyes inlaid with black, red and orange paint and served some ritual purpose.

Apart from these two areas, the team had also excavated the 'Hurrian' houses, three successive levels of mud-brick houses built between 1800 and 1500 BC. The excavations had produced a quantity of so-called Mitannian pottery, with designs in white paint on a black ground. The designs were predominantly geometric but there were also floral decorations, and depictions of birds. In the private houses of the Third Dynasty of Ur and earlier Sargonid periods, they made their richest finds of the season. A treasure trove in a clay vase produced a string of gold filigree pendants, gold, silver and carnelian beads, an alabaster bobbin, haematite weights and silver and copper bangles. They also found two complete cuneiform tablets and a number of fragments as well as many clay seal impressions.

On the way to Aleppo at the end of the season, the Mallowans travelled through the Balikh valley and spent two days taking a cursory view at likely mounds. Max was by now able to judge a mound by its appearance: too much solid masonry almost certainly meant Roman occupation and therefore the prehistoric remains underneath would not be easily accessible. Two that looked suitably denuded were Tell Jidle and Tell Mefesh, both of which he had mentioned to Henri Seyrig, who had indicated that permission to excavate at both these tells would be readily granted.

The Mallowans again went that June to Greece, from where Max wrote to Sidney Smith, sending him a sixteen-page typewritten report together with 70 photographs with typewritten labels. 'I hope you will agree with me that the season has been exceptionally interesting, and that we ought to go back again to Brak for a short campaign before the close of this year and before Seyrig loses his executive authority. You will see also that I suggest that we make soundings on the Balikh ... I am travelling slowly via Greece, Yugoslavia and Italy.' He expected to be back in England in the first week in July.

Max's intention was to return to Syria for a second season in October. He was keen to complete the excavation of the temple platform and if time allowed to go to the Balikh river to make soundings at the two small mounds which he and Agatha had looked at on the way back to Aleppo in early June. He reckoned he needed another five or six weeks to finish excavating the ziggurat plus three weeks on the Balikh. 'I feel this would round off the Expedition's work in Eastern Syria', he wrote on his report, 'and I would devote the whole of 1939 to the final publication of Tell Brak and the Balikh soundings'.

When Max arrived back in England that summer he had to set about once again raising money for the autumn season. Although he felt he had exhausted the generosity of the British School of Archaeology in Iraq, they did agree to sponsor this last season (his fifth in Syria), as did the Trustees of the British Museum, the Ashmolean and Sir Charles Marston as before. Mr A. L. Reckitt was another sponsor.

Sidney Smith had added his weight to the fund-raising by writing to the Director on 8 July on the subject of Mallowan's 'Proposed Excavations at Brak and on the Balikh River'.

> When I urged the continuation of the excavation at Brak ... last
> year, it seemed probable that this last season in the spring of
> 1938 would add very considerably to our Syrian collections,
> which, as you know, have been a very weak spot in the past
> owing to lack of opportunity to excavate. The expectation has
> been more than realised. Mallowan's report and illustrations of
> the finds enable me to form an estimate of the value of the new
> collection.

The collection now included:

> about 100 stamp seals, all of Jemdet Nasr period ... archaeolog-
> ically important ... take the form of animals or animal heads and

are themselves beautiful objects ... a unique collection, not
paralleled in any museum; ... about 100 amulets of the same
period, mostly in animal form ...; jewellery, amulets, weapons
and ornaments of the Agade period ... all purely Mesopotamian
in form ...; alabaster idols of early date, not otherwise paralleled,
... sherds, figurines and beads, of various dates. Two complete
tablets inscribed in cuneiform, and a few bronze weapons.

Shortly after this report, the Trustees agreed to grant a further £500
towards the expedition.

Max was also busy writing up a six-page report for *The Illustrated
London News*, published on 15 October just before the new expedition
set off. The article was entitled 'Revelations of Brilliant Art in North-
East Syria Over 4000 Years Ago – New Discoveries at the Great Mound
of Brak; A Palace Built by King Naram-Sin of Agade in 2500 BC and a
Tower-Platform of 3000 BC with a Hoard of Treasure Buried Beneath'.
Two pages of the article were taken up with a huge and beautifully
decorated table entitled 'Schematic Section Through the Mound at
Brak'. This showed objects, clearly drawn by Guilford Bell, from each
of the successive occupation periods, which numbered five.

The bottom period, dated about the fourth millennium BC, was the
prehistoric Tell Halaf level. Then *c.* 3000–2335 BC, Early Dynastic and
Jemdet Nasr level, then *c.* 2334–2154 BC, Sargonid level (the period of
the Naram-Sin palace), then *c.* 2112–2004 BC, Third Dynasty of Ur level;
c. 2000–1700 BC, Habur level, and lastly *c.* 1700–1400 BC, Hurrian level
(illustrated with a fine drawing of the face-vase). There were two more
pages of illustrations of objects found at Brak, including one that showed
as many different animal amulets as possible. A week later *The Illustrated
London News* printed another article illustrating Syrian craftsmanship of
about 2500 BC, with photographs of a number of small objects including
seals, more amulets, jewellery, tools, weapons and inscriptions.

By this time Max was at Brak, with Agatha, and once more with
Guilford Bell, described by Agatha as having a long, fair, serious face,
rather an innocent abroad, though an excellent artist. They installed
themselves in the expedition house and started work on the temple-
platform where they almost immediately made a lucky find, their first
piece of sculpture. This was a male head in white alabaster, some

18 cm high, belonging to the late Early Dynastic I, or early Jemdet Nasr period. Max wrote to Smith saying, 'Meanwhile amulets, beads and idols pour in: if we have another week like the first we shall have had a first class season as far as objects are concerned.'

In the end they spent only seventeen days at Brak, but they achieved most of what they had hoped to do and find. The great disappointment was the absence of any written material. They recovered no tablets at all. In the Eye Temple, the recovery of the plan proved to be extremely difficult as after the destruction of the temple the rooms had been hard-packed with clay which had then been stamped down. This was so hard that the workmen trying to smash it with pickaxes became physically exhausted and complained of pain in their arms and shoulders. The situation was made worse by the fact that others of their number had a far easier job to do: working in soft soil at the base of the temple-platform. To add to their sense of injury, these men were finding innumerable beads, amulets and other small objects which earned them *bakshish*. 'Thanks to a mixture of threats, cajolery, bribery, and punishment we succeeded in completing our task', reported Max to Smith in a later report.

Unfortunately, even when the task was completed the sense of simmering resentment went on among the workmen with the pickaxes. This led to a very serious incident in which two of them were killed during the interval for lunch one day, at a time when all workmen were forbidden to enter the excavations. They had surreptitiously entered one of the tunnels beneath the temple-platform and were looking for valuable objects, when the mud-brick tunnel collapsed on top of them and, as Max reported, 'they paid the extreme penalty'. This tragedy was resolved by Max, the local sheikh of the village from where the men came and the French security officer from Kamechlie, and the expedition was publicly exonerated from all blame by Sheikh Ali Sultan of the Habur, but it was clear to all that the situation in Syria was deteriorating and everyone was rather relieved when they moved on to the Balikh valley at the beginning of November. Agatha made no bones about it; taking a last walk down to the Jagjagha river, she admitted to herself that 'Brak has never had the hold on my affections that Chagar has. The village of Brak is melancholy, half deserted, and tumbling down.'

They set off for their 180 km journey westwards in Mary and their old Citroën taxi, laden with furniture, equipment, personal effects, Hiyou the dog and the servants who had looked after them so faithfully for all their seasons in Syria, having chosen for their headquarters a place called Tell Abyadh which lay just before the Syrian–Turkish border. The house they had taken looked charming but turned out to have been built on a marsh and was so damp that Agatha was soon so stiff that she could hardly move. Even Max began to complain of rheumatism and found it hard climbing out of bed. Guilford was still with them, and they had been joined by their old friend John Cruickshank Rose, whom they were very pleased to see again. Agatha started work on *Murder Is Easy*.

The survey was fun, but ultimately unrewarding. The main focus of their investigation was Tell Jidle, a mound 6 km south of 'Ain al 'Arus, the headwaters of the Balikh, on the west bank. It was a compact mound, some 15 m high with steep slopes. From the top there was a lovely view of the clear blue Balikh in which they could see fish swimming. A deep sounding which revealed eight levels was made. The site had first been occupied in the late fourth millennium and abandoned some time between AD 300 and 600.

They also looked at Tell Aswad, on a branch of the Balikh. It had some very ancient Neolithic arrowheads and evidence of extensive occupation during the Halaf and earlier periods. At the top of the mound, they drew the ground plan of a small prehistoric temple. Tell Sahlan, about a kilometre upstream, could be reached only by swimming so they merely took measurements of the mound.

At Tell Mefesh, they spent five promising days, looking at a mound that had last been occupied in the Ubaid period. They found pottery from that period and the Halaf period, and an interesting fragment of a sun-dried clay mother goddess figurine.

The general impression formed by Max was that a scarcity of metal implements meant that the Balikh valley was much less urbanized, and therefore much less interesting, than the Habur valley. He did not think it would be profitable to search for remains of the second millennium, as the soundings they had made produced remains of such poverty that they were hardly worth recovering. Reluctantly, he ruled out the Balikh valley as a future place of operations. His report of the survey was finally published after the War in *Iraq*, volume VIII, 1946, and was beautifully illustrated by John Cruickshank Rose.

Max and Agatha left Tell Abyadh just in time before the winter rains and had an eventful journey to Aleppo. They had been invited to breakfast at their former foreman's house and, hoping for a snack, were treated to a vast banquet, the last thing they felt like, especially as it took some six hours to produce. Absolutely exhausted, they staggered into Baron's Hotel, the last time they would stay there for many years. Already there were rumours of unrest in the air and they had uneasy feelings about the future. The Mallowans spent Christmas with Claude and Odile Shaeffer at Ras Shamra. C. F. A. Shaeffer had been excavating the great ancient site since Easter 1929 and had almost immediately been able to identify it as Ugarit, uncovering a necropolis area which revealed its cosmopolitan composition. It had flourished as a major Phoenician trading centre in the late first millennium. Over Christmas, Max walked over the excavations with Claude Schaeffer and Agatha spent her time bathing off rocks in the clear blue sea, just what she loved. From this visit, a firm friendship with Claude and Odile Schaeffer evolved. 'We are very glad in spite of the simple manner we had to receive Madame Agatha and you, you enjoyed your visit. Odile and I only regret that it was short.'

They left Beirut in the New Year of 1939 by boat. Agatha stood on deck looking back at the coast of Lebanon, taking a romantic farewell of what had been some of the best days of her life. She recalled the country, the people, the people they had worked with, both the Arabs and the Europeans, the jokes, the laughter, the mishaps, and the triumphs. 'I am thinking', she told Max, 'that it was a very happy way to live ...'

CHAPTER SEVEN

Reluctantly Cultivating Vegetables

The Mallowans had spent much of the summer of 1938, before their last season in Syria, at Ashfield, Agatha's childhood home in Torquay. Sometime during that summer, Agatha heard that one of the most perfect houses on the river Dart was for sale. She had known the house since she was a little girl and she clearly remembered her mother taking her to see it. On an impulse, she suggested to Max and Rodney Kannreuther, who was staying at the time, that they should go to see it. They went, and Agatha fell instantly in love.

Greenway House was a classic Georgian house, built in about 1780, with a graceful white façade which gazed down on to the river below. It was set in woods with fine old trees, and had a beautiful garden, rather overgrown, 33 acres in all. As Agatha sighed with hopeless desire to own this dream house, Max suddenly suggested that she should find out what the sellers wanted for it. Although Agatha thought they said £16,000, in fact they had said £6,000. This seemed an instant bargain, and, with Max encouraging her, she decided to buy it.

One of the deciding factors had been that her beloved Ashfield was very much changed from the halcyon days of her childhood. Then the large seaside villa had stood with two or three others on the outskirts of Torquay on grassy cliffs with a splendid view of the sea. Now, a secondary school blocked that view and at playtime the noise of the children was deafening. One of the neighbouring villas had been taken over by a nursing home for the mentally ill, and, on occasions, Ashfield's garden had been invaded by people who were clearly deranged, and occasionally extremely alarming. The spaces between these villas had been filled up with several smaller houses. In addition, Max had never really liked Ashfield, probably because it was associated in his mind with an Agatha whom he had not known, a child, a young married woman and a young mother. Rosalind was now grown up and they were spending less and less time there. But at the same time, neither of them wanted to break their links with Devon. Going there in the summer was very much part of the pattern of their married life, and they would miss the sea bathing and the nearby moors for walking and picnics.

Buying Greenway House seemed the perfect solution. The house as well as the garden was in a neglected state and would need much done to it to make it comfortable. Guilford Bell, who had been their architect at Tell Brak, came with them to see it and made the sensible suggestion that they should immediately pull half of it down. By this he meant that they should dispose of the Victorian additions, and restore the house to its original state. Guilford drew up plans for the alterations, and for the new interior, which was to include several bathrooms. The work was done, the whole house painted in plain white and the Mallowans took possession in late June 1939, three months before war broke out. In fact they were in the kitchen at Greenway, Agatha engaged in making a salad, at the time that they heard the momentous declaration of war.

Ever since they had been back from Syria in the New Year, the rumblings of imminent war had been growing louder. They had tried to maintain their normal way of life, commuting between Sheffield Terrace and Winterbrook House, with the summer in Devonshire, but there was an unsettled feeling to life. Max had been going to the British Museum and had overseen the arrival of four cases of antiquities from Tell Brak in February, and the Mallowans' friendship with Sidney and Mary Smith had progressed to the point where the Smiths were asked to dinner. But Max was uneasy, and when he was asked to attend an archaeological conference in Berlin in the summer he decided it would be better not to go. In the event, the conference was cut short and those attending scuttled home to their various countries.

Max had always said he intended to spent 1939 writing up his seasons at Tell Brak, and he tried to settle down in his spacious first-floor study at Greenway with its enormous windows looking down on the Dart, to do this. But with the declaration of war, this project was constantly being shelved as Max made determined efforts to involve himself in the service of his country. The problem was that authority did not really see it that way: with an Austrian father and a French mother, even though he had been born in Battersea, he did not qualify as really English. Those were suspicious times.

On New Year's Eve 1939, Max was writing to Sidney Smith in some despair:

> For the present I am one of the unwanted civilians, and having tried for several active service jobs have resigned myself to wait. I am now on the Reserve List for the R.A.F. Intelligence and the W.O. [War Office] and even trawlers have my name, but as nobody requires my services for the time being I am reluctantly cultivating vegetables and archaeology. Having missed the last War on account of extreme youth it seems that I may miss this one on account of extreme age. Meanwhile I am able to work on the Brak publication at my leisure and I anticipate that it will be finished in February and perhaps published in the autumn. I have twice been unlucky in finding you away from London but I hope I may see you some time in February when I bring up my MS and plates? ... I have very much missed the opportunity of discussing with you the great variety of topics which I have had to tackle in the Brak report ... I have perhaps been unduly long-winded, but I have at least concentrated my efforts on the catalogue of illustrated objects which contains a series of monographs. I have tried ... so far as possible to tie up the Brak finds with the related material on a considerable number of different sites.

He concluded by asking Smith whether he would read his manuscript when it was ready, and saying that he had decided to date the Eye Temple to the late Jemdet Nasr period and the objects buried beneath it to an earlier Jemdet Nasr period. This was the last letter of this kind that he was to write for many years.

Smith replied in an encouraging tone about Brak, and saying that he felt 'like a flat fish ... high and dry on a beach' himself, and very lonely since Mary had decided to take on their children's education herself, and had gone with them to live with her parents. Max wrote back to say they would all be welcome at any time if they wanted to come to Greenway. He added, 'Agatha is a trained dispenser and does part time work in the Torbay hospital making up poisons. Best wishes.'

By the end of the month, however, Max was in London, reporting to Smith:

> I am now an unpaid slave working all day and half the night as the Hon. Sec. to the Anglo-Turkish Relief. This is my first Sunday off for 3 weeks. I was in two minds as to where my duty lay – whether to finish Brak or take this job on, but apparently they were really stuck for a man and I decided to do it. Also there is a faint prospect of getting out to Turkey in the end and there may eventually be some work worth doing there. The highest point of Ararat would be a paradise after the office work I am now doing, for as you know a wretched secretary to a Committee gets all the kicks and none of the half pence! I don't know how you feel, but I take a very serious view of the pickle we are in, and the sooner we get rid of our complacent view of things and get to grips the better … I feel that anything we can do to ginger up Turkey is a step in the right direction. We have collected £20,000 in a week and already sent off enough clothing for 42,000 persons and 2 tons of medical supplies. Public generosity is outstanding.

The Anglo-Turkish Relief Committee had been set up after a catastrophic earthquake at Erzincan in the eastern part of the country. Its principal aim was to raise money for the relief of the victims, partly because there was genuine sympathy for the Turks and partly because it was considered in London that Turkey would be a valuable ally in a vulnerable part of the world. The Committee's offices were at 21 Albemarle Street and its president was Lord Lloyd of Dolobran, a powerful cabinet minister. The executive officer in Turkey was a colleague of Max, Professor John Garstang, who had dug with Flinders Petrie and Leonard Woolley, and founded the British School of Archaeology in Ankara. It was he who was responsible for Max's involvement. Agatha decided to come up to London too to keep Max company. They led a somewhat peripatetic existence as Sheffield Terrace was let. First they lived in Half Moon Street, then took a flat off St James's Street, then Sheffield Terrace became vacant again so they moved in there. It was not to be for long, however. On 10 November 1940, a blast from a land mine rendered the house completely uninhabitable, though it did not flatten it completely. They were able to remove the furniture and arranged for it to be stored in the squash court at Winterbrook House, which had been let for the duration.

Fortunately for Max, the Committee was much less busy because of the difficulty of getting ships out with relief for the Turks, though he did not expect to be formally dismissed till the beginning of the following year. But, homeless in London, it seemed to Max that he would try to work from Devon, and fit in some time for his archaeological work at the same time. He was still longing to be called up, however, telling Smith that both his younger brothers were in the army: 'I hope I shall be there too before the end of the war.' Meanwhile he had joined the Home Guard, 'doing a course of signalling which I find interesting. I imagine that a cuneiformist would learn the Morse Code in half an hour. It took me two nights.' Max had also become very interested in the garden at Greenway and spent much time, as well as money, ordering plants at his favourite nursery in Exeter, Robert Veitch & Son Limited. In October he bought a whole lorry-load of trees and shrubs, including eighteen rhododendrons, four judas trees, lilacs, and several different varieties of camellia and magnolia.

Agatha meanwhile had been acting as guardian for two children of doctor friends of theirs from Mosul, the Macleods. Crystal was Agatha's goddaughter. She was three, and her elder brother David was five. He was mad about aeroplanes, giving Agatha lessons on how to distinguish a Spitfire from a Hurricane and so on. One day he informed her happily that a Messerschmitt was coming over. She was dismissive, it dropped two bombs and David felt smug. That afternoon the two of them had a happy time looking for the craters. Shortly after this, a primary school a short way from them in the Dart valley was machine-gunned at playtime, and the Macleods decided to move the children to Colwyn Bay. Despite these odd raids, Greenway was then requisitioned as a home for evacuees from St Pancras. It did not take long for both Max and Agatha to decide it was time to leave.

Max's time on the Anglo-Turkish Relief Committee had its reward.

Lord Lloyd, who had taken a good view of him, weighed in to help him find a post in active service. Max had only one ambition, to get into the RAF, an ambition he felt was completely hopeless. Somehow Lord Lloyd managed to get him into the Intelligence Branch of the RAF, according to Max's account of events in his *Memoirs*. It is perhaps more likely that an inside influence smoothed the path. This would have been Stephen Glanville, whom Max had first met in the mid-1920s when they were both newcomers in the field of ancient history, Max working at Ur with Woolley and Glanville at the Department of Egyptian and Assyrian Antiquities at the British Museum.

Glanville, with the rank of Squadron Leader, was working in the Air Ministry in a department known as the Directorate of Allied and Foreign Liaison. He took Max under his wing and soon had him representing the Air Force on Lord Hankey's Committee which dealt with the co-ordinating the supply of equipment to Britain's allies from all three forces. The Army and the Royal Navy were represented on this Committee by a general or an admiral, but the Air Force seemed to think an officer of much lower rank quite adequate to represent them. Max found himself delegated to this task by Glanville and had to stammer his way through his first meeting, without the faintest idea of what he was supposed to be saying.

Thanks also to Stephen Glanville who already lived there, the Mallowans found a flat in a newly built avant-garde structure commissioned in 1932 by the furniture designer Jack Pritchard and designed by the modernist Canadian architect Wells Coats. They spent a contented year together at 22 Lawn Road Flats, from where Agatha went off to University College Hospital to work as a dispenser three-and-a-half days a week and alternate Saturdays, and Max to the Air Ministry, frequently walking home as the bombing of London had more or less destroyed public transport.

They saw various friends from their old life: the Seyrigs came over with their little girl, the Schaeffers and of course Leonard and Katharine Woolley, who had taken up residence at the Dorchester. Schaeffer reported to Max: 'I saw yesterday Woolley and Lady W! She asks him all sorts of services which really had to be done by herself and he … is like a kind obedient servant. They are both well and cheerful.'

Rosalind had recently married a Welsh Army officer called Hubert

Prichard, whom she had met at her aunt Madge's house. He was a friend of her cousin Jack. The wedding had taken place quite suddenly and Agatha had travelled up to Denbigh for the occasion, which took place in a Registry Office with only the best man and Agatha as witnesses. Now and again Rosalind would descend on Agatha in Hampstead, and Agatha went up to help Rosalind when she moved into her husband's family house at Pwyllwrach. These visits became much more frequent after Max left for the Middle East and Rosalind became pregnant.

After Max had been working for almost a year at the Air Ministry, the Directorate was asked to nominate two officers to go to Egypt to set up a corresponding Directorate for allied and foreign liaison there. Max had immediately volunteered, because he was still desperately keen to see some fighting and because he wanted to be back in the Middle East. He was promoted to the rank of Squadron Leader and posted to Cairo, where he was to report to RAF Headquarters. His role was to make and maintain links with Britain's allies, the Free French, the Czech and the Polish air force contingents. As a result of his liaison with the Poles in particular, Max conceived a life-long admiration for their courage.

Max lived first in the Continental Hotel, and later in a flat which he shared with his brother Cecil, who was by coincidence also in Cairo, unbeknown to Max, who encountered him on the terrace of the hotel drinking coffee. He was also living at the Continental. Cecil had been taken prisoner in Finland earlier on in the War, had been repatriated and then been sent out to the Middle East by the British Council. The two brothers, who had not seen much of each other in the recent past, now saw each other every day, eating most of their meals together. 'He often makes sarcastic remarks about my appetite', Max told their mother. In July they decided to move to a flat.

Cairo during the Second World War had a hectic and heady atmosphere. The central arena of the War in the Middle East, it had a constant buzz of excitement, with high-ranking people coming and going, and troops from all over the Middle East descending on it on leave, looking for excitement and distraction from the horror and boredom of their postings elsewhere in the area. The social life of that most cosmopolitan of cities had hardly been touched by the War; the same very civilized way of life continued with an added edge of excitement because no one knew how long it could last, or indeed how much longer they might be alive to enjoy it. The Gezira Club was open to officers: in its enormous and beautifully tended grounds, they could play polo, cricket, croquet and tennis. There was also a race-course and a swimming pool. Max regularly went to the Club in an attempt to keep his weight down, but so excellent was the local food that it was a lost cause. There were also concerts, dancing and cocktails (including one with the name of 'Suffering Bastard' invented by the White Russian barman at Shepheard's Hotel and the most effective hangover cure known to man), tea and ices at Groppi's.

Max was to be away from England for exactly four years, and during that time he wrote literally hundreds of letters in his small, neat hand. He wrote to Agatha every few days and to his mother almost once a week and these letters provide a clear picture of the daily round of his life. His duties at the Directorate were not onerous – in May he went off to Syria for a week and 'saw many old friends there including some archaeologists and we spent some time seeing the new Museum and discussing antiquities'. In September, he went to Palestine and spent a couple of days in Jerusalem, then went to Tel Aviv where he bathed from a fine sandy beach, much to the envy of Agatha. He had taken up learning written Arabic, and was taking up a new interest in Egyptology, buying books and visiting the Pyramids. There were archaeological contacts in Egypt too, in particular Eiddon Edwards, who later became the Keeper of Egyptian Antiquities at the British Museum. In Egypt, he was attached to the British Embassy.

Max and Cecil settled down to a comfortable routine in their flat with a 'first class Egyptian cook trained in American cooking. He makes beautiful ice cream.' The flat in a tree-lined avenue was cool and quiet, and Max much enjoyed his walk to and from work in the mornings and evenings along the Nile. In the evenings the two brothers often played chess or, less cerebrally, ping-pong. Sometimes they read. Max was always desperate for books. He set himself the task of reading the whole of Shakespeare while he was away, and hungrily devoured anything else that reminded him of home, or his past career. His letters home were full of literary criticism and discussion of what he had been reading, and he urged Agatha and his mother to do some serious reading as well, and report back to him what they thought. Max and Cecil also entertained once a week, their guests fellow officers or Max's archaeological friends, all of whom were envious of the Mallowan brothers' wonderful cook. 'How do you make a good French omelette?' he asked his mother. And a few weeks later, 'Tonight I am having some friends to dinner and have ordered a duck because the other day I went to see the Early Dynastic Egyptian bas-reliefs at Saqqara and saw many beautifully carved representations of ducks for the king's banquet. That shows the study of antiquity is not without profit!' Cecil kept teasing him about his growing waistline and, catching him eating a large bowl of banana ice-cream one day, said, 'If mother and Agatha could have a photograph of you eating that they would certainly have no anxiety about your fitness and appetite!'

Max and Cecil spent Christmas 1942 at the flat. Cecil had somehow acquired a turkey and a plum pudding and he made the Christmas decorations. They had six friends round to dinner. Max bought himself a copy of Thomas à Kempis as his present from Agatha, and he felt full of optimism about the future. 'We shall start off 1943 with high hopes and full of drive to push on to a victorious end.' His mother had entertained Agatha and Max's father for the day. Max's younger brother Philip had been seriously ill and was now out of the army and recuperating at home. He and Marguerite had been taking long walks in Kew Gardens, often with Agatha.

On 1 January 1943, Max moved into another flat, which he liked even better than his first one. It was lighter and had a fine view of the Nile from the front windows, and of the Gezira Club from the back. Cecil's work was regularly taking him away from Cairo, so Max was sharing with another man from the British Council, though Cecil used the flat too when he could. In February Max made another short trip to Palestine and saw the Dead Sea and the Sea of Galilee: 'green fields full of red and white anemones, cyclamen and irises. Mount Carmel was looking at its best. The Jaffa orange season ... in full swing ... I saw Nazareth and the church of the first miracle at Cana where you are shown the traditional site at which our Lord changed the water into wine.'

Back in Cairo, he decided to volunteer as a civil affairs officer in Tripolitania, as the country round Tripoli was called, where they were short of personnel who were familiar with the Middle East. He set off for his new posting towards the end of February, camping on the way, and much enjoying his open-air life, which was keeping him extremely fit. By the end of March, he was able to tell his mother that he had settled in and was finding his new job very interesting.

> I live in a charming Italian house on the sea, with tiled floors and tiles walls engraved with fish in all colours. Then I go about and see a lot of the country, the Arabs and the Italian grain and fruit farms. Where I am, there is a magnificent Roman ruin, perhaps the finest in Tripolitania with a large amphitheatre, forum, basilica, early Christian churches, streets and houses. I am seeing that the site is cared for and not altogether neglected during these troublesome times. Antiquities are international monuments and their care and maintenance has wherever possible to continue – war or no war … We drink peach brandy and once every six weeks – if lucky we see a bottle of beer! There are a pleasant lot of chaps working with me drawn from the usual variety of professions and my chief, a regular soldier, a Colonel, is a very able man and experienced administrator. He does what is necessary and wastes no time.

His new life was entirely congenial to Max. He liked his chief Colonel, H. C. E. Routh, very much (he reminded him of Campbell Thompson, 'the same honesty of mind and conviction as to what is right and what is wrong'), he enjoyed the work greatly, especially as it brought him once again into contact with the Arab world that he knew, and there was the added advantage of being in a beautiful place with interesting ruins, even if they were very late by his standards. One of the greatest pleasures of the job itself was going out on tour to make grain surveys. He spent his thirty-ninth birthday, 6 May 1943, riding on horseback from 5.30 a.m. to 7.30 p.m. through the corn lands of Tripolitania.

> It was one of the best days I have had, seeing nomad Arabs, talking to them, at lunch eating mutton and drinking sheep's milk. I was away for three days altogether and arranged my tour so that at midday and at night there was always a tent awaiting me. My

baggage camel was a sturdy beast. In all I rode about 70 miles in 3 days. It was pretty hot at mid-day, but I am now well used to the sun and in the pink of condition. No life could be more healthy.

Later on that month, Max was asked to take charge of an outpost in the Eastern Province of Tripolitania, at an oasis called Hon. Max left Tripoli on 19 May and had an interesting journey, visiting Leptis Magna on his way across the desert to his new posting. He was very excited to see the old quay walls clearly visible, with their stone bollards to which ships' ropes were once attached. In the marketplace there were stone store tables with measures marked out. Nevertheless, 'As artists the Romans were shocking. Debased Greek copies of sculpture and overcrowded stone friezes, meaningless columns in their buildings. But they were lavish, produced fine effects in coloured marbles, good hot and cold baths, fountains, lavatories and some fine coloured mosaics.' One aspect of military government with which unfortunately Max was not personally involved was the preservation and survey of antiquities in occupied countries. This meant that, since January 1943 when the Eighth Army entered Tripoli, the ancient cities and historical monuments of the area had become the responsibility of the British Military Administration, which had concentrated its efforts mainly on Leptis Magna and Sabratha, two sites with which Max was familiar. The Army Antiquities Officer was then R. G. Goodchild, and he worked in close liaison with the British School in Rome, whose director, J. B. Ward-Perkins, had been the first Army Antiquities Officer in the region.

Max reported home shortly after he arrived at Hon:

It is a small African oasis well to the south, well built European and Arab houses lying in a belt of palms ... I have a large and well furnished office at the end of the main street which is lined with an avenue of acacia trees. The Union Jack floats proudly over the city and I am monarch of the district! My house and living quarters are very pleasant. I have a large bedroom, bath-room and shower bath, office leading off my bedroom, dining room, sitting room, good kitchen with a range that burns wood,

and there is electric light which at present does not work ...
On three sides of my house there is a verandah where I can sit
in the cool of the evening ... a very pleasant garden which is full
of oleanders, at present in full bloom ... I have already eaten
asparagus.

Max found he was extremely busy in his new job, working a ten-hour
day, but there was in fact little else for him to do, except read. He was
still enjoying his domestic arrangements, dining out under the palm
trees in the evening among the flowers, in the company of a gazelle
and a mountain sheep that he had acquired, descriptions which no
doubt aroused severe envy in the breasts of his suffering correspon-
dents at home, for whom bombs and disgusting food were part of daily
life. His Arabic was now fluent. In due course he was joined by two
other officers, a Police Officer and a Medical Officer, and felt much
less lonely and much less hard-worked. As he said, the district was
beginning to run itself, and, with the harvest safely gathered in, he
turned his attention to making sure that the poor were given surplus
grain, settling an old tribal dispute (good for British prestige), making
sure Hon was clean and well-run, and its inhabitants reasonably
contented. The date harvest looked as if it would be a good one. He
now had time to study the history of the district, its traditions and
religious customs, and was giving English classes four times a week
for some of the Arab clerks. He went about the area on horseback
watching the Arab tribes ploughing and sowing. Occasionally his chief,
whom Max liked very much ('a most kindly man and a fine Arabic
scholar') would descend and have to be taken on a tour of the whole
district, excursions which Max much enjoyed.

I was travelling with my Colonel who is a most amusing character,
of Irish origin. He rarely stops joking ... He has spent a lifetime
among the Arabs and understands them, often a good deal
better than they understand him! He has no sense of time whatsoever and I am cast in the strange role of trying to make him
punctual ... we nearly always start a journey which was intended
to begin at dawn, in the pitch dark of the night ... On the
journey down I made the omelettes and he sliced the bread

professing always to be horrified by my appetite. His favourite food is marmalade which he consumes in large quantities out of a tin.

In March 1944, Max moved again, back up to the coast, not far from Sabratha where he had been before, to a place called Misurata. He reported home that, of all parts of Tripolitania, this was the most pleasant, because it combined the advantages of town and country. He had a large and comfortable house with he shared with one other officer, and it too had a garden, as well as a vineyard and an olive grove. He hoped to acquire three horses. He had also been supplied with a large and comfortable car for touring the more outlying parts of the district. He had already been to inspect, and found that there were wild flowers and fruit blossom everywhere. He had been asked to give a lecture to some of the army on the Arabs, 'a pleasing and amusing subject … with plenty of interesting historical material to ponder over'. Once a week he played bridge with fellow officers. Unfortunately this pleasant posting was very short-lived; by the end of March, he was moved back to Tripoli.

By mid-April, Max was sounding pretty cheerful again, writing from Tripoli that he had

> moved to a very beautiful house, built in the North African Turco-Moorish style, of the early 18th century and I have a room on a small quadrangle which looks rather like an old Oxford college, with bougainvillaea covering the walls and a lawn of mauve mesymbreanthemum in full flower. There is also a big garden, with palms, rose trees, tree lobelias and a large orangery. The food is first class as we have an Italian chef. I like the other members of the mess, they are all good friends and here one sees anyone of interest who happens to be passing through the country. My job is varied and deals with every type of problem – many of them insoluble!

Max spent his fortieth birthday 'riding 32 miles on horseback, drinking sheep's milk and feeding off some very tender mutton'. He was pleased to know that Agatha had spent the day with his mother and Philip and they had celebrated the day together. Agatha's birthday letter to Max began in her characteristic way, full of exclamation marks. 'Darling! You are 40 today! Hurrah! At last! *Lots* of love to you – It makes a big difference to me – I feel it closes the gap a little – When you were in the thirties and I had reached the fifties it was pretty grim.' Agatha minded more as time went on about the age difference between them. She had written a poignant letter earlier that year saying, 'If I had been so faint-hearted as not to marry you, I should have missed the best and the happiest 15 years of my life ... I think to be honest darling ... the wives of your friends were so young – much younger than their husbands – all with babies and young children and I minded – for *you* – that I should be so much older.' On two occasions at least she altered the date of her birth on official documents, but Max never seems to have minded the age gap at all.

Despite his interesting and busy life, Max was missing his work. His letters are full of what he might do after the War, and he worried incessantly that in a changed world there would be no room for archae-ologists, and he really did not know what else he could bear to do. His reading frequently included books about archaeologists, for example Sir Arthur Evans ('single handed he rediscovered the whole of the ancient Minoan Cretan civilization ... a little gnome of a man, gifted with considerable intelligence, will power and a flair for discovering the things he wanted'), and his letters make frequent references to his subject ('the whole house built on the Nazi system will crumble like a pack of cards, just as the Assyrian empire did in 612 BC'). On 2 July 1944, he wrote to his mother, 'It is strange to think that I have not done any archaeology for nearly five years and yet the subject seems to remain fresh in my mind, and I hope not to have too much difficulty in picking up the threads again. I want to finish off my publication of Tell Brak as soon as I can, but I reckon that there are still several months of work to be done upon it – so much to do and to examine and so much to read.' In response to a query from Max, Agatha wrote: 'You ask me what I have to say on future plans – I have a very strong feeling for your archaeological work – you have already done much – you certainly must publish Brak.' She hoped that they would have enough income for them to live as they wished without his having to abandon his archaeology. 'I want you to do what you want and feel a pride in doing ... You must NOT go to the BM!!!'

Agatha frequently cast her mind back to those halcyon days in Syria. She had been rewriting the book she had started then, *Come, Tell Me How You Live,* and the exercise had been giving her pleasure and pain in equal measure. On Whit Sunday, she went to early service in Hampstead, and wrote to Max,

> the air was very still and clear and had something of the feeling of Chagar Bazar on those mornings when I used to come up with you on the mound – that fresh untouched feeling of the empty smiling country. How lovely it all was – and the flowers! And thought what very great happiness I have had with you – Thank you, my darling, for all the love and beauty and sweetness you have brought into my life – I prayed, dearest, for us both ... I remembered a day in Alep when you comforted me on the anniversary of my mother's death – speaking with such faith and such sincerity – you were thinking of your friend Esme, I imagine – that friendship meant a lot to you and was a beautiful thing in your life – and what a friend you are, darling, so staunch, so true.

She told Max in June that she had been busy checking references for the book: 'only I *do* wish you could read it before I launch it on the world. Have been enquiring – but it would probably take 6 months or so to get an ms to you. Feel anxious that my references to you might not be as you like – but I have been careful to be quite off hand – *No* fond wife stuff. (Have promised R. who loathes idea of this book! That *no* reference to her will be in it!!)' In fact Max liked the book: 'The lighter side of archaeological life ... has ... never been more happily recorded.' In July the book was finished, and she wrote:

> Have been feeling very low all this week – I think really because I have finished the Syrian book and it's gone to be typed – and whilst writing it I was more or less living in those days again – and now suddenly I feel rather away from it all – and here, alone – terribly alone. No doubt about it, you are my other half ... What lovely times we will have when we are together again – how we shall eat!! ... chairs covered with books and a lot of laughing – And we will talk and talk and talk.

Meanwhile she was keeping as busy as she could with her work at University College Hospital, seeing her friends and Max's mother, and dashing down to Wales as often as possible to see Rosalind and her grandson, Mathew, who was born on 21 September 1943. She also made flying visits to Greenway and to Winterbrook House to see that everything was in order. Greenway was occupied by American officers. She was also acting as unofficial agony aunt to Stephen Glanville, their good friend and Agatha's close neighbour at Lawn Road Flats. He seemed always to be falling in love with unsuitable women and frequently sought Agatha's sensible advice. When it all became too much for her, she would take refuge in the flat and 'lie back in that funny chair here which looks so peculiar and is really very comfortable, close my eyes and say "Now, where shall I go with Max?" Often it is Leptis Magna ... or Delphi, or up the mound at Nineveh.'

Some of the friends Agatha saw were old friends from digging days. Early in 1944, Agatha took the Woolleys to see the dramatization of *Ten Little Niggers*:

> Was afraid Len wouldn't be allowed to come! But he was – and enjoyed it enormously – They are still at the Dorchester and K. has got the staff well trained – Waiters dither with nervousness when they bring in a tray!! However I hear she had a *small* cockroach in her coffee the other morning!!! Tremendous uproar and abject apologies and supplications – but I wonder! Could it be the drama of 'The Waiter's Revenge'?! K. was in grand form.

(But Katharine died, quite suddenly, in 1945.) Agatha had also seen Bumps and his wife, and a colleague of Max called Barbara Parker who was asked to find Max's copy of Herodotus which he urgently needed. Barbara was asked to call at Winterbrook House to see if she could find it there. She did, and Max was delighted: 'It is a great pleasure to me to have a copy of Herodotus with me and to read what he had to say about Africa. He is full of sound remarks and has a grasp of the essentials in any country.' Agatha went to dinner with their old friends the Keelings: 'all rather grand – actually *servants* – and dinner coming up in a lift, just the same as usual!! So used now to dining in the kitchen with my friends that I was quite upset.' She also kept in touch with Sidney and Mary Smith, near neighbours in north London.

Relations with Max's mother were not always easy, and Max was occasionally worried by news that his wife and his mother had quarrelled. Marguerite was having a difficult and lonely time. She was deeply concerned about her youngest son Philip, who was trying to resume a normal existence after being invalided out of the army. He had tried working on a farm, and had taken up teaching, but had not settled down happily yet. She was desperately worried about money, and at one point took in a lodger, whom she found she disliked. Max did what he could from Africa. He wrote to her frequently and tried to take an interest in her painting and her reading, and he reminded her of happier times, visits to Bossington and occasions when she had helped him with his work. He arranged for her to receive an allowance from him and he smoothed over troubled waters:

> Sorry to hear that you had a quarrel with Agatha! These family tiffs will always occur the world over, but I expect like everybody these days you were both feeling tired and the strain of the war ... But we must keep the peace in the family or how shall we keep peace in the world ... I won't make any change in instructions to the bank about your quarterly allowance because what Agatha sends you is from me also – we have a joint account at the bank anyway and you can look on your quarterly rent as all from me if you wish but she has been all kindness and care for you while I have been away and I hope you won't tell her that you refuse to accept it in the usual way because I think it would hurt her unnecessarily.

For her part, Agatha asked Max to write frequently to his mother as she was unhappy and prone to work herself into a frenzy when she did not hear from her beloved eldest son. Highly strung and temperamental, Marguerite was very different from her daughter-in-law. She did not scruple to tell Agatha she was wasting her talents and that she should write a serious book, a biography perhaps. Agatha took this in good part, being modest about her talents, and she continued to make regular visits to Marguerite in Hammersmith and share all her news about Max with her. Like Max, Agatha was convinced that Marguerite should be able to stay in her flat, knowing that she was happy there, and generously helped her to do so.

Agatha dashed down to Wales as often as she could. She greatly loved her grandson, writing to Max on 28 March 1944, when left in sole charge so that Rosalind could visit Hubert:

> I have got much too fond of him. You'd find him rather an early riser... the best time for breakfast, he thinks is 5.45. In fact he and the rooks start making noises together! Once the bottle is sucked to the last drop, M. is returned to bed and the idea is that we go to sleep again! But Mathew then starts trying out any new noises he has thought of – Produced one today like a very loud and explosive 'Ha' rather like an old man in a Club.

Life in Wales was hard work; apart from the baby, the large cold empty house was full of livestock: dogs and puppies, cats and hens. But it was fun. Then tragedy struck: on 16 August 1944 Hubert was killed in France, though Rosalind did not know this for certain until 9 October. Rosalind wrote to Max to tell him this, adding, 'You will be interested to hear I never think at all nowadays and never read a book ... I do not think you would find me a very interesting companion.' Deeply worried about her daughter, Agatha did what she could to help, but, as she said, 'The saddest thing in life and the hardest to live through, is the knowledge that there is someone you love very much whom you cannot save from suffering. You can do things to aid people's physical disabilities; but you can do little to help the pain of the heart.' Although she felt she could not help Rosalind to talk about the tragedy, she did feel she could help just by being there.

Stephen Glanville, Agatha's neighbour and a dear friend of both Max and Agatha, was lonely, his wife and children having gone to Canada. He was working in the Air Ministry and also writing. *The Legacy of Ancient Egypt* was published in 1942 and he was currently working on *The Growth and Nature of Egyptology*, which was published in 1947. Unfortunately neither his war work nor his writing prevented him from being vulnerable and he had a susceptible heart where women were concerned. Agatha was fond of him and ready to lend a sympathetic ear. She also looked after his sick father when he came to stay at Lawn Road Flats. Stephen had always taken an interest in her writing, helping her with the plot of her play *Akhnaton*, and making useful suggestions for *Death on the Nile*. Towards the end of 1943, he suggested to her that perhaps she might set one of her novels in ancient Egypt. He supplied her with a fascinating and original source: the letters and accounts of a man called Heqanakht found in the tomb of a vizier Ipi at Deir el-Bahri near Luxor in Egypt during the 1921–2 excavation season, conducted by the American archaeologist H. E. Winlock. The expedition had received a surprise visit from the English Egyptologist Battiscombe Gunn, and he had made a preliminary translation, a later version of which was published in the *Bulletin* of the Metropolitan Museum of Art for December 1922, where doubtless Glanville had read it. The papyri gave a vivid picture of the squabbles Heqanakht was having with his family, including five more-or-less troublesome sons, his mother, his second wife, a favourite daughter and various other family members, friends and neighbours. Agatha had drawn freely on her source and produced an ancient Egyptian murder mystery story which, according to Glanville, in a reassuring letter to Max, worked both for the layman who felt that the action could all have taken place in Pimlico, and also for the Egyptologist who needed to feel that it could all have taken place in Luxor. The book, entitled *Death Comes as the End*, was dedicated to Professor S. R. K. Glanville, who was thanked for the patience with which he had answered questions and for the time and trouble he had taken. Agatha had cooked him many dinners by way of reward.

This and *Come, Tell Me How You Live* were by no means the only books Agatha wrote during this prolific period while Max was away. Her application to her craft must always provoke wonder and admiration but at this time in her life that intense application was also an escape, from the harsh realities of war-torn London with all its privations, and from her own personal loneliness. She wrote a Poirot book and a Miss Marple book, to be called respectively *Curtain* and *Sleeping Murder*, and put them in cold storage, in case anything should happen to her, to Max or to Rosalind. The copyrights of the two books were assigned to the two people she loved best as an insurance against the future. She wrote *The Moving Finger*, *The Body in the Library*, *Five*

Little Pigs (also dedicated to Glanville) and *Towards Zero*, and drama-
tized several of her novels including *Ten Little Niggers* and *Moon on the
Nile*. Agatha became quite excited about the theatre, attending
rehearsals in seaside places such as Brighton and Salcombe. By the
time Max finally arrived home in May 1945, she had written another
novel and had started thinking about her next.

Max's return had long been anticipated by them both. At the end of
September 1944, Max had been promoted to the rank of Wing
Commander but he did not think that it would be long before he
exchanged his new uniform for a pair of grey flannel trousers. He
started writing positively about coming home in January, and from
then on his impatience to be home runs like a thread through all his
letters. In mid-March, he was told to be prepared to return home, and
became more restless and impatient every day. In April, he spent a
weekend doing all his heavy packing, going through old papers and
tearing most of them up and tying up all the loose ends. By the end of
the month he had done his last real day of work and decided to
concentrate on antiquities. He was given a copy of a letter written by
Colonel C. R. Gormley, Acting Chief Administrator to the Chief Civil
Affairs Officer, which read, 'I wish to take this opportunity of writing
to record that Wing Commander Mallowan has performed his duties
as Staff Officer with zeal and efficiency, and it may be useful to him if
the R.A.F. is informed that his conduct has been entirely satisfactory.'

Meanwhile Agatha was making her own preparations for his return
and had gone down to Greenway at the end of February, reporting that
'The house of course looks awful – now that they are out of it, it looks
worse … sporadic WCs "all in a row" … rows of washbasins … I've
refused to accept anything – so they have to "put it back" as it was.' By
late March she was sounding much more cheerful: 'Chaos at present
and lots of problems. But Oh! I did wish you could have been there –
for it was the perfect time with the white magnolia below the house –
and the stellata – the camellias out and primroses everywhere … And
2 days of perfect weather.'

As the weeks wore on, Agatha became completely unnerved. In
May she suddenly decided she must go to Wales for the weekend to
get away from the flat. She took a train back on the Sunday evening,
failed to find any sort of public transport, took another train to north

London and then staggered back to the flat carrying her suitcase and a couple of kippers for her dinner.

I got in, weary and cold, and started turning on the gas, throwing off my coat and putting my suitcase down. I put the kippers in the frying pan. Then I heard the most peculiar clanking noise outside, and wondered what it could be. I went out on the balcony and I looked down the stairs. Up them came a figure burdened with everything imaginable … clanking things hung all over him. It seemed impossible that anyone could be hung over with so much. But there was no doubt who it was – it was my husband! Two minutes later I knew that all my fears that things might be different, that he would have changed, were baseless. This was Max! He might have left yesterday. He was back again. We were back again. A terrible smell of frying kippers came to our noses and we rushed into the flat … What a wonderful evening it was! We ate burnt kippers, and were happy.

CHAPTER EIGHT

What about a Site? Erbil, Kutha, Der, Nimrud?

In an interview for *The Illustrated London News* in March 1966, Max recalled how it felt to pick up the threads of his old life. He said, 'When I came back to Syria after the War and five years in the R.A.F. Volunteer Reserve, I had an interesting and instructive experience of reading my half-written-up Syrian findings as though they were the work of a complete stranger. It took about six months of painful work to get back into it all.'

But even before this, Max had to make the enormous adjustment from the life of comparative ease that he had enjoyed in Tripoli, to the harsh privations of London in the grip of rationing, ruin and despair, despite the joy he felt about being with Agatha again. He had been very much his own boss in Tripolitania, and now he was back at the Air Ministry for a final six months, working under an Air Commodore he disliked. It felt rather pointless especially as there did not seem to be anything for him to do. On Christmas Day 1945, while they were staying with Rosalind in North Wales, Greenway was at last derequisitioned. Max and Agatha went down as soon as they could, arriving in bright cold sunshine. The place they loved so much looked as ravishing as ever 'but it was wild, wild as a beautiful jungle. Paths had disappeared, the kitchen garden, where carrots and lettuces had grown, was all a mass of weeds, and the fruit-teees had not been pruned.' Inside, the house was not quite as bad as they feared, though the kitchen was quite indescribably filthy and they had acquired a row of fourteen lavatories in the stone passage behind it. They were not sure what would become of Greenway, if they would be able to afford to live in it, but they were determined to bring it back to its former beauty and live there if they could. Meanwhile they decided to give up Lawn Road Flats and move back to Cresswell Place.

During the spring of 1946, Max started work on his Brak report. He was finding it hard work, not only because he had lost the thread of what he wanted to say, but also because he felt curiously detached, living down in Devon isolated from stimulating colleagues. In May, Sidney and Mary Smith came to stay, and to distract and inspire him Smith suggested to Max that he might write a monumental history of Babylon, a project he thought might take five years. It did not appeal. Max wanted to be digging. On 7 June, he wrote from Greenway to Smith asking his advice about the selection of a new site in Iraq after Sir Edgar Bonham Carter had contacted him about a possible joint expedition by the British School of Archaeology in Iraq and the Iraq Museum in Baghdad, to take place some time in 1947. Max had thought about the finances of it and decided that, if the Iraq Museum could put up £1,000 towards workmen's wages, and salaries for technical assistants from the Museum, the School might be able to meet the rest. But where?

> What about a site? I think we can now well afford to give the prehistoric and protohistoric periods a rest. My own inclination would be to go for remains ranging from Hammurabi to Sargon of Agade – an interesting pendant to my work at Brak, but for that matter anything between early dynastic and Achaemenid can still provide a surprise. I like the idea of digging in the Zab area, which needs opening up … Erbil, Kutha, Der, Nimrud? I know not.

Smith replied from the British Museum on 14 June:

> I shall be delighted to talk with you about possible sites at any time. You will not get me to budge from certain general principles viz (1) that the choice of a site should depend on the problem which is to be solved not on the whims or tastes of an individual (2) that the successful digging of a site depends on getting the right team for that particular site (3) that the habits formed between 1920 and 1938, of raising some sum for a dig, allowing

some specific person to do any dig with the money he chose in any way he could, are thoroughly rotten ... And a site not protected by late remains is not worth digging. All the best sites were always occupied down to the Roman period. For that reason it is nonsense to plan digging for one season: nothing much less than 10 years continuous is any good. Digging without prior reconnaissance is childish.

To this onslaught Max replied, 'You sound on good form!'

Max went back to his writing, but his mind kept returning to where and how he might dig again. In July, the Mallowans went back to Winterbrook House and there too spent much time and energy trying to restore it to the house they knew before the War. As Max told Smith, 'If all else fails I feel I can now reasonably apply for a job as cleaner of silver and brass.' In September, he accepted a commission to write a contribution to the *Cambridge Ancient History* about prehistoric sites in Syria and took the manuscript into the British Museum for Sidney's comments. 'Too many subjective interpretations', was Smith's verdict, and he was not sure that eye symbols were necessarily personal dedications. Substitutes for something else? At least Max had the consolation of seeing volume VIII of *Iraq* with his report on excavtions in the Balikh valley. Looking back at the year at Christmas from Rosalind's house in Wales, Max felt it had not been one of his most enjoyable or successful.

Early in 1947, he and Agatha felt they could not bear to stay in England any longer and set off for the Middle East. They went to Eridu, Basra and the Persian Gulf, before going to Baghdad, from where Max wrote to Rosalind to tell her that 'I am keeping my eye open for possible mounds to dig, and it is obvious that there are hundreds of plums waiting to be pulled out of the rich Iraqi mud-pie'. They were luxuriating in being looked after, wallowing happily in clean laundry and cold drinks. Seton Lloyd was the Technical Adviser to the Directorate-General of Antiquities for the Government of Iraq in Baghdad, and Leonard Woolley was already back at Alalakh, where he had been excavating before the War. Max was delighted to find that the faithful Hamoudi had been awarded the King's Medal for Service in the Cause of Freedom (KMS) for services to British interests during the War.

In London, Max had submitted his Tell Brak report to Sidney Smith, who had decided that he must help Max to find some sort of academic post. He consulted V. Gordon Childe, the Director of the Institute of Archaeology, and they decided to approach Agatha, who readily agreed to sponsor a new chair of Western Asiatic Archaeology at the Institute. Max was forty-three but it was generally felt that his experience in the field had been long and varied enough to merit the honour. He was also admired for his grasp of his subject and the prompt way in which he published his archaeological reports. The Institute had been founded in 1934, and formally opened in 1937: it operated from Bute House in the Inner Circle of Regent's Park. Max's colleagues, apart from Childe, whom he greatly liked and admired, were Mortimer Wheeler, the Professor of Archaeology of the Roman Provinces, and Kathleen Kenyon, Lecturer in Palestinian Architecture, in Max's new department. He was very friendly with Wheeler, but his relationship with Kenyon was later described by David Oates, his future colleague at Nimrud, as one of 'armed neutrality'.

Max's terms of employment were not strict, because he had made it clear that he wanted to be able to be absent for five months of the year to pursue his archaeological interests in the field. He was required to teach, though this was entirely at a postgraduate level. He found that he rather enjoyed this part of his new post, and some of his pupils made gratifying progress.

On 16 October 1947 at 5 p.m. the new Professor of Western Asiatic Archaeology delivered his inaugural lecture, *The Legacy of Asia,* to an invited audience, including Agatha swelling with pride. They had changed their domestic arrangements again: Agatha let Cresswell Place and bought a flat at 48 Swan Court, in Flood Street, off the King's Road in Chelsea, which was to be their London home for the rest of Agatha's life. She made it very attractive, with black and gold papier mâché tables and chairs, and deep pale blue sofas into which Max could thankfully sink at the end of a long day at the Institute. The Mallowans' homes were always places of refuge for their friends and colleagues. The rooms were cluttered with books and interesting objects, Agatha was an imaginative cook in those days of rationing, and Max poured generous glasses of claret.

Early in February 1948 Max and Agatha escaped once more to

Baghdad for warm sunshine and cooling breezes, as he told his mother. The purpose of the visit was for Max to prepare a course of lectures for the Institute for the coming summer term on the foundations of civilization in Western Asia. By the end of the month, he had written two introductory lectures on the geographical background

> in which I attempt to explain the physical conditions of Persia, Mesopotamia, Turkey, Syria, Palestine, Egypt and Arabia, and to show how the mosaic of ancient and modern history fits into that kaleidoscopic background. As a result I have become so fascinated with my own descriptions of southern Arabia with its exotic mountains, its frankincense trees, and its spices, that I feel impelled to go and see the country which I pretend to know so well ... the day after tomorrow Agatha and I have planned a trip up to the Persian frontier. We go to a place called Mandali where I happen to know that there is a wide variety of ancient mounds to be examined. After that a few more days in Baghdad and then a trip to the north of the country to examine more ancient remains within the district of Assyria ... It seems a pity that we have to leave here about the middle of April ... wandering about the Asiatic countryside is infinitely preferable to the stuffy atmosphere of a University class room.

A month later they were back in Baghdad, but about to go to Turkey for a fortnight, staying with Professor Garstang in Ankara. Max's lecture series was more or less complete and he and Agatha would both be returning to work 'like giants refreshed'. He recommended to his mother a new book by Seton Lloyd, *Foundations in the Dust*, 'a fascinating tale of human skill, perseverance and ingenuity'.

Apart from his lecture series and teaching, Max's only publication was in *Iraq*, where he had written a short account of a copper rein-ring from southern Iraq, a privately owned object which he had been shown in London the year before but which had been found at Nasiriyah in 1922. Max was sure it had originally come from Ur or Kish.

In 1949, Max was made the first Director of the British School of Archaeology in Iraq, as his plans for finding a major site to dig there became more concrete. The School had been formally founded in 1932 as a memorial to Gertrude Bell, but the first moves to establish it had been made some three years earlier when a group of her friends and others who were interested in archaeology in Iraq had met to discuss the project at a meeting presided over by Sir Percy Cox, Gertrude's esrstwhile chief. They had appointed a committeee which was to draw up plans for founding the British School of Archaeology in Iraq. Its purpose was (1) to encourage research and excavation, (2) to provide travelling scholarships, (3) to publish a journal, and (4) to co-operate with archaeological work done in Iraq by other countries. The committee pledged themselves to raise £44,000 to add to the £6,000 legacy by Gertrude Bell.

Max's search for the perfect mound had now crystallized with the site of Nimrud, the capital of the Neo-Assyrian empire at its height in the ninth to eighth centuries BC. It was a place redolent of history for the British since it was the scene of many great archaeological endeavours, foremost being that of Austen Henry Layard himself. He had excavated between 1845 and 1851, mainly around the ziggurat, and discovered a series of palaces along the western side of the acropolis. His best-known excavation was that of the so-called North West Palace, built by the king most associated with the site, Ashurnasipal II (883–859 BC). The famous Black Obelisk of Shalmaneser III now in the British Museum had been one of his major finds. In 1853 Hormuzd Rassam had excavated the temple of the god Nabu, and found statues dedicated to the god by Adad-Nirari III (810–783 BC). W. K. Loftus on behalf of the Assyrian Excavation Fund dug there in 1854 and 1855, uncovering the so-called South East Palace, where he found a large number of ivories. After a twenty-year gap occasioned by the Crimean War, George Smith returned to the site and in the Nabu Temple found parts of the historical texts of Tiglath-Pileser III (744–727 BC). Hormuzd Rassam came back in 1878 and excavated a building near the ziggurat and a temple dedicated to the goddess Ishtar. The site had then been abandoned for some seventy years. It was believed that perhaps Nimrud was exhausted, but Mallowan thought not. And it seemed to meet the criteria of Sidney Smith's letter of 14 June 1947. In February he had inspected Khorsabad, Nineveh and Ashur but none of them was as appealing as Nimrud. And, as he told Cyril Gadd, 'we have at least an ancient name to conjure with: it is much more difficult to raise money for an unknown site.' He had applied for and been given permission to excavate by the Director General of Antiquities in Baghdad.

That autumn, Max asked the School to offer his old friend and companion R. W. Hamilton a fellowship with the School and the post of Secretary/Librarian at the School in Baghdad. Hamilton had been released from his previous employment as Chief Inspector of Antiquities in Palestine with the ending of the British Mandate there in 1948, and was currently semi-retired in Suffolk, 'minding geese and hens and a garden'. His first responsibility in his new employment was to find a suitable large house in Baghdad for the School to use as its central base of operations, a place where staff could sleep, live and work.

Hamilton was an almost exact contemporary of Max. He had been a scholar at Winchester and a demy at Magdalen College, Oxford, and achieved a first in Greats, an outstanding clacissist of his generation. He had also taken up the study of classical Arabic during his time in the Middle East. His drawing talents he owed to his mother, who painted in water colours. Like Max, he had been drawn into archaeology by Leonard Woolley and had subsequently dug at Jerash, Megiddo and Meydum, and at Nineveh with Reginald Campbell Thompson. He had then been in Jerusalem from 1931 to 1948.

In October 1948, Hamilton left for Baghdad, and in one of his first letters home reported, 'I think I have found just the house for the School – a "Turkish" house round a courtyard, overlooking the river, many rooms of various sizes – some of them very nice, a bath in existence; many lats., of diverse categories; an ancient bread oven and a steam bath heated by a furnace in the kitchen ... in exceptionally good order for Baghdad'. The house also had a long narrow upstairs room with one side almost entirely made up of high glass windows overlooking the courtyard. Hamilton thought it would make an excellent library and reading room.

Regular letters home to his wife in Suffolk provide an amusing record of Hamilton's attempts to get the house ready for occupation. He described his various set-tos with the landlord over repairs, repainting and so on, visits to lawyers, shopping for household items and the hiring of a cook. Seton Lloyd and his wife were about to give up their house and were prepared to let the School buy their furniture at a low price. By the New Year 1949, the house was nearly ready:

> I have just completed a terrific day of whizzing around Baghdad, buying aluminium saucepans, and doormats, and Harpic, and sardines, and teacups … The house is by no means clear of carpenters and painters … tomorrow the Lloyds are letting me have half their furniture … I have engaged a servant, but one day has pretty well convinced me he is no use: an impossible jabberer … I shall have to sit on top of him with a rhinoceros-whip … I got desperate about the kitchen, which was as dark as Styx, and stank … so I decided to have it replastered at our expense.

He spent his first night at the house on 6 January: 'It is perishingly cold, and there is a faint smell of paint, but I am wrapped in a vast number of blankets … on a new mattress made to my order, in a room cleaned (more or less) by my newly-engaged servant, and have had a hot bath (so-so) in the bathroom next door, with water heated by a patent water heater downstairs (after a fashion).'

Part of the rush was the imminent arrival of the Mallowans, on 18 January, in a dust-storm. Luckily, 'They are overjoyed with the house … Agatha somewhat hampered by arthritis, and finds our steep staircase a trial. To my dismay, she shows no inclination to participate in household affairs.' Luckily, this was short-lived.

On 15 February, Max and Robert Hamilton set off for Mosul. They had acquired a Dodge station-wagon, vast and dilapidated, and they took it in turns to drive. They stopped for a picnic lunch on a deserted ridge behind Kirkuk, drove on past Erbil ('perched upon an ancient tell, ancient itself, ringed with walls like a city in Assyrian sculptures … all built in brick'), reached Mosul and stayed with the Antiquities Guard. They had various projects. One was to see whether they could appropriate any equipment from an old American dig house at Khorsabad. Another was to find suitable accommodation for themselves near Nimrud. In pouring rain, and with chains attached to the Dodge's wheels, they set off to accomplish these projects. The only suitable building near Nimrud was a mud-brick farm surrounding a vast courtyard, currently full of dung, but it would have to do.

Back in Baghdad, they organized themselves for the expedition but also embarked on a round of socializing. They had several dinner parties and a house-warming cocktail party: 'It will be one of those horrible affairs stiff with big-wigs, which we all detest ... but the entertainment allowance must be earned.'

On 14 March, they left for Nimrud, the Mallowans by train and Robert Hamilton in the Dodge, which soon broke down in a Kurdish village. The weather was atrocious, and when Robert finally reached Nimrud he found the Mallowans marooned. The courtyard was one vast lake, the mud-brick rooms around it literally melting like chocolate ice-cream and the lavatory inaccessible 15 m away across the lake. The Mallowans went into Mosul to get money and supplies and were unable to get back, probably to their great relief. Nevertheless, work started on 18 March.

With 22 skilled men from a nearby village, work began high on the western flank of the mound where excavations had started some hundred years before, but where were there still many patches of ground completely untouched. Most of the eastern sector of the mound was undisturbed. As Max wrote, somewhat theatrically,

The pickmen themselves had about them an air of excitement and expectancy and, as the third generation of skilled workers in the field, a sense of their historic mission ... The shades of Layard were in their midst; he stood invisible like Banquo's ghost, and pointed to the last of a long line of Assyrian kings whose realms had once embraced the landscape.

The weather fortunatly improved and they were able to appreciate the beauty of the ancient city, situated on a bluff overlooking the Tigris. From the top of the mound there was a clear view of the great agricultural plains of Assyria, stretching northwards to Nineveh and southwards to Ashur. To the east could be seen the mountains of Kurdistan. They concentrated their efforts of re-excavating parts of the North West Palace dug by Layard and Loftus, and found many fragmentary ivories. They also worked on the Governor's Palace, as they called it, and laid bare the main outlines of the building. Several rooms were paved with bricks inscribed with the names and titles of Shalmaneser III.

The Mallowans spent the summer at Greenway, and in October were delighted to be informed, once more at the last minute, that Rosalind was to marry again. They were invited to the wedding, if they wanted to come, but there would be no reception because the newly-weds had to get home to feed the dogs. Agatha and Max became devoted to Rosalind's husband, Anthony Hicks, an amusing scholarly man whose interest in life was Tibet but who had all sorts of other interests including several, like wine and gardens, that appealed to Max, and travel that appealed to Agatha.

The year of 1949 set a pattern that was to change very little over the next decade. Soon after Christmas, Max and Agatha would set off for Baghdad where they would stay for about two months before the Nimrud season started, early in March, lasting till about the time of Max's birthday on 6 May. The School's house in Baghdad became very much like another outpost in Agatha's empire-building, acquiring her unmistakable imprint. They had decided though that nothing would induce them to spend another season in the waterlogged farm, and it was proposed that a proper expedition house be constructed. Barbara Parker, a former student of cuneiform of Sidney Smith at the British Museum, had now taken over as Secretay/Librarian in Baghdad, and it became her responsibility to supervise the building of this, which began in the autumn of 1949.

The 1950 season also began in bad weather, so that Max and Robert Hamilton had rather a trying time slithering through mud and forging *wadis* to reach the site. When they arrived they found that their fine new mud-brick house was built, to be used for meals and working. There were tents to sleep in, two to each tent. If a bath was required, it could be taken in a round tin tub in the privacy of a tent, the same tub that was used for washing potsherds, but emptied and cleaned out for the purpose. An excellent new cook had been engaged. He made delicious rice dishes with lamb and chicken, and a neighbouring sheikh supplied them with a bucketful of sheep's yoghurt and flat folds of Arab bread every day. There were to be three extra members of staff that season: Barbara Parker, who arrived with Agatha the next day by train, Donald Wiseman from the Department of Egyptian and Assyrian Antiquities at the British Museum, as epigraphist, and Margaret Munn-Rankin, Max's former pupil at the Institute and now a lecturer on ancient history and archaeology at Cambridge University.

Hamilton had known Barbara for many years and described her as 'the faithful, ever-industrious and resourceful member of the School and its dig at Nimrud ... Her deceptively indolent ejoyment of life, concealing a really stoical capacity to put up with trying circumstances, made her the good-natured butt of Max's occasional satirical humour.' Donald Wiseman, who arrived a week later, had also been in the RAF with the rank of Group Captain, and had recently become the father of a daughter. He was described by Hamilton as being 'one of the most faithful and useful members both of the Nimrud expeditions and ... of the British School itself ... He was one of those talented and industrious people who could read a cuneiform text as easily ... as the *Daily Mail*; and could transcribe it in an immaculate cuneiform hand. He contributed to the social life of the dig a kindly and constant interest in his colleagues' personal well being.' Margaret Munn-Rankin was then about forty, a 'rather nice' spinster. There were also two representatives from the Iraqi Antiquities Department, Sayyid Izzet Din and Dr Faraj Basmachi. Max took great pains to make them feel included in the family atmosphere and to help them with their training.

The season was short and work was the priority. On Wednesdays, however, there were days off, always spent in exploring the neighbouring countryside with a picnic lunch, sometimes to see ancient sites, sometimes medieval churches and one memorable special overnight trip to see the Rowanduz gorge, a treat paid for by Agatha. They celebrated Easter Sunday with poems written by Agatha on their breakfast plates. There was plenty of good-natured badinage, teasing by Agatha and in-jokes presided over by Max with his satirical grin.

Towards the middle of April, the pace speeded up and Hamilton could barely keep up with all the drawing that needed to be done. He still had the most difficult slope of all, round the ziggurat, to plan and was not sure if he would have time.

Then we have cleared a lot of rooms and corridors of a huge palace partly dug by Layard – and all that has to be planned: very awkward as the floors are very deep, and none of the walls are vertical, so you can't take measurements at ground level, but must do them at the bottom of the pits ... Then I seem to be the only person capable of drawing pots etc., of which we have quantities to do ... cleaning and mending ivories etc.

They were all back in Baghdad on 5 May and enjoying running water and proper beds. Max and Agatha had invited the Hamiltons and their children to come down to Devon for a week in August, an invitation which they accepted with alacrity. In September, Agatha celebrated her sixtieth birthday with a splendid lunch party at Greenway. 'Though rain pours down, eating is always eating!' she told her publisher, who had arranged a party in London for her. 'Thank you for asking me to meet Agatha Christie', she replied to the formal invitation to the event.

The 1950 season was promptly written up for volume XII of *Iraq* and set another precedent from which Max was seldom to deviate, that of publishing his results at once and however summarily. As he explained, reports would have to remain provisional until a time when a large amount of comparative material was available and it could all be properly collated. But quick publication enabled specialists in all fields to make use of the relevant material with the minimum of delay.

The long article started with an essay on the historical importance of Nimrud, known to the Assyrians as Kalhu, and its topography. Max introduced his team by name and described the work each one had done during the season. He then went on to describe the excavations. Once more they had largely confined their work to the eastern sector of the mound, where an early sounding had revealed an imposing mud-brick building partly faced with burnt bricks, the Governor's Palace. This was likely to be the administrative office of Assyrian governors of the eighth century BC, for in one corner they found an archive office with a collection of 150 clay tablets. This building had a large central courtyard, and two great audience halls to the north and south. The walls of one of these halls were decorated with frescos, simple geometric designs in a brilliant cobalt blue with black and red and white. They made further soundings in the South East Palace and continued their re-excavation of the North West Palace, where their object was to re-open a selected number of chambers dug by Layard so that they could be properly examined and photographed. Max's chapter was followed by Wiseman's on the tablets, the first 76 from the Governor's Palace, the first article, he hoped, of a long series on epigraphic finds from Nimrud.

The season was also described in *The Illustrated London News* on 29 July in a four-page article, copiously illustrated. The two best finds had been an ivory figure of a cow and a translucent cylinder seal of mauve chalcedony. On 16 August, the magazine had a romantic cover entitled 'Winged, Harnessed and Poised to Guard the King's Majesty of Assurnasirpal the Second: One of a Pair of 11 Foot High Monsters (*c.* 880 BC) Recently Discovered in the Most Important Assyrian Dig at Nimrud Since Layard's Time a Hundred Years Ago'. Inside was another four page-article.

In August, Wiseman wrote to Max in some despair. Gadd was on leave and he was about to go on leave himself. Would it be all right if J. V. Kinnier Wilson from Durham University took over the rest of the Nimrud tablets and catalogued them in January 1951? Max was firm: 'Will you please impress upon him that as and until the division is effected, they are the property of the Iraq government; it is most important that they should be kept in safe custody. They should not be entrusted to the post and should be kept under lock and key when not in use.'

Max's third season at Nimrud in 1951 was overshadowed by the death of his mother. Max had arrived in Baghdad on 19 January and Agatha on the 28th. They were enjoying their time, Max in the Museum, reading books and writing articles, including another chapter for the *Cambridge Ancient History*, and both of them seeing friends and preparing for Nimrud in March. Two new rooms had been built on to the expedition house, and they were looking forward to seeing them. Then a letter came from Max's younger brother Philip to say that their mother was in a nursing home, and was seriously ill. Max had thought that she was recovering from the bronchitis she was suffering from when they left, and it was a terrible shock to discover that she had cancer. He was deeply concerned. He tried to cheer her up with news of what they had been doing and what would be happening next. On 6 February, he wrote her a last letter, uncharacteristically emotional:

My darling Mother, Just a few lines to tell you that I think of you every day and am closely with you in thought at this time. You have always been a dear mother to all of us and we miss you when we are away. We are very well and enjoy seeing the beautiful river Tigris outside our window. I was very happy to have your short letter with your loving wishes. My dear love to you darling and Agatha sends hers to you also. I will write again soon Max.

She died soon after receiving the letter. Max had always found it hard to express his feelings. Marguerite had adored her eldest son and taken great pleasure and pride in his work, even making drawings in the Assyrian Galleries of the British Museum to please him. Donald Wiseman was once asked by Max to take his mother round the Assyrian Galleries at the Museum, and she was absolutely thrilled to see the evidence of his work in glass cases before her. Unlike Max, she was a person who gave full expression to her feelings, to the occasional discomfiture of others, but she had a truly loving and generous heart.

Early in March the team assembled in Baghdad. Robert Hamilton had flown out from Amsterdam where he was visiting friends, and had sat next to an agreeable young American called Kelly Simpson, who turned out to be from the Metropolitan Museum of Art in New York, new and generous sponsors of the Nimrud dig. He was on his way to Nimrud: 'a young, willowy fellow, careful of many things such as the right length of socks to take on a dig'. The plane was met by Agatha and Barbara, who took them back to the house to meet the other new members of the expedition, Neville Chittick and Diana Kirkbride. They travelled by train to Mosul,where Donald Wiseman joined them, and their Iraqi colleague from last year, Sayyid Izzet Din.

Hamilton's letters to his wife and children in England fill in the gaps left by the official reports. He tells of innumerable visits from other archaeologists in the region, the new British consul in Mosul, Mr and Mrs Allen Lane of Penguin Books, and so on. He also reported the arrival of a bulldozer lent by the Iraq Petroleum Company:

It arrived today from Kirkuk, transported on a 20-ton trailer; a monstrous engine, weighing 15 tons and furnished with a

gigantic steel pusher, with which it can push the top off a small
hill with irresistible force. It is not very usual to do archaeological
excavation with a bulldozer, but here there are various important
buildings which have been prodded and probed by earlier
diggers a hundred years ago, and we wish to get rid of their old
dumps quickly ... it really displays a diabolical power.

He tells of the Wednesday jaunts, to the stone acquduct built by
Sennacherib, to Hatra, and of trips to Mosul for shopping and haircuts,
but the letters that year lack quite the air of unalloyed fun of the
previous years.

This was probably partly to do with the fact that the 1951 season
was a busy and successful one with some major finds. There were also
far more archaeologists on the dig, and inevitably the company was on
less intimate terms. How busy they were is reflected in the account of
the work in *Iraq,* volume XIV. It was the third continuous season at the
site, and Max began by describing the newcomers: Neville Chittick of
Cambridge University who catalogued the pottery and acted as general
field assistant, Kelly Simpson who had 'deft fingers in extracting
ivories', and Diana Kirkbride from the University of London. Their
principal efforts had been directed towards the North West Palace,
where they had made substantial additions to the ground plan, and
discovered a massive stela of Ashurnasirpal II as well as a collection
of ivories, 'a notable addition to the nucleus first discovered by Loftus
in 1854'. To the south side of the South East Palace they had made
further excavations at the eastern gate into the inner city, where they
had found the remains of a massive stone gateway with a gypsum
lion in relief. This extra activity had been made possible by generous
sponsorship from the Metropolitan Museum in New York. Donald
Wiseman described the Esarhaddon Cylinder, which had been
discovered in three separate fragments and put together to form one
large octagonal cylinder, and continued with his presentation of the
Nimrud tablets. *The Illustrated London News* published articles in July
and August with many illustrations, of the principal find of the season,
the massive stela of Ashurnasirpal, and of the ivories. The stela,
surmounted with a portrait of the king holding a battle mace and with
two daggers in his belt, described the banquet which was laid on for

the city of Kalhu at its inauguration. The number entertained was a precise 67,574 people.

During the following season, the fourth, in 1952, Max was pleased to have Cyril Gadd with them. Gadd had entrusted himself to an aeroplane, 'an awful type of machine ... not fit for human conveyance' as he reported back to Edwards at the Museum. He had spent three days with the American expedition at Nippur and been much intrigued by their 'tablet factory', their method of baking, cleaning and moulding the tablets they uncovered, in particular the cleaning process. This was done by means of a 'sand-spray', a jam-jar filled with fine sand which was released under pressure and neatly removed the accumulated débris of the millennia. Then the tablets went to be moulded. A cellulose solution was applied to the clean surface and over this a covering of latex which, when dry, was peeled off. Latex 'squeezes' were then sent by the boxful to Chicago. Back in Baghdad, Gadd reported on 2 March:

> We have here at present Max and Agatha, Miss Parker, Reid (drawing ivories in the Museum), Saggs (at the moment absent and presumed to be wandering in the southern desert with an American girl, Miss Joan Lines, who was determined to see Ur (which is easy) and Warka (which is said to be not)). Hamilton is expected tomorrow and we are going up to Nimrud, though not all together in the course of this week.

Work started on 8 March. Max and Robert Hamilton drove up ahead of the others who arrived by train, and were able to do the tedious business of sorting out tents, camp beds and so on. Once she arrived, Agatha took over the domestic arrangements, which were up to her usual standard that year with ever more inventive ideas. Her efforts were much helped by the loan of a refrigerator by the Iraq Petroleum Company. Max was absolutely shameless in borrowing items of equipment from the Company, whose only reward was an invitation for its employees to come and see the dig in progress on their days off. It was thought by some that they really came to see the famous crime novelist at work, but Agatha was prepared to put up with this for the advantages involved for Max.

The team that year was a happy one, as described by Robert Hamilton. He was sharing a tent with Cyril Gadd which he enjoyed, 'an agreeable scholarly type with a pleasant quiet humour'. John Reid was an architect who helped with surveying, 'a nice fellow', and Joan Lines 'very jovial and quite pretty in a solid, blonde, blue-eyed, rosy-cheeked way: nice, gay, competent, intelligent', who was to catalogue the pottery and do general field work. H. W. F. Saggs, a former pupil of Sidney Smith, was expected, described by Max somewhat unkindly as 'Saggs at the knees', 'a sad, prayerful, reserved type'.

Max had three main areas of operation in mind: the Burnt Palace, the North West Palace and an administrative wing of the palace to the south side of the ziggurat, which they called the ziggurat terrace. The Burnt Palace soon began to produce considerable quantities of carved ivory fragments from beneath its covering of charred wood ash and baked earth. They were mainly representations of female heads and animal figures. In April, they borrowed a great tripod and winch from the Iraq Petroleum Company and began emptying out an Assyrian well which Layard had abandoned during his excavations in the North West Palace. This was Max's third well; one had been too dangerous to clear, and a second had collapsed suddenly at the bottom, narrowly avoiding tragedy. Before its collapse, however, it had yielded a group of ivory and wooden writing boards, which had once been covered with beeswax. The boards were familiar from representations on Assyrian sculpture, but none had been found before. Donald Wiseman clearly remembered an afternoon when two boards came up from the depths: they fitted neatly into each other at the hinge and, having put them together, he was able to read the inscription at once.

In Max's third well, more real treasures began to come up, in quantity, miraculously preserved in the sludge that lay at the bottom. One that became well known was the ivory face of a woman, instantly called the 'Mona Lisa' as she had something of that same enigmatic smile. Max wrote in an article in *The Illustrated London News* published in August:

It was indeed a thrilling moment when we saw this lady emerge from the deep waters of the well where she had laid immersed in mud for more than 2600 years. Carefully we wiped away the dirt from her face, her hair and her crown. What we beheld was a thing of beauty still radiant with life. The warm brown tones of the natural ivory set against the dark black tresses of hair that framed the head combined with the soft rounded curves of the face to give an extraordinary impression of life. The slightly parted lips appeared to have a light reddish tint; the dark pupils of the eyes were encased in dark lids.

Agatha too recalled that 'most exciting day of all – one of the most exciting days of my life – when the workmen came rushing into the house during the period of clearing out an Assyrian well, and cried: "We have found a woman in the well! There is a woman in the well!" And they brought in, on a piece of sacking, a great mass of mud. I had the first pleasure of gently washing the mud off in a large basin.' But the ultimate pièce de résistance was a pair of almost identical ivory plaques which showed an African being savaged by a lioness under a hedge of lotus flowers. These were some of the finest objects to emerge from ancient Assyria, the artistic composition and the brilliant workmanship combined to create masterpieces. The ivory had been inlaid in places with gold, carnelian and lapis lazuli. The 'Mona Lisa' was followed by another large ivory portrait called the Ugly Sister. 'This lady is no beauty, perhaps because the mouth was left unfinished ... The nose is broken.' Agatha had her part in the conservation of these 'delicate, exquisitely fashioned ivories ... I had my own favourite tools as, I think, every craftsman always does have. An orange stick, possibly a fine knitting needle – one season a dentist's tool which he lent – or rather gave me – and a jar of cosmetic cleansing cream for the face which I found more useful than anything else for gently coaxing the dirt out of the crevices without harming the friable ivory ... How thrilling it was! The patience, the care that was needed; the delicacy of touch.'

From a building at the foot of the ziggurat terrace, excavated during the last few weeks of the season, emerged tablets in great quantity but in a state of fragility, so a kiln was built in order to bake and stablilize them. They were interesting documents, many being letters to Ashurnasirpal from governors in distant parts of his empire. It was good to have an expert such as Gadd on hand. He was also thrilled to be present when 'we uncovered a fresh series of ninth century sculptures on the north front of the North West Palace, a set which had not been seen since Austen Henry Layard had buried them a century ago'. Gadd was immediately able to tell them of the order in which these reliefs had once stood.

The finds of this wonderful season were given good publicity in *The Illustrated London News*. 'Mona Lisa' was shown life-size on the cover of 16 August, and in the same issue there was also a full-page colour illustration of the 'Lion Killing the Nubian in a Field of Lotuses', also life-size. A fortnight later, the magazine printed a second article about some of the smaller objects and written documents. There was a fine illustration of two winged colossi that flanked the gate to the second main entrance to the North West Palace which they had exposed that year. There was a small Nimrud exhibition at the British Museum, which moved on to the Ashmolean in Oxford.

The fifth Nimrud season began as usual in Baghdad at the beginning of March 1953 with members of the expedition meeting at the School, and setting off by different means to the site. Donald Wiseman was back and went off with Max in the Dodge 'looking like a circus turn'. Agatha, Barbara, John Reid and Robert Hamilton travelled up the following night by train. There was a new face (rather a pink one, according to Hamilton) belonging to Peter Hulin from Oxford University, who had come to help Donald Wiseman.

It was a very wet start to the season: Max and Donald Wiseman had to abandon the Dodge by the side of a river where a bridge had been washed away, hitch-hike to Kirkuk, and then borrow a five-ton break-down vehicle with a winch to tow the Dodge through the water. The wet weather lasted till the end of the month, hampering operations, but they did again borrow equipment from the Iraq Petroleum Company, two motor-driven winches, together with a trained operator this time. None the less it was frightening when the great machines began to tilt over in the mud. The plan was to investigate another 15 m well: this involved first removing an enormous stone slab which covered it, and which had broken into three fragments. Apart from the wells in the North West Palace, their aims that season were to complete the plan of the Burnt Palace, to excavate the quay wall, the ziggurat terrace and private houses to the north-east end of the mound, and to look at the outer town, north of the ziggurat, where they dug five trial trenches, which gave disappointing results of poor remains of private houses and scattered burials. Then they came across the ruins of yet another palace, at the north-west corner of the outer town about a kilometre from the outer wall of the acropolis, a large and imposing structure probably covering about an acre of ground. Inscribed bricks identified it as belonging to Adad-Nirari II (810-783 BC).

There were plenty of jolly excursions to view the countryside, and shopping trips to Mosul. Under Joan Lines's influence, Robert Hamilton bought a length of rich ruby-red cotton for pyjamas, and everyone bought brightly coloured Kurdish cloth for trousers or table mats. One day the whole expedition was invited to lunch with the old uncle of their neighbouring sheikh and regaled in Arabic with tales of the discovery of the Balawat gates by Hormuzd Rassam. As usual there were plenty of visitors to the site, some who came to stay, including the Lanes again, and the Altounyans, old and dear friends from Aleppo. Ernest Altounyan was the son of a distinguished brain surgeon and was, according to Agatha, 'almost the ugliest man I have ever seen. He was a tall man with a great head, a face of corrugated knobs, wild hair, eyes sparkling with fanatical excitement behind glasses; he was always in a state of supreme exhaltation and exuberation, of passionate feeling of some kind'. Dora Altounyan was the daughter of the Oxford philosopher and historian R. G. Collingwood, and was quite the opposite of her husband, being quiet, silent and, Agatha said, 'with a singular absence of any kind of enthusiasm'. Dora painted a particularly charming portrait of Agatha mending pottery at the exhibition house at Chagar Bazar in 1936. Others came for the day, such as the annual visit by the British Council, dreaded by everyone since the party numbered about eighty and all had to be entertained, and given tea and cakes.

Max wrote up the season in *Iraq*, volume XVI (1954). Most of the volume was taken up with Nimrud: there were articles by Barbara Parker on the business documents (most of which had been discovered during the 1952 season in the Governor's Palace) and by Joan Lines on Assyrian palace wares, and Cyril Gadd reported on inscribed prisms. *The Illustrated London News* showed on its cover the 'Mona Lisa' ivory as it looked after cleaning and repair, and a week later reported on the whole season, commenting that a five-year excavation plan was now completed and that the fortunes of the city between 883 and 612 BC had now emerged.

The Mallowans particularly enjoyed their homecoming that year since Agatha's grateful publishers, Collins, had decided to lavish a car on her. Before leaving in January, she had looked at various ones before deciding on a Humber Imperial. Max loved cars too. The Humber Imperial had seven seats and was ideal for their particularly generous way of journeying through life. There was room for books, dogs and produce from the garden, as well as huge picnic parties and all the hampers that went with them. And as Agatha said to her publishers, 'You've no idea the amount of things that archaeologists take with them.'

Max had had had it in his mind for some time that he would not excavate in 1954. He had tried to be meticulous about keeping his reports up-to-date, but so successful had been his first five seasons that he needed to take a year off and devote it entirely to writing. He settled himself into a rountine of spending working weeks at Swan Court, weekends at Winterbrook House and holidays at Greenway. He reported to Donald Wiseman in February that he had already written forty thousand words. Meanwhile Barbara Parker was living in the house in Baghdad and running the School while also writing up her epigraphic finds. Now and again frantic letters would arrive at the British Museum: 'WHERE is my little green note book?', and Barbara's long-suffering aunt would be sent round to collect it.

It was a glorious summer that year and as usual Rosalind and Anthony brought Mathew to stay. Both Max and Agatha were devoted to the boy and Max spent happy hours teaching him cuneiform signs and playing cricket with him. It was a sadness to him not to have children of his own and at one stage he became so involved in Mathew's upbringing that Rosalind felt she had to assert her own rights as his mother. Later, Max and Agatha took a similar interest in Cecil's sons.

The sixth season at Nimrud (1955) had a specific object: to rediscover the great temple dedicated to the god Nabu, and the library which it almost certainly had, somewhere at the south-west corner of the acropolis. 'The results exceeded our most sanguine expectations', Max wrote in *The Illustrated London News* of 31 January 1956. Their biggest problem, initially, was that when they found it the temple was buried under huge dumps of the nineteenth-century excavations. It was once more a case for an Iraq Petroleum Company bulldozer. Once the spoil heaps were removed, they were able to plan the temple, which had attached to its south side another palace, containing a throne-room with a pedestal. In this room were literally hundreds of fragments of engraved ivory panels. As two were nearly complete, they were able to reconstruct others, which depicted the king receiving tribute from his subject peoples. Robert Hamilton described the technique of saving the ivory: celluloid dissolved in acetone was applied to the fragments and then strips of gauze bandage were gently pressed down, which stiffened as they dried so that the ivory could be picked up. There were also a great many fragmentary tablets, mainly treaties made by the king with foreign princes, one in particular being a long treaty made by Esarhaddon with a prince of the Medes, some six hundred lines long and inscribed on the observe and reverse in four columns. Assyria was then at the height of its power, though it was to be only sixty years later (612 BC) that those same Medes, with the Babylonians, were to sack Nineveh. Max surmised that they then came on to Nimrud and destroyed Esarhaddon's palace shortly afterwards.

The team that season consisted of Agatha, Robert Hamilton, Barbara Parker, Sayyid Izzet Din, John Reid, and a newcomer, David Oates, an experienced archaeologist who in the previous season had been in Jebel Sinjar, looking at Roman remains. There were two volunteer assistants, as well as colleagues from the Iraq Antiquities Department. Max was beginning to think that there ought to be formal training in their own history for these enthusiastic young men. He wrote to Cyril Gadd on 7 February to ask him:

> Can you think of anyone who in about one or two years' time might like to come out to the University of Baghdad and teach Akkadian language, elementary Sumerian, and some literature? By that time teaching in those subjects may be needed for one of the arts degrees ... someone like Saggs would be the answer, Kinnier Wilson or the like?

Working conditions that year were bad: a severe drought and high winds which brought swirling dust. In the last week of April, there was a hurricane which blew down their tents and nearly took the roof off the expedition house. Agatha was ill at the end of March and had to be driven to hospital in Kirkuk by Max. They had electricity for the first time, both in the rooms in the expedition house and also in their tents, though someone had to stay up to turn it off at night. The Iraq Petroleum Company had been generous again that season with the loan of a bulldozer ('not exactly an orthodox archaeological tool'), and an electricity generator with an engineer in attendance.

Robert Hamilton, whose last Nimrud season it was, thought it was going badly:

> I think the dig is being rather unproductive at present – and what with Agatha's illness and some trouble of his own, I feel Max isn't coping with operations quite as successfully as usual. Also he is affected by Mortimer Wheeler's sarcasms about Near Eastern archaeologists, and consequent efforts to be more 'scientific' are tending to upset the balance of work, and lead us nowhere.

Agatha was then nearly sixty-six and her illness that season had doubtless left Max in no doubt that he could not expect her to spend many more springs in a tent in inclement weather in quite primitive conditions, especially in regard to hygiene. The arrival of younger men, such as David Oates, who had been professionally trained and were much more 'scientific' as Hamilton said, was perhaps a blow to Max's confidence, though he was quite capable of defending his own record. He may well have felt that his status as leader was being unintentionally undermined. Gone too for ever were the carefree days when Max and Agatha ran digs rather like private house-parties in exotic settings. In those days, their assistants had been selected by them, and were generally novices being given a first chance to see what they would make of the work and the life. Agatha reigned supreme. Now as she sat changed for dinner in the expedition house at Nimrud, her long fur-trimmed sleeves knocked over the glasses, and she looked, and, being sensitive, doubtless felt, out of place. There were many more people in the team, most of them young, and they spent their free time together, pushing off after dinner to do things on their own. Max had his work, an increasingly heavy burden, and Agatha spent much time in her own little writing-room on her books. She was not really at the centre of things in the same way, though she still helped greatly by cleaning ivories and mending pottery and took much pleasure from doing it so well. The work had indeed become more 'scientific', a much more technical approach was required and the old jolly amateur days were a thing of the past.

Max had plenty of time to reflect on this back in London. Apart from writing up the last season, he had lectures to give at the end of the year. Richard Barnett (now Keeper in the Deapartment) reported to Barbara in Baghdad that Max had been in fine form and that 'There was a record crowd at the Schweich lectures when Max certainly produced material to make us all think, especially statistically concerning the estimated population of Assyria'. There were also the plans for the celebration of the School's silver jubilee to be considered, an exhibition and a book. Max himself had been elected to the British Academy.

Max's main contribution to the School's jubilee was the book. It was entitled *Twenty-five Years of Mesopotamian Discovery* 1932–56, and described with pride the sites at which the School had excavated since its inception, gratifyingly all of them ones in which he himself had participated. He described the excavations at Arpachiyah, Chagar Bazar, Tell Brak, his soundings in the Balikh valley and finally his first six seasons at Nimrud.

The Mallowans were back in Baghdad in March 1956 for the seventh expedition with Barbara Parker, David and Joan Oates (as Joan Lines had now become) and various other colleagues from several academic institutions. They concentrated on three main areas on the mound: the temple of Nabu, the Ninurta temple, last touched by Layard in 1850, where they uncovered a colossal pair of winged lions, and a town wall above the bed of the Tigris, where they found a large mud-brick construction which they thought was a palace belonging to Ashurbanipal, Esarhaddon's son. The season was mainly remembered, however, for the re-excavation on the mound of Balawat, where in 1878 Hormuzd Rassam had found a pair of enormous embossed gates from the time of Shalmaneser III. The Nimrud expedition was fortunate to discover another two more pairs of gates, belonging also to

Ashurnasirpal II. They too were wonderfully ornamented with scenes of the king hunting wild animals, and leading his battle-troops. A colleague from the Institute of Archaeology, Marjery Howard, was in charge of the Balawat excavation and she later made a fine reconstruction drawing of the gates.

Although the season was reported in *Iraq*, volume XIX (1957), the most important article in the journal that year concerned the exhibition at the British Museum given by the School for its jubilee. The exhibition was opened by Leonard Woolley on 14 November 1956. Exhibits had been lent by the Metropolitan Museum in New York, the Ashmolean and, most importantly, by the Iraq Museum in Baghdad. All the sites described by Max in his book were represented by exhibits, the star of them all being undoubtedly the chryselephantine plaque of the Nubian from Nimrud.

On 26 July, Richard Barnett had written to Max saying, 'we should include such material as we can find, bearing on the history of Assyriology in this country. There are manuscripts of Layard and Rawlinson and Rassam in the Museum; the original maps and drawings of Boutcher and Layard.' Max was enthusiastic; between them they decided to display the portrait of Lady Layard wearing the magnificent necklace, bracelet and earrings of cylinder seals which Layard had presented to her on her marriage and subsequent anniversaries.

The exhibition began with a bust of Layard and drawings showing him at work, and concluded with Rassam's Balawat gates, with Max's own discoveries very much set in context. It attracted fourteen thousand visitors. Max made an opening speech in which he told the audience that 'only a moron could fail to be roused' by the splendour and variety of the exhibits, a remark felt to be typical of him. There was also a smaller celebration at the School's premises in Baghdad.

In February 1957, Max and Agatha were back in Nimrud. Work began on the south-east of the mound though rain was torrential and results disappointing. Max reported to Richard Barnett on 24 March: 'Digging very deep for the plan of Layard's building at the s.e. end of the mound ... but it is much plundered. Many ivories but alas all plain panels.' Little did he know what lay just around the corner. Max described to readers of *The Illustrated London News* in November how it was.

Whilst walking round the outer town towards the beginning of the season I was attracted to some high-lying ground which with its undulating outlines obviously contained within heavy walls. As luck would have it we noticed, at a point not far from a gap which seemed to indicate a gate, an inscribed brick of Shalmaneser III ... From that moment we resolved that at the first opportunity we should move half our workmen to this rich-looking cover which we named in anticipation Fort Shalmaneser ... So promising were our first efforts in this direction that we soon felt constrained to move all the rest of our men and make a supreme effort to reveal the ground plan.

That ground plan, which four weeks' work revealed, showed a building which covered nearly 6 hectares in area, was entered by a single narrow gateway and had four courtyards. In it was a mass of magnificent and extraordinary ivories, making the Nimrud collection of them the richest ever recovered from the ancient world. The ivories from Fort Shalmaneser were distributed over several rooms, embedded in heavily packed mud-brick. It was Joan Oates to whom Max gave the great credit for their extraction. Out they came, piece after piece: feasting court women, suggestive courtesans, men of magic, a dog-like lion, a prince picking a lotus (reproduced on the cover of *The Illustrated London News* on 23 November), 'beautiful and enigmatic'.

In May, the Mallowans flew straight to the United States because Max had been awarded a gold medal by the University of Pennsylvania, a ceremony which gave them both enormous pleasure. They then spent three days at the Grand Canyon, and then they went to Los Angeles, where Agatha's play *Witness for the Prosecution* was being filmed. Back home, they spent their usual sort of summer at Greenway, and before Christmas went to Barbados. After Christmas, they went to Baghdad. They both knew that they were coming to the end of these annual visits, and the pleasure of being back was tempered with sadness.

It was the discovery of Fort Shalmaneser that had set the crown on nearly a decade of achievement at Nimrud. It also marked the turning point in Max's career. With this under his belt, he felt the moment had come for him to retire from the field. He had been thinking about it since 1955 when Agatha had been so ill, and now it seemed appropriate to hand over to a younger generation who would need all the energy and enthusiasm they could muster for the massive task ahead of them. Max made his resignation plans clear to readers of *Iraq* in volume XX, though he did take part in the 1958 season with David Oates as Director. Max wrote up the ivories for *The Illustrated London News* in January 1959 in an article with two full-page coloured illustrations showing a winged sphinx wearing an Egyptian double-crown, pectoral, uraeus and kilt, and a figure of a golden-haired winged boy with polychrome incrustations. A third coloured page showed four further ivories including the so-called 'Woman at the Window'. Max wrote one more article about the Nimrud ivories for the magazine in January 1960, but after that his long association with the magazine, begun in Arpachiyah days, ended.

If Max regretted his resignation from the field, he gave no one that impression. He was as busy as ever, full of projects, to keep him from regret. Foremost of these, and the one which was to make his name as famous as that of Woolley, and of Layard, was his definitive account of the Nimrud years.

CHAPTER NINE

In the Grand Manner

Retirement from the field did not bring Max to a more leisurely way of life; in fact, he became busier than ever as his academic commitments increased. Agatha continued to play her part in supporting him, taking great pride in his achievements. In the New Year's Honours List of 1960 he was awarded a CBE and shortly afterwards by way of celebration he and Agatha took Rosalind, Anthony and Mathew to Ceylon for a short holiday. This was very much to everyone's taste as there was an ideal mixture of interesting ruins and fine sea-bathing. Afterwards, Max and Agatha departed by themselves to India and Pakistan, a trip that was as enthralling as it was exhausting. In her seventieth year, Agatha travelled some five thousand kilometres to the Khyber Pass from Bombay, visiting digs and museums on the way, and everywhere she went being fêted by the local people, to whom she was something of a legend. Agatha Christie novels were very popular in India. In Iran, Max was working: the British Academy was considering the setting up of another British School in Tehran, and Max had been asked to do some preliminary work in preparing the way.

The Mallowans were still abroad when they heard of the death of Leonard Woolley on 20 February, so they were unable to attend his funeral service. They were, however, back in time for his memorial service at St Martin-in-the-Fields, which took place on 14 March. Max was asked to take charge of the fund set up in memory of Woolley and to edit the forthcoming *Festschrift* in *Iraq*, volume XXII, a task which involved contacting many former colleagues from a great number of academic institutions, those who wished to pay tribute to the outstanding British archaeologist of the ancient Near East of the century. The volume was entitled *Ur in Retrospect*, and it was a generous and affectionate collection of articles in Woolley's honour, Max himself contributing the first, entitled 'Memories of Ur', which described his arrival at the site as a complete novice in 1925. In November, Max delivered the first Woolley Memorial Lecture on Ur of the Chaldees at the Annual General Meeting of the British School.

He was also still publishing records of the ninth campaign at Nimrud, specifically huge ivories from a royal bed discovered in one of the rooms at Fort Shalmaneser. His last article on the ivories for *The Illustrated London News* was published in June 1960. And he was planning his great work on his decade of work at Nimrud, to be a definitive account of the discoveries.

Max and Agatha received an invitation from the Headmaster of Lancing, John Dancy, to be present on Founder's Day, 18 June, at the inauguration of the new open-air theatre. John Dancy was hoping that Agatha might be persuaded to say a few words on the occasion, but this was something she declined to do, hating public speaking, and, as Max explained, she would not want to offend others to whom she had declined to give speeches in the past. But she was willing to cut a tape and even light a flame on the Greek altar of the new theatre, provided she did not have to do too much standing.

Glorious weather attended the event, and in the evening the Mallowans sat through the evening's performance of Marivaux's *Le Préjugé Vaincu*, some English verse, and the last part of *Oedipus Tyrannus*, mostly in Greek, with great enjoyment, despite the midges. Max wrote to Dancy afterwards, 'I little suspected in my callow youth that I should one day enjoy such a happy return to the School.'

That September, Agatha's seventieth birthday was celebrated on many fronts. She and Max went to Oberammergau to see the Passion Play, a long-held ambition of hers, and the whole family went to see Wagner's *Rheingold* at Covent Garden. Max took her on holiday to Ireland, and the day itself was spent at Greenway, with her favourite dinner, hot lobster. Her chair had been decorated with flowers so that it looked like a throne. Max's nephews, Cecil's boys John and Peter, were frequent visitors to Greenway, since their parents were abroad. They had become great favourites of both Max and Agatha, who took them out from school, Balcombe Place at Hayward's Heath, and, later on, from Downside. In the holidays, Max took them sailing in the

Greenway boat, the *Golly*, a glass-fibre dinghy with a 10 hp outboard motor, and played tennis and cricket with them.

Towards the end of the year, the British Academy's investigations into the feasibility of the new School, the British Institute of Persian Studies, were complete, following a visit to the country by Mortimer Wheeler and Sir Maurice Bowra. In January 1961, Max went out to Tehran to talk to David Stronach, who was to become the Director of the new School. He was then the British Academy Attaché with the British Council. On 15 February in London, the Council of the British Academy officially appointed the governing council of BIPS, nominating Max himself as President. Later that month, the School project was gracefully referred to at the time of the royal visit of the Queen and Prince Philip to Tehran. The Chancellor of the University of Tehran was thanked by the Queen for the University's hospitality to the new School, which was to be presented by the University with a house containing enough accommodation for up to nine people, in a large garden with a swimming pool, the house to be rent free and supplied with heating and lighting, for a period of five years. The arrangements regarding the house were the work of David Stronach. Richard Barnett at the British Museum was rather worried by Stronach's appointment, however, writing to Max that he thought him 'very young and somewhat inexperienced'. Max showing great foresight wrote back on 27 March:

> I daresay you do not know him as well as I do. He has already spent a year in Persia and is the only man I know who has dug in Anatolia, in Iraq, in Persia and in Pakistan where his work was highly approved of by Mortimer Wheeler, and there could be no more exacting master of archaeological technique … we have all been impressed with the methodical and practical way in which he set to work.

Max's visit to Tehran had been marred by a slight stroke which he suffered on 3 March during the royal visit to the University of Tehran. He was fifty-seven. He came home unassisted, however, and there was little relaxation in his schedule. The archaeological Schools were dear to his heart; in his *Memoirs*, he wrote:

> These institutions have for me been the most rewarding part of
> my participation in Oriental archaeology, for not only have they
> yielded a multitude of friends, but this form of international
> involvement has conferred mutual prestige on our country and
> the host country concurrently. We have in this way helped each
> other to take a pride in the past ... and by sharing excavations
> have aided in the building up of the great Museums and national
> collections ... the consciousness of involvement, of a sharing
> with our foreign friends in a common task, and of helping with
> technical training ... has been ... most rewarding.

Max's interests were wide-ranging. On 28 June, he was writing to *The
Times* regarding the saving of the great temple of Ramesses II at Abu
Simbel from the building of the Aswan high dam: 'a unique, incompa-
rable monument, a massive architectural and sculptural achievement
which for over 3000 years has enshrined the spirit of ancient Egypt,
and is the heritage not of one country but of all mankind'.

That summer Agatha was reported by UNESCO to be the world's
best-selling author in English. Her books were sold in 102 different
countries. It was also the summer of a film based on her 1957 book *The
4.50 from Paddington*. The film was called *Murder She Said*, and the
entire Greenway party piled into the Humber and set off for the Regal
Cinema in Torquay to see it. It was a sad disappointment: even the
little Mallowan boys knew it was not quite as it should have been.
Exuberant Margaret Rutherford was nothing like the precise and
spinsterly heroine, Miss Jane Marple. Fortunately other film adaptations
of Agatha's books were to be more acceptable to their author.

Max had been fund-raising for BIPS, whose first project was to be
three seasons' work at Pasargadae. He was vigorous and successful,
and raised £17,000. Work at the site started in October 1961 and Max
and Agatha went out in the autumn to inspect. On 10 and 11
December, the official ceremonies for the opening of the new School
in Tehran were held. Max said in his speech that the new Institute
would not confine its energies to the art and archaeology of antiquity
but would endeavour to provide facilities for the study of Persian civilization 'in all its length and breadth, from the remote past to present
times, in many aspects, in different disciplines'.

In March 1962, Max wrote to Rosalind from Winterbrook House with some exciting news.

> I tell you for your private ears until such time as it is published in *The Times*. It is that I shall be vacating my chair in London, when I resign my professorship in October, having been elected to a fellowship of All Souls for the next seven years until the age of 65. I answered an advertisement for it in *The Times* last October, and understand that I came top out of seventy candidates, and that astonishes me ... It is a coincidence that Mathew and I will be going up as new boys together in the autumn.

Max had been championed in his election to All Souls, that acme of academic achievement and privilege, by Lord Salter, whom the Mallowans had known in Baghdad, and who later became the President of the British School in Iraq. The Warden was John Sparrow. Max's rooms were in the Old Quadrangle which dated to the fifteenth century, quite modern by Max's counting. None the less, he used to wonder 'how long it took for the news of the fall of Constaninople to reach the infidel in Oxford' and other such latter-day events. Max himself was immersed in the eighth and ninth centuries BC as he finally had time to tackle his seminal work on Nimrud. He had been asked at his interview if he would help with the new Oxford edition of Herodotus, but it seems that his other labours left no time for this. Being at All Souls gave Max untold pleasure. Whenever he could he wrote letters on All Souls writing paper, took an active part in College life, and entertained graduate students to (usually) magnificent lunches (though young Lambert was given a terrible egg curry and ancient cake on the occasion of his visit) after which he invited them to read their dissertations to him, frequently nodding off, even when the subject was as interesting as Nimrud metalwork. As he said, 'I felt that I had through the efforts of my life-work, recovered from the lack of academic distinction in my youth', something that he minded about more than he often revealed.

Agatha spent more time now at Winterbrook House with the faithful housekeeper Mrs Belson in attendance. Max came home at weekends and they fell into a pleasurable routine of shared rituals, such as collecting silver, a piece for every year from 1700 to 1800, which meant turning down many pieces they might have liked to own. Another was the long search for the perfect rice dish (culminating in the purchase of a magnificent Song dynasty bowl from an Oxford dealer who could not quite believe his ears when he heard what it was to be used for). They went often to London, though Agatha did less cooking at home and they usually entertained at Boodle's or at the Detection Club, where Max played second fiddle and was quite content to be Agatha Christie's husband. They still spent as much time away together as they could, going in late August once more to Bayreuth, where Mathew joined them as he too loved Wagner. Agatha greatly enjoyed reading the scores of the evening's performance with him and on one occasion Friedelinde Wagner, the composer's granddaughter, took them behind the scenes in the opera house.

In November that year they went again to Baghdad, and back to Nimrud so that Max could re-examine the ground and check some of the information he needed to complete his book on the excavations. They went on to look at Persepolis, returning in time for the Tenth Anniversary Party for *The Mousetrap,* which was held at the Savoy. It was one occasion on which Agatha did manage to make a very short speech and felt extremely proud of herself afterwards.

The next year, 1963, saw the twenty-fifth volume of *Iraq,* which was devoted entirely to Nimrud, and began with an article by Max on the so-called Mona Lisa of Nimrud, the haunting ivory portrait that he had found in a well in the North West Palace in 1953. Its exciting discovery was recalled: how as they struggled to remove the water in the well, it surged up even more swiftly so that they had to work the pumps all day and for part of the night. The editorship of *Iraq* had passed to Donald Wiseman, who persuaded Max to confront one of the perennial problems of the cuneiform texts: how their accounts related to similar accounts in the Old Testament. The result of this was an interesting article in the following year's journal, 'Noah's Flood Reconsidered'. Max was still battling on with his great work on Nimrud, but also found time to contribute his volume to the Library of Early Civilizations, *Early Mesopotamia and Iran,* published in 1965 to good reviews.

That summer the Mallowans went to Lake Annecy, to Talloires, then on to Austria and Switzerland. They had left behind them another long-term problem, Agatha's battles with the Inland Revenue. It suddenly declared that she owed them £100,000 in unpaid tax, a gloomy but not unexpected outcome to a long battle. For such a prolific and internationally popular best-selling author, she was constantly worried about her financial position, being plagued by demands from the tax authorities both in Britain and in the United States.

At the end of 1965, Max eventually finished his two-volume magnum opus on Nimrud and took Agatha to the Ritz in Paris after Christmas to celebrate. The book was called *Nimrud & Its Remains*, a quite deliberate choice of title to reflect an earlier highly popular work on Mesopotamian excavation, that of Austen Henry Layard's *Nineveh & Its Remains*. The first volume described the excavations on the acropolis, including the ziggurat, the Ninurta and Nabu temples, the North West Palace, Ezida and the private houses, and the second was entirely devoted to Fort Shalmaneser. The volumes were reviewed in *The Times* on 24 February 1966: 'two well-written, well-produced and well-illustrated volumes do the fullest justice to the excitement of the excavation ... they present close-up glimpses of that part civilized, part-barbarous people, the Assyrians'. The paper's only cavil was the price: 16 guineas for the two boxed volumes including separately bound maps, plans and sections.

On 15 March, *The Illustrated London News* ran a long article about the book and about Max himself under the headline 'Professor Mallowan Tells the Story of Nimrud, Ancient Military Capital of Assyria'. It reminded its readers that throughout the 1950s they had been treated to annual accounts, 'rich, full and fascinating', of the treasures discovered by the British School of Archaeology at Nimrud. Now they had the full story, which had been well worth waiting for and was a model of what such things should be: informed, detailed, full of the love of the subject, and most of all readable. The archaeological editor Edward Bacon particularly liked the fact that every illustration had a full caption on the same page, and was printed on the same page as the text that mentioned it. The magazine also published a fine picture of Max in his study at Swan Court, with the caption 'Writing is the Most Painful Part of any Excavation'.

Cyril Gadd also wrote about the book in *The Times*, managing to say a great deal about the history of Assyria but practically nothing about the book itself, and there was a particularly good review in *The Times Literary Supplement,* prompting an unusually friendly letter from Max to Richard Barnett:

> I really want to thank you ... for a review of *Nimrud and its Remains* which I recently read ... This was a most generous tribute and a great encouragement which I most warmly appreciate. It was replete with learning and written by a savant and must, I think, have been the work of your pen.

Max's publishers, Collins, gave a lavish party.

A lecture tour in the United States took place in autumn 1966, and both Max and Agatha very much enjoyed the hospitality of their generous hosts during a fairly gruelling itinerary that took them to Cleveland, Washington, to universities in New England, then to Texas and Dallas. Texas reminded them both of Baghdad, and how of sad they were to be missing the opening of the new Iraq Museum on 9 November. The Iraqi Ambassador in Washington gave a large lunch party to celebrate, and Max was the guest of honour. In Baghdad, there were a thousand guests from all over the world, and two of Max's most magnificent ivories from Nimrud were prominently and proudly displayed, the 'Mona Lisa' and the 'Nubian in the Lotus Thicket'.

The indefatigable Mallowans returned to spend Christmas with Rosalind in Wales. Agatha was completing her autobiography, and Max was involved in the forthcoming volume of *Iraq,* to be dedicated to Sidney Smith on the occasion of his seventy-seventh birthday. There were various good reasons for doing this, as Max reminded Richard Barnett who was unenthusiastic about the tribute. Smith had been the founder of the journal and its first editor. Friends and former pupils were anxious to express their recognition on his birthday.

> No-one believes that he was ever an easy man and his last days in the BM were as I well know sad [but] ... he set high standards both for himself and others. You have forgotten his *Early History of Assyria* which was a solid contribution at the time and is

still a mine of information. Everything that he wrote had quality and his chronicles of Esarhaddon, Nabonidus, Cyrus, and his chapters in the *Cambridge Ancient History* on Assyria are masterly and still hold their own. For his pupils, he took endless pains; he was a most stimulating teacher, and I have always admired the originality of his mind.

Max was right to honour Smith. Barnett had never been an admirer of Smith, whom he believed to be anti-semitic. He described him as 'gaunt, arrogant, aggressive, inflexible but rather able ... When World War One broke out ... he was wounded in the back and invalided out. He recovered but not to fight again, except on paper and to dramatize.' He was at his best as an historian of the ancient Near East. Some believed his troubles were the result of worry about his wife Mary who had had periods of nervous breakdown.

Once the journal had been achieved, in the spring, Max and Agatha went abroad again, to Iran with Mortimer Wheeler to inspect the work of BIPS. Then, in May, they had the excitement of Mathew's wedding to Angela Maples, after which Max and Agatha went to Yugoslavia. They spent most of the summer at Greenway, then went to Spain, then Max went back to Iran in October. It is perhaps not surprising that he should have suffered his second stroke there (aged sixty-two), while delivering a lecture, and, though he managed to carry on to the end of his talk, he was flown home as soon as he was able to travel.

It was decided at this stage that Mathew, now he was married, should move into his ancestral home at Pwyllwrach and that his mother and stepfather Rosalind and Anthony Hicks should move down to Greenway, particularly now that both Max and Agatha were not as robust as they had been. The Hickses moved into Ferry Cottage on the Greenway estate, though Rosalind spent most of the time in the big house when Agatha was there being an invaluable help on the domestic and administrative side.

In June that year (1968) Max was knighted for services to archaeology, an honour which pleased him greatly, not least because it meant that Agatha also received a title. Other new knights in the same list included the football manager Matt Busby and Barnes Wallis, the inventor of the bouncing bomb. Max now devoted most of his energies to writing and reviewing. To *Iraq* volume XXI he contributed an article entitled 'Rediscovered Skulls from Arpachiyah', which related the sad history of his case of skulls that arrived at the British Museum in the summer of 1934, and was stored in the so-called Carthaginian Basement. When Max came to sort out that season's finds, he dispatched the case of skulls to the Royal College of Surgeons in the care of two stout porters, who wheeled the case down Great Russell Street to the College, hauled it up the steep steps, and then lost control of it, so that it crashed over, smashing most of the contents. The Royal College then informed Max that the skulls were far too damaged to bear examination, so the case was wheeled back to the Museum, where it rested until long after the Second World War. Max had managed to persuade Dr Hilda Linford at the Natural History Museum in the Cromwell Road to take an interest, and her recent investigations were the subject of the article. Max must have reflected on how things had changed since those carefree days.

Both Max and Agatha were considering their past achievements. They did a little gentle travelling, to Cyprus and later to Ober-ammergau, but they were really saving their energies for Agatha's eightieth birthday celebrations in September 1970. There were various commemorative projects that Agatha dreaded but undertook with her usual good humour: an official photograph for the National Portrait Gallery and a portrait by Oskar Kokoschka, which she liked very much indeed, rather to her surprise. Godfrey Winn was granted the privilege of the one interview Agatha could bear to give, to the *Daily Mail,* and the family tried not to show their secret delight when he was bitten by Agatha's rather tiresome and nervous terrier, Bingo. The celebrations themselves took place at Boodle's, at All Souls and at Greenway where on the day there was a huge family picnic on Exmoor with five dogs in the party, and a grand dinner with Agatha's favourite hot lobster and blackberry ice. Collins also gave a huge party, with an enormous chocolate cake, and *The Times* had a picture of Agatha in the feathered hat she had worn to cut it.

In the 1971 New Year's Honours, Agatha was made a Dame Commander of the British Empire, and Max took her to Paris to celebrate. She was asked to sit for a waxwork at Madame Tussaud's. It was very sad for Max and Agatha that a fall in June, when Agatha broke her hip, should come at such a peak moment in her long career, when she was really at the height of her fame and success, truly a national treasure but recognized worldwide. Her recovery from the fall was slow and painful; even by December, at the time of the state visit of the King of Afghanistan, Max had to write to Buckingham Palace to ask for help for Agatha with the stairs. The celebrations were gruelling by any standards, a state banquet at Buckingham Palace on 7 December (*Consommé Madrilène, Suprême of Turbot Waleska, Selle d'Agneau Rôtie, Pêches Toscane*) followed by a state luncheon at Lancaster House on 8 December (*Oeufs Cécilia, Poularde Chimaq, Bombe Glacée Montreuil*), but Max enjoyed such occasions greatly and Agatha liked to keep him company. In fact, throughout those years of his fellowship at All Souls Max's papers bear witness to the vast number of colossal dinners in all manner of august institutions that he attended, and at which he spoke or introduced other speakers. Apart from these official occasions, he loved to entertain friends and colleagues at home, and the visitors' book at Greenway is a fascinating record of the world of archaeology in the mid twentieth century. Both Max and Agatha were particularly kind to the young, and visits from Max's students and novice archaeologists at the Institute were frequent. These (usually) penniless young people were swept down to Greenway (or made to drive Max down in his own car while he issued instructions on how to drive it) and treated to weekends of sailing and walking and copious meals.

It gave Max a feeling of proud achievement to be appointed a Trustee of the British Museum in August 1973. He was appointed by Margaret Thatcher, the Minister of Education, to represent the British Academy and he replaced his old friend and sparring partner, Sir Mortimer Wheeler. The appointment was for a term of five years, and he felt honoured to be part of an institution which since boyhood had been his 'intellectual and spiritual gymnasium'. Now very much the grand old man of Near Eastern archaeology, his seventieth birthday in 1974 was marked by his colleagues with the dedication to him of the whole of volume XXXVI of *Iraq*. 'In Honour of Sir Max Mallowan' ran the frontispiece, with a fine photograph of Max, and there followed tributes from all Max's closest colleagues and his contemporaries. Richard Barnett wrote about the beginnings of Assyriology, Oliver

Gurney on the topography of Babylon, and Robert Hamilton on thuribles (bronze censers) 'offered in admiration to Sir Max Mallowan, and as a reminder of bumpy but delightful journeys to certain ancient monasteries in the Mosul area where such objects will have been used'. Seton Lloyd wrote about Eridu 'dedicated to Max Mallowan, whose interest in Eridu has been and is as great as my own ... offered as a token of gratitude for his unfailing help and friendship during the past many years'. Rachel Maxwell-Hyslop contributed a chapter on Assyrian sources of iron, Margaret Munn-Rankin (Max's former pupil) on two reliefs of special interest to Max, and David Oates on Balawat. He said in his dedication that it was characteristic of Max that he was careful of the reputation of his predecessors in the long line of British excavators in Assyria, among whom he held a place of honour, and that it had been a privilege to work in his company. Joan Oates wrote about late Assyrian temple furniture, Barbara Parker on a middle Assyrian seal impression, and André Parrot on a cylinder seal from Mari. He wrote about 'Une amitié vieille de près de quarante ans nous lie aussi solidement que le bitume des constructions sumériennes: Arpachiya après Ur, Chagar Bazar, Brak et pour finir, ce feu d'artifice de Nimrud avec cette fabuleuse moisson d'ivoires, quelle magnifique succession de victoires! Impossible pour un fouilleur de souhaiter mieux.' He went on to recall their first meeting in 1935 at Beirut at the Hotel Bassoul et d'Orient, when Max was on his way to Chagar Bazar and he on his way to Mari, and even at the time of writing he could not pass by the hotel without thinking of Max, and indeed Agatha to whom he paid a special tribute. H. W. F. Saggs wrote on the Nimrud Letters, recalling how on arrival at Nimrud in 1952 Max had shown him round the excavations. 'He had the gift of making every chamber in the Burnt Palace, every fragment of ivory, every slab and every sculpture, breathe with life as though there had been drawn back the curtain of two and a half millennia.' Saggs spoke of his debt and gratitude to a great Assyriologist. Other contributions included one from Claude Schaeffer on a cylinder from Chagar Bazar, a posthumous tribute from Henri Seyrig, David Stronach on an Achaemenid village at Susa, and Donald Wiseman on 'Murder in Mesopotamia', a piece about regicide and homicide, as a small tribute to Agatha. There was also a full bibliography of Max's publications up to 1973.

The introduction to the volume must have given Max particular gratification since it spoke of qualities that he had tried very hard to cultivate and instil in himself as a regular discipline. It spoke of the manifold contributions Max had made to the study of the ancient Near East, and his support and encouragement of others. His career after the War had been a happy combination of academic teaching and research, with practical training of young archaeologists, six of whom had gone on to become Directors of British Schools of Archaeology. It spoke of his insistence that it was a scholar's duty to present without undue delay a clear and meaningful interpretation of his work to the wider world of scholarship, and not least of his fruitful co-operation with his colleagues in the Iraq Antiquities Service and his very practical help to young students from Iraq when they came to London.

The volume was formally presented to Max at a celebration in Oxford, at which Agatha was present. The following month she suffered a heart attack, which left her very frail. In December she had a bad fall at Winterbrook House and cut her head badly. She spent much of her time in bed, and had become very thin and fragile. None the less she was able to be present in the summer of 1975, at the première of *Murder on the Orient Express*, the film that brought her name to the attention of a whole new generation of enthusiasts. The book made a splendid film, and the cast included just about every star in the cinema firmament. Agatha's last outing was in December, to the annual party for *The Mousetrap*. She was by then more or less confined to her bed, which had been moved downstairs at Winterbrook House. Max sat with her when he could and friends and relatives braved the fangs of Bingo to sit with her too. A night nurse had been engaged to watch over her. Algy Whitburn's nephew, Richard Quick, recalled bringing his uncle, five years younger than Agatha, who was then eighty-five, to lunch. Though she sat with them, she ate very little and was quite silent, but was none the less an endearing presence. And she readily agreed to sign a book for Richard's son. *Come, Tell Me How You Live* had been reissued in a new edition in the autumn, and recalling those happy days did give her pleasure.

In 1976, twelve days into the New Year, Agatha died, quite peacefully after lunch at Winterbrook House. Her death made front-page news worldwide and *The Times* published an obituary the following day. Max was overwhelmed with letters and telephone calls, and requests for official tributes. The funeral took place on the 16th at the church nearest to Winterbrook House, St Mary's in Cholsey. It was a small family occasion. Agatha's memorial service took place on 14 May, at St Martin-in-the-Fields, and was a great gathering of family and Max's colleagues, all of whom had held Agatha in great esteem and were well aware what Near Eastern archaeology owed to her. Max's old school-friend Humphrey Trevelyan, later ambassador in Baghdad, read the lesson and Sir William Collins, of Agatha's publishers, gave the address. The guest list was a roll-call of the luminaries of Max's world: Mortimer Wheeler, Kathleen Kenyon, H. W. F. Saggs, Roger Moorey, Donald Wiseman, Claude Schaeffer, Robert Hamilton, Seton Lloyd and Oliver Gurney. The congregation was invited to contribute to the Agatha Christie Memorial Fund which had been set up to help two causes dear to her heart, the very old and the very young. Hughes Massie Limited, copyright agents, were to divide the amount raised between the Little Sisters of the Poor and the Agatha Christie Trust for Children. Agatha left a modest £106,000 in her will, but provisions for the disposal of her estate had been made long before her death. Max and Rosalind were the chief beneficiaries.

Agatha's death prompted many tributes but the one that she would have appreciated most would doubtless have been the chapters about her, her work and his pride in and devotion to her that Max wrote in his *Memoirs,* which he had just finished writing when she died. Her death, he said in a postscript, 'came as a merciful release, though it has left me with a feeling of emptiness after forty-five years of a loving and merry companionship. Few men know what it is to live in harmony beside an imaginative, creative mind which inspires life with zest.' In that year's *Iraq* journal there was an obituary of Agatha by Donald Wiseman in which he described her as a much-loved founder member and one of the School's most generous and devoted supporters. All at Nimrud would remember her wit and charm as she presided over the expedition dining table, a kindly and charming personality which contributed so greatly to the team-spirit. He also reminded members that she had given the copyright of one of her books, *A Pocket Full of Rye*, to the School in 1953, which they acknowledged with pride and gratitude. The copyright was almost immediately assigned to a trading company which paid an annual sum to the School for five years, and had helped finance the excavations at Nimrud.

Agatha's posthumous tribute to Max was her *Autobiography*, published in 1977, in which she described the way in which she and Max had met, and decided to marry, and what had happened since. For such a very private person, it was a revealing and intimate account, from which her deep love for her husband was quite apparent. Max's own *Memoirs* followed soon afterwards. A *Times* review, entitled 'Last of the Giants', mentioned particularly his loving account of his wife's achievements, 'the only person for whom his affection and respect was absolutely unequalled', a contrast with some of his more trenchant views on members of his profession.

Max felt completely lost and dreadfully lonely without Agatha, who had been the centre of his existence, the pull which brought him home, whether it was to Swan Court, to Greenway or to Winterbrook House, and the person who attended to all his comforts and whose happiness was her first concern. His domestic arrangements became rather erratic. The roof of Winterbrook House was leaking badly and, although the housekeeper did her best, the house too seemed bereft without its mistress. Max and Agatha's old friend Barbara Parker made it her business to come to the rescue, coming down every weekend from her flat in London to do what she could to cheer Max up and cook him simple meals. There was nothing she would not do for him, whom everyone knew she had always adored. Rodney Kannreuther arrived one day to find her massaging his frozen feet. Perhaps he felt beholden to her, certainly he was fond of her, but it came as a great surprise to his family, and to their archaeological colleagues, when in September 1977 Max married Barbara. *The Times* carried a small announcement, describing Barbara as 'also an archaeologist'.

Max had of course known Barbara Parker for a very long time. She was perhaps an unusual convert to Near Eastern archaeology, having started her career as a mannequin at the couture house of Worth and afterwards studied Chinese art at the Courtauld Institute. It was in the library there that she saw an announcement on the notice board about a new course in Near Eastern archaeology. What made her enrol as one of the first students at the Institute, when Max first met her, no one really knew, but she was a keen student and trekked readily to classes in deciphering cuneiform with Sidney Smith at the British Museum, and to lectures at King's College and University College in Assyriology from her bedsit in Wellington Square. After the course ended, she went out to Lachish, where J. L. Starkey was excavating. He was shot dead on his way to the opening ceremony of the new Palestine Archaeological Museum in January 1938. Barbara returned home and at the outbreak of war she joined the London Fire Brigade and served with distinction through the Blitz. After the War ended, she became for a short time a civil servant in the Ministry of Works, before being appointed Secretary/Librarian at the British School of Archaeology in Iraq in 1949. It was she who was responsible for the extensions to the expedition house at Nimrud. She had added a terrace for afternoon tea 'paved and walled with Assyrian bricks and with a superb view of the snow-capped Zagros mountains to the east'. It was Agatha who had suggested that the terrace be edged with flowering cherries, and, ever dutiful, Barbara bought the trees in Mosul and borrowed a Jeep from the Chief of Police to drive them to Nimrud, over a track which had become a quagmire in the rain. The trees were planted, began to flourish, and were eaten by goats when nobody was looking.

At Nimrud, Barbara had been the photographer, taking over from Agatha the developing and printing of films in a dark cubby-hole. She was then promoted to epigraphist with a special interest in seals. One distinguished colleague later said that she could have been a fine scholar had she been better taught, a sideswipe at Sidney Smith, some of whose ideas about grammar are now thought eccentric. In fact it is more likely that it was Barbara's rather disorganized and somewhat slapdash approach to her work, added to a rather endearing quality of stopping whatever she was doing in order to accommodate the needs of others, that stood in the way of real scholastic achievement. In Baghdad, where she ran the expedition house, she was extremely kind and hospitable to all comers, neglecting her work in the process. Her notebooks of the period have a harried look about them; in a large rounded hand her cuneiform signs and their transliterations look rather rushed and there is much crossing out.

Barbara was popular with the Iraqis and it was said that she often knew what was going on in government before some of its officials. In

1961 she returned to the Institute of Archaeology as Lecturer in Mesopotamian Archaeology, and lived in her nephew's flat in Scarsdale Villas in Kensington. This was doubtless the time when her path crossed so frequently with Max's. Since Max was known to use junior and female colleagues mercilessly as dogsbodies, and Barbara was one of the people he leaned on most heavily, they spent much time together. This has given rise to suggestions that there was more to the relationship than a shared and deep interest in their subject. No one closely related either by family or work believes this, and indeed the immense surprise caused by Max's marriage to Barbara rather proves the point. What was abundantly clear to everyone was that, while she was alive, Max's life revolved around Agatha. He certainly had neither the time nor the inclination to involve himself with anyone else, though he was susceptible to a pretty face, as many men are.

Poor Barbara had never been taken terribly seriously by her colleagues though she was respected by them for her published work on seals and tablets. By making herself indispensable to Max, she acquired a reflected status in the small world of Near Eastern archaeology. She was Max's slave; she ran errands, found things he had mislaid, sorted out his papers, looked up references, found photographs and so on, readily putting aside her own work for the time being. She became an amalgamation of a secretary, an old friend and a nanny. When Agatha was dying, it was Barbara who rushed down to Wallingford at weekends to relieve the pressure on Max. And when Agatha died, it was Barbara who took over the domestic side of Max's life, as well as those other duties. First his mother, then Agatha, and now Barbara had made sure that Max was properly looked after.

How much pleasure Barbara derived from her subsequent marriage to Max is hard to gauge. She certainly did not have long with him, and throughout their short married life he was in poor health. But since it was generally accepted that she was a very lonely person, and adored him, her marriage did give her life a great focus. Max left her a generous settlement when he died (£40,000 in cash and the house in Cresswell Place, with a life interest in Winterbrook House), so her chronic money worries were eased. Inexpert financial advice added to the rampant inflation of the time meant that Barbara was never very rich, but she was secure. She soon moved out of Winterbrook House, which was too expensive for her to repair and maintain. She settled down in a pleasant house in the same town, and thereafter made Oxford her main base for work. She was often to be seen hard at work in the Oriental Institute there, brightly dressed and elegantly turned out, for she retained her slender figure and long straight back to the end. She was for fifty years an opera buff, and was a knowledgeable source of information on this subject also. As Lady Mallowan, she had a special place in the British School of Archaeology in Iraq's hierarchy, becoming its President, and she was held in great affection.

Max did not mention his second marriage in his *Memoirs*, and the reviews of his book did not mention it either. Many people felt he had betrayed Agatha's memory in marrying so soon after her death and preferred to think of him as the grieving widower; if they referred to his marriage at all, it was as a marriage of convenience.

In July 1978, Max had an operation on his hip from which he did not recover properly. Barbara took him to Devon on holiday, and it was there on 19 August that he died. A notice in *The Times* described him as 'beloved husband of Barbara'. His funeral, like Agatha's, was held at St Mary's, Cholsey, and his coffin was laid beside Agatha's under the same enormous tombstone decorated by Seton Lloyd's wife, Ulrica. At the funeral service on 24 August, the congregation sang 'All People that on Earth Do Dwell' and the reading was taken from Ecclesiastes.

There were handsome tributes and obituaries to Max in *The Times* and academic journals, which gauged the measure of the man with some success, emphasizing his good qualities though not glossing over some of his less attractive traits. Max's strengths were the result of his self-confidence, a deep-seated belief in himself which had been engendered by the unqualified devotion of his mother, and enhanced by the deep love and admiration of his first wife, her 'own dear friend and lover' whom she so honoured and respected, 'for your integrity of character and the absence of anything petty and small about you', as she had once written in a letter to him.

In November, the Annual General Meeting of the British School was preceded by a Memorial Service for Max at St James's, Piccadilly, at which Seton Lloyd gave the address. Lord Trevelyan read the lesson for him too, and a mass of colleagues were present from all the archaeological schools and institutions with which Max was associated.

Max believed in himself, and this belief could lead him to behave arrogantly. He wrote what were described as some of the 'rudest letters ever penned' but quite often they were mitigated by a 'simultaneous and very friendly telephone call'. He was described by one pupil as 'infuriating but lovable', by another as someone who considered the British School as a personal fiefdom, his to order like an Assyrian tyrant. He could be quite staggeringly mean with money, perhaps remebering a time when it had not been so plentiful. On the other hand, he was an extremely generous host, summoning colleagues and pupils to Boodle's, to All Souls, to Greenway and Winterbrook House for vast and delicious meals and splendid wines. He was generous with his time too, taking infinite trouble with pupils who interested him, and getting them to do things they thought they were incapable of doing. He brought out the best in people.

Max had quite a presence, and he sometimes liked to project sides of himself that he thought would impress others: 'quite a showman'. A colleague recalled Max at Nimrud asking the current epigraphist to translate a cuneiform inscription running across limestone slabs just revealed, and then noticing that, when visitors arrived later, Max scrolled his stick over the inscription and gave his awe-struck audience a fair rendition of what it actually read. Max in his senior position on various academic bodies often presided over lectures and seminars and liked to reminisce in a casual-seeming way at the end, 'Now when I was a young man at Chagar Bazar ...' Few knew that these remarks had been carefully prepared in advance.

There was much disappointment over the disposal of Max's library after his death. Max had a magnificent library, since money had never really been an object with him since his marriage to Agatha, and he had bought books whenever he wanted them. (In fact he had always loved books and started collecting them at Oxford using Christmas and birthday subventions.) In addition, many of his books had been presented to him by the authors, and signed by them. When he died, the books were in his library at Winterbrook House and thus Barbara had a life interest in them, apart from the several specific bequests to the Institute of Archaeology (three hundred volumes to be chosen by them), to his former pupil Margaret Munn-Rankin and to Donald Wiseman. Since Barbara could not live at Winterbrook House, a sale at Sotheby's was arranged, somewhat hurriedly, and the books were sold in large lots, with only the first three properly described, so that it was impossible to find out what was in each lot unless a personal visit was made to the auctioneers. The division of the books into lots seems to have been made without any real attention to detail: thus his magnificent original set of *Délégation en Perse* was broken up and doubtless cannibalized for its prints. As many of Max's books were first editions presented and autographed by their authors, they fetched unnaturally high prices and ended up in smart booksellers' shops, way beyond the means of Max's colleagues, who were those who really understood what the books were about. Since the proceeds of the books were split into four parts, to Max's residuary legatees, no one made much monetary gain from the sale, and the three great institutions with which Max had been so involved all felt that they had been cheated of acquiring a great resource, for which they would doubtless have been prepared to offer some recompense. Another sad loss was a fine portrait by William Coldstream of Max for which he had been sitting at the time of his death. It unaccountably disappeared from the house in Wallingford after Barbara's death, and has never been found, much to the disappointment of Max's family and colleagues.

Max's strengths lay in his ability to communicate ideas and enthusiasm, his energy in getting things done and not allowing obstacles to impede that progress. He had a broad view of what should be achieved and he did not permit detail to obscure it. In general he got on well with his colleagues, and inspired enormous affection and respect, with very occasional reservations. He was at his best as a field archaeologist in the tradition of the great ones of the nineteenth century. He himself knew that his methods had been superseded by the end of his career, but he continued to look back to the old days with pride and with ill-concealed scorn on the earth-grubbers of the scientific present. As he said in his *Memoirs*, 'When I review my archaeological life, I am impelled ... to compare past with present ventures ... I have been fortunate to practise ... for the first three decades of my career ... in the grand manner, on a grand scale.' He compared then with now: then big expeditions were worked with huge labour forces numbering in excess of two hundred men, and each season hundreds of thousands of tons of soil were shifted. The results could range over six thousand years and produce a catalogue register of some twenty thousand objects. He was prepared to admit that, because of the speed of such excavation, some evidence was lost, but he infinitely preferred such progress to the slow and painstaking modern method which found only about a tenth as much. He knew that the archaeologists of bygone days were scientifically less well-equipped than their successors; they used native common sense to arrive at the truth, 'but truth is no longer acceptable unless determined mathematically by computation ... I am therefore ... an unashamed supporter of the bygone days of digging, the last of the Romantics.'

Max's strong sense of the narrative of modern archaeology, his undoubted genius for picking his site, his wide-ranging historical knowledge, his elegance of literary style and his wholehearted and unswerving devotion to Near Eastern archaeology: these were his great strengths and the reasons that he became a giant in the annals of his own heroes, particularly Layard, in whose tradition he so squarely stands. The reading chosen from Ecclesiastes for Max's funeral service summed up the life of a great archaeologist:

Man goeth to his long home, and the mourners go about the streets: Or ever the silver cord be loosed, or the golden bowl be broken, or the pitcher be broken at the fountain, or the wheel at the cistern. Then shall the dust return to the earth as it was: and the spirit shall return unto God who gave it.

Further Reading

Amory, Mark, *The Letters of Evelyn Waugh* (1981)

Annan, Noel, *Roxburgh of Stowe* (1965)

Carew, Dudley, *A Fragment of Friendship* (1974)

Christie, Agatha, *Absent in the Spring* (1944)

Christie, Agatha, *An Autobiography* (1977)

Christie, Agatha, *Appointment with Death* (1938)

Christie, Agatha, *Come, Tell Me How You Live* (1946)

Christie, Agatha, *Death on the Nile* (1936)

Christie, Agatha, *Murder in Mesopotamia* (1936)

Christie, Agatha, *Murder on the Orient Express* (1934)

Christie, Agatha, *They Came to Baghdad* (1951)

Curtis, J. E. (ed.), *Fifty Years of Mesopotamian Discovery* (1982)

Hamilton, R. W., *Letters from the Middle East* (1992)

Hastings, Selina, *Evelyn Waugh: A Biography* (1994)

Lloyd, Seton, *Foundations in the Dust* (1947)

Mallowan, Max, *Nimrud & Its Remains* (1966)

Mallowan, Max, *Twenty-five Years of Mesopotamian Discovery* (1956)

Morgan, Janet, *Agatha Christie: A Biography* (1984)

Pryce-Jones, David, *Evelyn Waugh and his World* (1973)

Rowse, A. L., *A Cornishman at Oxford* (1965)

Winstone, H. V. F., *Gertrude Bell* (1978)

Winstone, H. V. F., *Woolley of Ur* (1990)

Index